Waterstones
29.7.96
£ 14.95

WITHDRAWN

The Practice of
Advertising

The Marketing Series is one of the most comprehensive collections of textbooks in marketing and sales available from the UK today.

Published by Heinemann Professional Publishing on behalf of the Chartered Institute of Marketing, the series has been specifically designed, developed and progressively updated over a number of years to support students studying for the Institute's certificate and diploma qualifications. The scope of the subjects covered by the series, however, means that it is of equal value to anyone studying other further or higher business and/or marketing related qualifications.

Formed in 1911, the Chartered Institute of Marketing is now the largest professional marketing management body in Europe with over 21,000 members and 20,000 students located worldwide. Its primary objectives are focused on the development of awareness and understanding of marketing throughout UK industry and commerce and in the raising of standards of professionalism in the education, training and practice of this key business discipline.

OTHER TITLES IN THE SERIES

The Practice of Advertising

Edited by

Norman A. Hart, MSc., FCAM, FIPR, FCIM

Third edition

Published on behalf of
the CAM Foundation
and the Chartered Institute of Marketing

Heinemann Professional Publishing

Heinmann Professional Publishing Ltd
Halley Court, Jordan Hill, Oxford OX2 8EJ

OXFORD   LONDON   MELBOURNE   AUCKLAND   SINGAPORE
IBADAN   NAIROBI   GABORONE   KINGSTON

First published 1978
Reprinted 1981
Second edition 1983
Reprinted 1984, 1985, 1986
Third edition 1990

British Library Cataloguing in Publication Data
The practice of advertising. – 3rd. ed.
1. Great Britain. Advertising
I. Hart, Norman A. (Norman Arthur) *1930*
II. CAM Foundation   III. Chartered Institute of Marketing
659.10941
ISBN 0 434 90796 0

Typeset by Hope Services (Abingdon) Ltd.
Printed in Great Britain by
Billings & Sons, Worcester

Contents

Preface to the Third edition

Since its initial publication in 1978, *The Practice of Advertising* has secured a place on the reading lists of many courses both in the United Kingdom and overseas.

With the fast changing nature of the advertising business, it was thought necessary to produce a completely revised edition so as to be right up-to-date. With this in view, some chapters have been rewritten, with new authors, others substantially changed, and the balance updated.

Thanks are due to the many contributors for their helpful assistance in producing a third edition of what I hope has become a standard text.

NORMAN HART

Biographical notes

ANN BURDUS is senior Vice President, Marketing and Communications, Olympia & York Canary Wharf Ltd. Before taking up this appointment in 1989 she was a Director of AGB Research plc. Most of her career has been spent in advertising and until 1983 she was Director of Strategic Planning at Interpublic in New York having moved to this position from being Chairman of McCann & Co. Before joining McCann-Erickson in 1971 she was Research Director of Garland Compton. She had her initial training in research and advertising at Ogilvy Benson and Mather which was called Mather and Crowther when she first joined. Ms Burdus was on the Council of the Market Research Society and later for six years on the Council of ESOMAR (the European Society of Marketing and Opinion Research) where she took special responsibility for seminars and conferences. Before going to the United States in 1978 she was on the Council of the Institute of Practitioners in Advertising and chaired the Professional Standards Committee. She also held the position of Chairman of the Advertising Association for a year from July 1980.

ALAN COPAGE is Head of Research at TMD Advertising Limited, one of the largest of the media independent companies in the UK, and one of only two such companies to be publicly quoted on the USM. Copage is an avid supporter of the advertising industry, and currently sits on eleven industry committees, ranging through JICNARS, BARB, JICREG and Media Research Group. A frequent writer of articles for the advertising trade press, he has lectured for the Media Circle, Market Research Society, Media Research Group, Industrial Society and Advertising Association. Copage is a member of the Market Research Society, the Chartered Institute of Marketing and Communications Advertising and Marketing (CAM).

MAURICE 'MO' DRAKE joined Young & Rubicam in 1959 as Copy Supervisor. He became an Associate Director in 1964, Creative Group Director in 1966 and subsequently Head of Copy. He joined Grey Advertising in 1972 as Creative Director, and became Creative Director of Lintas London in 1975. He is a fellow of the IPA and of CAM and is a member of the Creative Circle, of which he was President in 1977 and 1978. In 1979 he became Executive Creative Director and Deputy Chairman of Lintas. In 1984 he left to open a creative consultancy 'Drake Associates'. He also in 1987 joined with others in starting BDFM, a full-service advertising agency.

DAVID HANGER joined *The Economist* in 1969 as Advertisement Sales Executive. He was appointed Advertisement Manager in 1975 and Advertisement Director in 1979. Prior to joining *The Economist*, he spent four years with East Midlands Gas Board in Leicester as a management trainee. Educated at Wellingborough Grammar School, he holds a Diploma in Marketing and Management Studies, is a member of the Chartered Institute of Marketing, is Chief Examiner, CAM Diploma in International Advertising and Marketing, President of the UK Chapter of the IAA, a Freeman of the City of London and a member of the Worshipful Company of Marketors.

NORMAN A. HART is currently Managing Director of Interact International Limited having previously been Director of the CAM Foundation and Chief Marketing Executive of IAB Marketing, a government-sponsored management consultancy. He was earlier at Roles & Parker Limited on the account service side, and was Group Chief Executive when he left to join a Unilever company, Thames Board Mills, as Publicity Manager. He subsequently became Marketing Manager, and finally went into publishing with Morgan Grampian, where he was Divisional General Manager. A frequent speaker both in the UK and overseas on industrial advertising, Mr Hart is author of a number of books. He is also a visiting fellow of the University of Bradford and holds a Master's Degree in Management Studies.

JOHN JOSLING has spent his whole career in the advertising agency business, and has worked in a number of leading London advertising agencies. He was Chairman of Interlink, then Alliance International UK, and is a former main board director of Lopex plc. He has served on a number of advertising industry committees, including the Chairmanship of the Advertising Association Courses and Seminars Committee. He is also a non-executive director of Alliance International (UK) and of Social Service Advertising Limited (an agency totally devoted to charity clients). He is a past Chairman of the Lord's Taverner's (an active charity raising funds for a wide range of needs in addition to cricket) and is a Deputy Chairman of the Governors of St Albans School. He has contributed to standard publications in the advertising business in addition to a number of press articles and is a member of the International Advertising Association and of the Marketing Society.

VIVIENNE KRIEFMAN has a BSc in Sociology and Psychology from the University of Bath. She is currently a lecturer in marketing, advertising and sales techniques at the Henley College, as well as at other venues and institutions. She took her CAM certificate in 1977 and was given the Daily Express Rosebowl Award for top marks in the media paper. She obtained the CAM diploma in 1981 with distinction in the Public Relations paper. She has worked as an account executive for KH Publicity, as a PA to the Director of the CAM Foundation, as a director of Kudos Conferences which specialized in the marketing and legal environment. She has written booklets in careers for the CAM Foundation and the London Chamber of Commerce.

MARK R. C. LOVELL is President of Groupe Innova Inc. in Montreal, and a Director of The Creative Research Group Limited, the parent company in Toronto. His research experience began in England, where he joined the British Market Research Bureau in 1959. This was immediately after graduating from Jesus College, Cambridge, with a double first in classics and psychology. In 1963 he moved to Marplan, where he was appointed to the Board. From 1966 to 1975 he was in charge of market research at the LPE Ltd (later Leo Burnett Ltd) in London. He joined The Creative Research Group Limited on arrival in Canada in January 1976. Since this time he has organized a wide range of different research projects of all kinds. He has spoken at various conferences including ESOMAR, British Market Research Society, and the American Marketing Association. He co-authored *Assessing the Effectiveness of Advertising* (Business Books, 1976) with Jack Potter. He is also the author of a number of books on child psychology including *Saturday Parent* under his pseudonym Peter Rowlands. He is a Past President of the Professional Marketing Research Society (of Canada); and he has been President of the Montreal Chapter of the PMRS.

KENNETH MILES is Director General of the Incorporated Society of British Advertisers, the business association which advises companies from all kinds of industry on advertising and related subjects, and speaks for them to Government, the media and other interests. He completed his education at Oxford University and then joined Unilever Limited where he worked in a number of marketing posts, both in and outside Britain. This included five years in India where he was involved in the development of new media for the rural areas, as well as the launching of new products. In 1968 he joined Watney Mann Limited, a leading brewery group in the UK having responsibility for all marketing and advertising activities. He was subsequently a Marketing Adviser to ICI Limited and Head of Marketing at the Central Council for Agricultural and Horticultural Co-operation. He joined the ISBA as Director in April 1979 and represents advertisers through the ISBA on many organizations and committees in Britain and internationally. He is a member of the International Chamber of Commerce (ICC) Commission on Marketing and Distribution, a member of the Management Committee of the World Federation of Advertisers (WFA) and Chairman of the Consumer Affairs Panel of the Confederation of British Industry (CBI). He is also Chairman of the Exhibition Liaison Committee which brings together all parties in the exhibition world in Britain; a Council member of the Advertising Association (AA) and a Governor of the Communication, Advertising and Marketing Education Foundation Limited (CAM).

PETER SIMMONS started his sales promotion career with the Young & Rubicam below-the-line company, G. L. H. Marketing Services. This was followed by seven years with the Marketing Triangle becoming a Director in 1979. In 1983 he co-founded Team, a Sales Promotion and Communications consultancy, of which he is now Managing Director.

GEOFF SMITH now runs his own marketing and strategy development consultancy. He had for many years been a member of the top management team in 3M United Kingdom with responsibility for central marketing and new business ventures. He has served two terms as Chairman of the Marketing Society as well as being its Honorary Secretary for a number of years. He is a Fellow of the Marketing Society. He serves as Chief Examiner in Management and Strategy for the Diploma of the CAM Education Foundation. He is also Chairman of the Sales Promotion Committee of the Incorporated Society of British Advertisers.

JOHN STANDISH is a business and technical product media consultant to the industry. With a background in accountancy he joined agency life in 1954 on the advent of commercial television, working first at Masius Wynne-Williams where he built up and developed the agency's expertise in TV planning and buying, and then at Everetts Advertising where he was seconded to plan the IPA submission for, and subsequently set up, an area ITV contractor. However, it was in 1964, when he joined Adgroup as Media Head of Roles & Parker, Stuart Advertising and Creative Workshop that he developed his fascination for industrial and business media and later, as a director of Parker Research, industrial research. After the Adgroup merger with Charles Barker in 1981 he joined the board of Ayer Barker, leaving in 1986 to take up an appointment as Media and Research Director of the Carter Matanle/Interact Group. Grammar school educated in Devon, he has served as a CAM examiner, on the ABC council, the IPA Media Advisory Panel, the MDF and the BRS steering committees and is a member of the Industrial Research Association.

PETER THOMSON was Director General of the Advertising Standards Authority and Secretary of the Code of Advertising Practice Committee until 1989. He was educated at Oxford, where he gained an MA in Jurisprudence, and subsequently became a barrister, Middle Temple. Mr Thomson joined ASA/CAP staff in 1968 after experience in industrial relations and management of a promotional organization. Mr Thomson is now Director General of the Institute of Purchasing and Supply.

ROY TOPP is Commercial Director at Ogilvy & Mather. He served on the Print Technical Panel of the IPA and is past Chairman of the Creative Services Association where he is still very active. A frequent speaker at seminars and conferences, he also sits on the PIRA Print and Information Technology Division Committee, concerned with standards and developments in the printing industry. His career spans over forty years with advertising agencies such as Foote Cone & Belding, SSCB:Lintas and Allen Brady & Marsh as Production and Print Executive, TV Administration, Account Management, Control Group Head, Control Manager and Board Director. He is a Member of the Institute of Practitioners in Advertising and an Associate Member of the British Institute of Management.

DAZ VALLADARES is a partner of one of the fastest growing media independents – Bygraves, Bushell, Valladares & Sheldon Limited, a company with the greatest number of syllables in its name – at least amongst media independents. In the past, Valladares worked with agencies such as Masius Wynne-Williams – now known by the less pleasant sounding DMB&B Limited. He has been the Media Director of agencies such as Pembertons, PLN, Allardyce-PLN and MWK. He is deeply involved in advertising education, having been Chief Examiner of CAM for ten years and is a past Chairman of the prestigious Media Research Group.

MIKE DE VERE is Resources Director, Zenith Media Buying Services. His career started in 1971 as a trainee media buyer in Masius Wynne-

Williams. Following this three year 'apprenticeship', he joined Hobson Bates as a television time buyer. During 1975, he started what was to be a ten year association with Benton & Bowles. During this period, he worked across all media and was ultimately made a Director of the in-house media buying service – Mercury Media Limited. In 1985, Benton & Bowles were involved in a worldwide merger with Masius Wynne-Williams which led to a number of directors forming a new media independent – Ray Morgan and Partners. RMP opened its doors in 1985 with clients including General Foods Ltd, Richardson-Vicks, Vidal Sassoon, Johnson Wax and Crookes Healthcare. The business grew rapidly and was ultimately second in size to TMD, with annual billings of around £80 m. In 1988, Saatchi and Saatchi decided to pool the buying of the three major agencies within the group – KHBB, Dorland and Saatchi and Saatchi. The combined billings of approximately £600 m represented about 15 per cent of the media marketplace. The scale and significance of this volume has enabled the company to forge a new order of media buying. RMP was bought in to form the nucleus of this enterprise. Mr de Vere's current responsibility is the management of Zenith's radio buying and negotiation together with the coordination and development of broadcast sponsorship.

Introduction

Ann Burdus

One simple but precise definition of advertising is 'the action of calling something to the attention of the public, especially by paid announcements'. This is an important definition, because many people think of advertising mostly in terms of selling manufacturers' consumer goods, soaps, toothpastes, food and so on. This is the most obtrusive and conspicuous kind of advertising, and certainly it is important, but it is by no means the only kind, and now it probably accounts for less than 40 per cent of all the money spent on advertising.

People have for centuries communicated their ideas and their needs to one another through advertisements. They have sold houses, acquired servants, found lost dogs, expressed ideas, bought land and engaged in a wide range of social and economic activities through advertising. Government communicates with the people, politicians with their constituents, corporations communicate with the city and their shareholders, employers announce job opportunities and persuade people to come to them, and charities exhort us to support their many causes. The uses of advertising are many, and advertising is a constructive part of our social fabric.

Advertising is an agent of choice. One of the most important benefits of advertising is that it facilitates the consumer becoming an active rather than a passive agent in the economic cycle. In order to make purchasing decisions or social decisions, the consumers must be informed. Ideally, they should receive information from a variety of different sources, and the paid-for advertisement is one of these sources.

We are surrounded by manufacturers who are continuously trying to improve their sales, and one way they do this is to make the product better fit the consumer's needs than the competitive product. The consumer must know about the product improvement and the manufacturer, therefore, buys advertising to inform the consumer about the changes made and to tempt the consumer to try the product once. If the product does not live up to the expectations aroused by the advertisement the consumer will not buy twice.

Sometimes the individual product improvements may seem small and the claims exaggerated, but the products will only be bought and continue to be bought if they match up to their claims and meet the consumer's needs.

This link between the manufacturer and the consumer through advertising has important economic consequences, but advertising has additional social significance. If people are to play a full role in society, they must be able to exercise choice, and that choice must be based on a multiplicity of sources of information. Advertising contributes to this process in two ways. First, it is a source of information in its own right. The recipients of the information know that someone paid for the time or space to communicate with them and take that into consideration when evaluating the information. Second, advertising provides revenue for the media.

It is important that we should have more than one source of television, and commercial television is supported totally by its advertising revenues. It is important that we should have more than one newspaper. The national newspapers get nearly half their revenue from advertising, and most would certainly go out of business without this income. The quality Sunday newspapers get three-quarters of their revenue this way, and most consumer magazines and particularly trade and technical journals are heavily dependent on advertising support.

Interestingly, advertisements also make a positive contribution to the content of the media in which they appear. One survey showed that more people liked the television commercials than liked the programmes! When the Advertising Association asked women if they would like their magazines to appear without advertisements, there was very considerable agreement that they would not. The entertainment and informational value of advertising is appreciated.

Although people use and approve of advertisements, they are often critical of advertising in the abstract. Yet, again, careful research has shown that advertising is something they accept as part of their lives; they don't talk about it as much as other issues, they don't criticize it as much as other issues, and they don't see it as much in need of reform as other things which impact on their lives.

This is partly because the role of advertising is understood by the public and partly because the whole advertising industry works towards maintaining the confidence the public can have in advertising communications by maintaining high standards and trying to make sure that the public are not misled.

Although advertising has been with us for a long time, and is likely to remain with us if the right to advertise is protected, it is subject to continuous evolution and change.

There is no question but that advertising has a future, because people will always want to communicate their ideas and to inform other people about products and services they may have to offer.

In many parts of the world, advertising is increasingly under attack from people who would prefer government control of the media to what they consider to be undesirable commercial influence. Many others, however, are still convinced that commercial and other interests are a valuable source of funds for the multiplicity of alternative information which should be available in a free society. They believe anyone should be able to buy time or space to communicate across and within national boundaries, providing the message communicated is responsible and true. Protecting the right to do this and having the opportunity to do this will be a continuous battle for the advertising business into the future.

Advertising is going through many changes which will be accelerated. These are being led by new media developments and primarily by new developments in the electronic media. Mass media advertising and broadcasting as we know it are changing towards more specific targeting (called 'narrowcasting') because of the needs of communication and because the media are becoming available to make this possible.

Several things are happening at the same time. The commercial use of satellites for transmitting broadcasts and advertising messages across boundaries is a reality in many parts of the world and has raised challenging copyright and other legal issues.

Since it is becoming possible to reach both wider and narrower audiences, people are also turning to cable television and videotapes and discs for programmes which relate more specifically to their personal interests and needs. This suggests a fragmentation of the media which may raise problems for the funding of the making of programmes. It is possible that the pressure on funds will lead to a change in the quality of programmes and eventually to a further change in the reading and viewing habits of the general public.

It is not only in the electronic media that audiences are becoming fragmented. Although we still have strong national newspapers and magazines in the UK, there has been a growth in publications directed at specific groups with very specific interests. Slimming magazines, magazines relating to particular hobbies, or particular parts of the country are all gaining, whereas some of those targeted to a more general audience find it difficult to survive.

Advertising information will still be important, perhaps increasingly so, to these publics who look for information relevant to them, their interests and their hobbies. As living patterns change, there may be an increased reliance on advertising. Already, much shopping takes place in a mute marketplace with no sales person to help with the decision process – if anyone is going to sell to consumers or give them information on which to base decisions it will be advertising, point-of-sale material and, to some extent, specialized editorials to be found in the new media.

We can see that in the future people may increasingly shop from their own homes. There is a growth in the use of direct off the page selling through newspapers, colour supplements and magazines. People can also call up product and service information on their television screens and then make their purchases either by telephone or directly through a home computer. In the selling of products and services in this environment, advertising becomes more and not less important.

Increasingly, manufacturers are looking for specific targets within larger market units. Some already see Europe as a single market, and they are asking for advertising that can be used across the continent, or at least across several countries. In some European countries, there is already considerable media overlap, so that consistency of presentation between countries is important.

Such international advertising and marketing activities will come much more swiftly in some fields than others, but they will raise interesting new creative challenges and specific challenges for advertising regulation.

Advertising will be different in the future, because almost everywhere there is a trend towards increased expenditures on social messages and services, rather than products and brands, and this will continue.

However, the role that advertising plays in our lives will remain significant. The form and the content of the messages will change with time, but the need for people to communicate with each other through paid-for time and space will remain with us.

1

Marketing and the function of advertising within it

Geoff Smith

The term marketing is used in a number of different ways. It can describe a department within an organization and in so doing sets that department or function apart from other company functions such as production, research and development, finance and administration.

It can also be used to describe a set of techniques such as market research, advertising, sales promotion and customer relations. These activities are frequently aggregated under the general umbrella of marketing.

The marketing concept

Most importantly marketing describes the concept which total enterprises can and should adopt and by which they should operate. This can lead to defining marketing, as Hugh Davidson succinctly proposes, as '. . . the process of balancing the company needs for profit against the benefits required by consumers, so as to maximise long-term earnings per share.'

The successful marketing organization will therefore:

1   Develop strategies which aim to meet the battery of needs of target markets more effectively than competitors.
2   Integrate all company efforts in market orientation so that all management decisions are taken in the full understanding of how they will affect the customer and his or her perceptions of the company and its products or services.
3   Ensure allocation of resources to build sustained profitability working within the financial and other constraints incumbent upon any organization.
4   Operate in ways which are consistent with the legitimate concerns of

employees, suppliers and the communities surrounding company operations – consistent also with the well-being of the environment – as well as meeting the reward aspirations of shareholders.

It follows that within the structure of such organizations there is likely to be a marketing and/or marketing services function but that the marketing concept is held paramount throughout management and especially by the chief executive. The outstanding global success of so many Japanese companies has been based on just such an approach. It is open to any motor manufacturer, for instance, to understand that among the needs of consumers seeking to purchase cars reliability and corrosion resistance are likely to rank high. Responding effectively to such needs – by making appropriate decisions throughout the organization (research and development, component sourcing, production and so on) has brought outstanding success in most markets around the world to which the Japanese makers have been allowed access.

It is commonplace for individuals to insist on the differences between marketing products or services, consumables or capital items in the different markets in which they operate. It is undeniable that the marketing approach – the strategies which are developed – should be specific and appropriate to the particular situation. The marketing principles to be followed, however, remain very similar in all situations and can be properly promulgated for all organizations. This is true even for non-profit organizations which should equally be concerned with meeting the battery of needs of those they serve while balancing that aim with operating within the resource constraints imposed upon them and making the most productive use of those resources of people, skills and money.

What, then, is the process by which these marketing principles are put into effective practice? It is important, first, to define the business and its basic objectives – its mission. Definition of the broad market to be served follows together with careful selection of target segments within that broad market.

Even to go so far it will be clear that information is important if marketing decisions are to be well-founded and have a good chance of success. For those already operating in a marketplace there will almost certainly be much valuable data in existence within the company – data about sales of different products or services within the range offered, sales through different types of distributive outlet, sales to different regions, data about seasonalility and other cyclical factors.

Further information about the market – its structure, its size, growth or decline may be available from published sources, such as government statistics, trade associations, trade publications, commercial research organizations and others. But to understand clearly what motivates customers to buy products or services, to define the benefits they seek to acquire and enjoy it will often be necessary to undertake some form of market research. Research studies may take many forms. They may carry high costs or be relatively inexpensive. The sample may need to be truly random in order that it represents the subject universe (e.g. total adult population or all companies with mainframe computer installations) or it may be selective in some way which reduces costs but compromises statistical validity. The questionnaire may be strictly followed word for word or it may, in a discussion group or in some industrial research, be a topic guide which the researcher uses in order thoroughly to explore important aspects of the subject. Interviewing may be face-to-face and be at the informant's home or place of work or in some location to which suitable informants are invited to view products or advertising or concept boards illustrating either of those. It may be carried out over the telephone – this is likely to save costs when compared to face-to-face interviewing and it is increasingly the method chosen in much industrial market research. In the field of consumer research it is only valid if all target informants can be reached on the phone. Postal questionnaires are occasionally used but suffer greatly from the strong element of self-selection in the sample – those who respond may well be unrepresentative of the total target sample.

Other methods of gaining market research information may involve participation in syndicated studies offered to all companies in a particular industry sharing costs between them or in 'omnibus' studies which are carried out regularly and use large randomly drawn samples from the total population – they consist largely of questions from all participating companies who are charged on a per-question basis.

Reliable market research agencies will advise on the most suitable research method to provide the results needed and on what can be achieved within the available budget. The Market Research Society will willingly suggest candidate agencies guided by specialization and location. The Industrial Market Research Association will also be helpful in the area of business-to-business markets.

In undertaking market research the marketer must be clear about his or her objectives, the uses to which the desired information will be put as well as the time and budget constraints which apply. In such ways it becomes possible to acquire information for sound marketing decisions. These may fall within the scope of a number of analyses important to the development of an effective marketing plan.

The important areas for analysis are:

1 *Market analysis*
   - How attractive are alternative markets (size, growth, competition, profitability)?
   - Do we have the capability to compete effectively (matters of market share and position, cost effectiveness, technical capability, marketing and distribution strengths, future requirements)?
2 *Customer analysis*
   - How is the market segmented?
   - What are the needs of each segment?
   - How are purchasing decisions made?
   - Who makes the key decisions?
3 *Competitor analysis*
   - Who are the key competitors?
   - What are the strategies of competitors?
   - How are we positioned as competitors?
4 *Environmental analysis*
   - What trends are apparent in political, social, economic or technological areas which may impinge on our marketing freedom to act?

Our purpose initially is to put together the outline, at least, of a marketing plan. This will define requirements for the product – size, colour, shape, its desired levels of quality and reliability, its performance characteristics and the target selling price, which should represent value to the consumer for the benefits provided. It will assess the extent of desired distribution and how this can be achieved. It will outline the needs for advertising, public relations, merchandising and sales promotion (the range of marketing communications activities).

From such an outline plan it is possible to attempt a draft financial plan. This will incorporate revenue estimates based on forecast sales volume and cost estimates covering research and development, production, warehousing and distribution, the cost of sales effort and of providing pre-or post-sales services and the marketing communications costs. The financial plan will need to allow for the costs of providing the required level of production capacity – including the costs of new plant and equipment if the sales volume expectations demand it. Inherent within the outline are the resource requirements – of finance, of people and various types of expertise. The financial plan will assess contribution margins at particular levels of production and sales. This leads on to management determination as to whether the planned project meets overall financial objectives measured in terms, variously, of return on investment, return on capital employed or, possibly, return on sales.

Marketing management will, in all likelihood, have been instrumental in drawing up the outline plan and the draft financial plan often with the help of accountants from the company's financial and administrative personnel. Every function within the company is likely to be affected by the proposed activity. Research and development and/or purchasing groups may be involved in developing product and packaging best suited to meet customer needs. Production units will be guided both on the volume of product required and on the quality and reliability standards which need to be met and maintained. Warehousing and distribution management will have clearer understanding of inventory-holding requirements and of the projected timing and volume of product movements into distribution. Personnel management will learn from the plan of the numbers of people required to meet the needs of the plan in all its operations and, therefore, of the needs for new recruits, for new skills and for relevant experience.

Thus the marketing process involves all parts of the organization; those responsible for its implementation have to ensure the coordinated cooperation of each and every function. Marketing directors, therefore, have to undertake responsibility for effective action in many areas where they have no direct authority as well as directing the work of those operating within marketing functional areas. In the most effective organizations which follow the marketing concept all functions are guided by the needs of the marketplace. They will make decisions in their own functional areas always holding in mind the effect those decisions will have upon the ultimate consumer and aiming to enhance the benefits provided.

The marketing mix

The fact that the ultimate consumer of products seeks far more than the bare product features when considering purchase – ease of availability and perceived value for money come to mind as examples – means that a number of elements demand consideration when putting together an effective marketing plan. These elements are often grouped under the heading of the 4 Ps:

- Product
- Price
- Place
- Promotion

Consideration of the streams of activity which fall under these headings should be undertaken in the fullest possible understanding of consumer needs and of competitors' strategies for meeting those needs. This is important in order to have some chance of success in seeking to differentiate your product or service from your competitors and in ways that come closer to the needs of your target market – points of competitive differential advantage.

Product

1 By range or variety
2 By features
3 By packaging, design or practical aspects
4 By branding

Price

1 Possibly by lower or higher price
2 By payment terms
3 By trade-in allowances
4 By lease/purchase schemes
5 By extended credit

Place

1 By use of non-traditional outlets
2 By direct marketing
3 By more intensive distribution

Promotion

1 By developing unique brand character
2 By building warm and friendly familiarity ⎫
   from continued advertising impact   ⎬ Marketing
3 By developing novel selling approaches   ⎭ communications

In product marketplaces in which the physical differences between brands are minimal – and many of the fast-moving consumer goods markets have this characteristic – advertising becomes a vital means by which differentiation can be brought about. This is achieved by attributing character to a brand by means of those who are featured enjoying it after purchase or via the environment in which it is consumed. These aspects of the brand in its advertised use represent aspiration in the minds of target consumers – buying the brand brings, by association, the calm after trauma that comes with a Hamlet cigar, for example.

In developing a marketing plan each of the elements of the marketing mix is considered fully. Within this consideration it is important to assess where the company's strengths and weaknesses lie. How well do the strengths relate to the customer's needs? Do the weaker areas need converting to greater strength because they would otherwise leave the company vulnerable to competitive onslaught?

The marketing environment

Important also is the consideration of the external marketing environment, influences upon it and trends within it. The company must take into account a range of variable demand factors. It must understand the stage in the market life cycle in which it is operating since it must, by changing emphasis in the marketing mix, distinguish between markets at an early stage of building awareness and confidence, those during the phase of fast growth as greater numbers of consumers show allegiance to the product category or those which are static or declining because saturation has been reached and there is a diminishing number of faithful brand purchasers. Marketing activities will have different emphases in each of these phases.

Within the environment there are a number of areas of influence which have potential significance for marketing planning. The initials PEST provide a useful memory jogger:

- *P = Political/legal.* Are there political influences at work likely to lead to legislation which will restrict or open up marketplace opportunities? Restrictions on the media in which tobacco products can be advertised or legislation enabling the use of reflective materials on vehicle number plates are a couple of examples.
- *E = Economic.* What are the global, national and regional economic trends? Are there business cyclical movements likely to affect your marketplace? Monetary control measures, interest rates, tax changes – they may all represent opportunities or threats.
- *S = Social.* Movements under this heading tend to be long term. They nevertheless demand consideration since social trends in a country may well represent opportunities to be exploited by the astute. Such trends may, for example, relate to an increasingly important market among the elderly – since this group, predominantly female, is continuously growing in size, absolutely and relatively, in many developed nation populations – or to the greater disposable income of young unmarrieds.
- *T = Technological.* Whereas most social trends occur gradually and

can, for the most part, be readily forecast, technological trends are characterized by an ever-increasing rate of change. Technological forecasting is often fraught with difficulties. It can, however, be of crucial importance to many significant management decisions. Frequently the decision to lay down capital equipment at high cost has to be taken with the considerable chance that technology development could soon make obsolete the product about to be newly marketed. It is for this reason that in many fast-moving industries, such as consumer electronics, intelligence about technological development is vital and commands considerable sums of money while efficient and swift market penetration by the products of existing technology carries a high premium.

Central to the external marketing environment in which you operate and demanding close attention are the activities, the strategies and the likely responses of competitors. Competition may be direct and arise from competitors who meet the needs of the marketplace broadly in the same way that you do. For example, a restaurant is likely to be seen as a direct competitor to another restaurant in the same locality. Or competition may be indirect, where the customers' needs are met by a different form of product or service. Indirect competition for the restaurant may well be a variety of other 'evening out' entertainments competing to fulfil the market's need for leisure activity. The company marketing paper clips needs to be aware not only of the strengths and weaknesses of other paper clip marketers but also of the companies marketing staples and staplers. They additionally need to be alert to the threat from such an innovative product as 3M's Post-It Notes – a product which has done so much to revolutionize the way in which notes are transmitted within companies and on internal and external correspondence.

Keeping a vigilant eye on competitors is an important task for the marketing man or woman. Direct competitors may be able to steal a technological march on you or demonstrate their sensitivity to changes in fashion, develop strengths in their organizations in converting earlier weaknesses or in other ways threaten your market share. They will gain advantage unless you are alert to the need for change.

Indirect competition is more difficult to assess than direct. It may represent a force that will always take a relatively consistent share of the market which is thereby closed to you. There may in many markets, though, be an innovative company, not competing directly with you, which revolutionizes a marketplace and totally disturbs the traditional pattern of market shares. Failure to recognize such threats and the movements they cause until too late has been the downfall of many apparently well-established companies. Examples are many: the American railroad operators described by Theodore Levitt in defining 'Marketing Myopia', or the diecast model vehicle manufacturers who held sway in the toy market and failed to respond to the thrust from electronics into that market.

Another aspect of competitive activity which demands attention is the likely nature of competitors' responses to your actions. Are your major competitors leaders or followers, aggressive or slow to change course, innovative or likely to match each action of yours, broad market competitors or keen on avoiding direct competition by seeking less-occupied segments to exploit? If you are able to determine your marketing plan with a general understanding of the likely environmental consequences the greater the chance of your being successful; you will have thought through the potential problems arising from your marketing decisions and will have contingency solutions at hand. You will have refrained from actions which are likely to be damaging in terms of the responses they prompt.

An obvious example might lie in the area of pricing strategy. It might be thought self-evident that it is distinctly dangerous to adopt a price-cutting stance if your major competitor is supported by a lower production cost structure than you are. It is strange how often such a mistake is made in many markets even when it should be clear that, if prompted, competitors will use their economic production advantages to squeeze the initiator's profit margins and do immense, possibly terminal, damage.

The marketing plan

As we have seen, the marketer's aim must be to put together a marketing plan which encompasses consideration of each element in the marketing mix and concentrates on strategic issues based on competitive differential advantage. These are likely to be found in areas where the company recognizes that its strengths lie and will be directed at market sectors where those strengths are considered relevant to consumer needs.

Included within the plan, therefore, will be the fruits of careful consideration of the following aspects of marketing:

1 Product:
   (a) The product lines to be offered, the range and variations – qualities, design features and functions.
   (b) Product development policy – product ideas for future exploitation and research and development or technology search activity required to provide them.

(c)   Range rationalization – concentration on the most profitable mix; decisions on product lines to be dropped.

2   Market:
(a)   The broad market at which product or service are aimed.
(b)   The target market segment(s) where needs are most closely matched with the company's ability to provide benefits.

3   Branding:
(a)   Policy relating to the use of the company name/individual brand names.
(b)   Applicability of the brand name in overseas markets at which the company aims.
(c)   Private label opportunities/unbranded product sales.

4   Packaging:
(a)   Product protection.
(b)   Product display.
(c)   Promotional packs.

5   Channels of distribution:
(a)   Policy regarding direct sales/via distributor sales.
(b)   Distributor motivation.
(c)   Multiple retailer cooperation and the means to promote it.

6   Personal selling:
(a)   The emphasis to be placed on sales force activity in selling to:
    (i)   End users
    (ii) Distributors
    (iii) Key accounts
(b)   The use of specialist sales forces with expertise related to the needs of particular sectors of the market.

7   Display:
(a)   The emphasis to be placed on display at point-of-sale.
(b)   Use of merchandising techniques to enhance display.
(c)   Deployment of specialist merchandisers.

8   Marketing communications:
(a)   Target audiences for communications activity – end users, distributors, decision makers, influencers, etc.
(b)   Communications phase – awareness, inducing trial, motivating repeat purchase, consolidating brand loyalty.
(c)   Relative importance of main media advertising, sales promotion, public and press relations, direct mail, etc.
(d)   Media choice for advertising – television, press, radio, cinema, outdoor.
(e)   Corporate and product positioning – the image you wish to be projected.

(f) Use of sales promotion techniques for trade cooperation, for end-user objectives.

9 Services:
   (a) Provision of pre-sales services, e.g. feasibility study, test run, free trial.
   (b) Point-of-sales services, e.g. delivery, installation, user manual.
   (c) After-sales services, e.g. breakdown servicing, preventative maintenance, spare parts availability, supply of consumables after the installation of equipment.

10 Physical handling:
   (a) Warehousing.
   (b) Inventory levels – the need to sustain availability at an economic inventory financing cost.
   (c) Distribution logistics.

11 Data collection, analysis and measurement:
   (a) Determining the means of acquiring data relating to market, customers and prospects, competitors.
   (b) Data relating to quantified objectives within the marketing plan to allow for periodic progress measurement – from internal company and external sources.

These headings suggest a wide range of decision-making areas relevant to a marketing plan for product or service. Not all will apply in all circumstances – an obvious example would be the irrelevance of point-of-sale considerations for an industrial capital equipment sale. Nevertheless, the basic elements of the marketing mix remain constant for almost all marketplaces and marketing situations – fast-moving consumer product, industrial component or financial service. What varies from situation to situation, product type to product type is the emphasis placed on each element in the mix. Thus great stress is likely to be placed on advertising and sales promotion in marketing plans for frequent-purchase consumer goods while industrial products may well concentrate much more heavily on achieving differentiation in product features and on the importance of the sales force in communicating with customers and prospects.

The development of modern marketing

The primacy of the consumer was clearly recognized as far back as the last quarter of the eighteenth century when Adam Smith was writing that 'Consumption is the sole end and purpose of all production'. Yet the modern concept of marketing has only been developed in recent decades.

Changes during the nineteenth and the first half of the twentieth centuries have been well documented – they moved Britain and much of continental western Europe from being composed largely of agrarian communities to the developed nations we see today. It is the more recent changes in marketing and the marketing environment which are interesting to look at briefly. It is among these that we shall find issues which exercise the minds of marketing people today and into the foreseeable future.

The pace of change

A significant contrast between earlier times and the present day lies with the rate of change in the marketing environment. Social, economic and, particularly, technological change occurs at an ever-increasing pace. Business decisions have to be taken swiftly and with a degree of flexibility in approach which was unheard of a few years ago. Japanese consumer electronics companies are reported to be carrying out new product development at a frenetic pace – no longer does the competitive scene allow for sequential activities, each sequence marked by go/no go decision making before moving on to the next. In order to increase the speed with which the company can arrive at a viable end-product the development team divides its activities among individuals working closely together who carry out as many as possible of the activities either simultaneously or with considerable overlap. Good communication continuously within the team means avoiding most of the problems which might be expected from such an approach. The rewards of being ahead of competition with the newest technological advance may be immense, particularly if swift and effective marketing action is taken to build sales before competitors can respond.

Such speed of change puts great pressure on marketing management. It demands of them closer monitoring of the marketing environment, swift attention to brand development, a shorter timeframe within which to show profitable returns from marketing investment, constant reappraisal of the competitive scene – manufacturing capacity with the advantage of low wage rates shifts from country to country, e.g. Japan to Taiwan to South Korea with the possibility of a swing towards Brazil or elsewhere in Latin America. Altogether an alert flexibility is, and will increasingly be, vital for successful marketing.

Environmental concerns

Growth has been an important objective in recent
however, voices are raised about the impossib
greater consumption in a world of finite resource
ingly with ethical problems posed by the contr
produce mountains in the western developed world and ...
of diet among the Third World nations.

Closely allied questions are posed about the effects of our actions in
pursuit of commercial objectives upon our global environment – green-
house effects from fossil fuel burning for electricity production and the
powering of motor vehicles, holes punched in the protective ozone layer
by CFCs in aerosols and refrigerators.

That such concerns are being more widely recognized in the developed
world is evidenced by the proportion of votes cast for the 'Greens' in
many parliamentary elections in Western Europe in the late 1980s.
Marketers will ignore such concerns at their peril. Socially-responsible
marketing, as it might be called, will have increasing relevance. It will
strike a chord with growingly important market segments. Influential
consumers may well put more stress on good value in products and
services which show environmental sensitivity than on conspicuous
consumption. Politicians will bow to the pressures and tighten the legal
constraints within which manufacturers have to operate.

Self-regulation

Legal constraints arc important in the world of advertising and sales
promotion. In Britain self-regulatory controls are also of significance. The
Advertising Standards Authority publishes the Codes of Advertising
Practice and of Sales Promotion Practice and exercises a watchdog
function over adherence to the provisions contained within them. These
Codes are regularly revised to reflect changes in public opinion and to
ensure that as industries newly employ advertising and sales promotion
techniques the provisions of the Codes are extended to ensure continu-
ance of protection of consumer interests.

The Codes also have international influence. The British Codes and the
International Codes published by the International Chambers of Com-
merce have much common ground. This increases the likelihood of the
British Codes bearing considerable weight in discussions about regula-
tion which will undoubtedly take place in Brussels or elsewhere as the
'Single European Market' becomes a reality.

e retail scene

This is an ever-changing area of crucial importance to the marketing community. As the number of independent retail outlets diminished and the multiple retailers took a fast-increasing share of fast-moving consumer goods trade the problems of the branded goods marketer have multiplied. Demonstration of the speed of change is given by the fact that the number of grocery outlets halved between 1971 and 1985; whereas independents controlled 42.5 per cent of all commodity turnover in 1971 their share had fallen to 18.3 per cent by 1985. Conversely multiples increased share from 44.3 per cent to 70.1 per cent despite a fall in the number of grocery outlets they operated from just under 11,000 to 4500 by 1985. In 1985 the top 10 per cent of shops held 80 per cent of all commodity turnover in the retail grocery trade. Sales per square foot of shelf space per week in multiples increased from £2.90 to £9.24 between 1977 and 1986 at current prices, a change of almost 220 per cent over ten years.

This concentration has put tremendous pressure upon branded goods suppliers. Their problems – and possibly opportunities – have increased further as multiple retailers have aimed to promote their own brands. By December 1986 28.7 per cent of packaged grocery turnover consisted of private label brands; paper goods, at 40.1 per cent and dairy products, at 38.5 per cent, saw private label share in those commodity sectors well above the average.

This concentration of power in multiple retailer hands has brought restriction of distribution for many manufacturers since in many commodity fields the retailer will give shelf space only to the brand leader, one or two others with considerable advertising budgets and to its own-label product. In response manufacturers have greatly increased the proportion of their communications budgets which is spent on sales promotion techniques of various kinds – these tend to place emphasis upon impact at the point-of-sale while many are tantamount to 'buying' distribution by offering special financial inducements to retailers thus increasing their margin or enabling them to undercut their competitors.

Another response has been to direct product and marketing effort not at the broad market but at specialist segments within it. In this way the modest broad market share holder can perhaps become brand leader in an important segment of the market for whom the retailer finds it profitable to cater.

Market segmentation

This is not a brand new, freshly-minted aspect of marketing. It is, however, a facet of marketing expertise which has been growing in importance in recent years and which it is vital to understand for success in the world's increasingly competitive markets. It is dependent upon detailed understanding of consumer needs – but, then, all astute marketing is that. What that understanding will bring is alertness to the existence of groups of consumers characterized by relative homogeneity of need within each group. The needs of different groups will in some ways – often subtle – be different.

A good example might be the tea market. The broad marketplace is dominated, very competitively because it is not one of the young, fast-growing markets, by a number of major brands – PG, Typhoo, Brooke Bond – and price competition is intense. But brands such as Ridgways and Twinings have carved successful niches for themselves at significantly enhanced price levels by appealing to segments of the tea market which are keen to drink, or to be seen to be drinking, regularly or on special occasions, specialist teas from named growing areas. They are prepared to pay a premium price for the pleasure of doing so.

Valid segmentation for marketing purposes can be based on various types of differentiating factors: demographic – age, sex; socioeconomic; lifestyle – characteristics based upon the shape and composition of the household; psychographic factors – all to do with the individual's self-projection and how he or she wishes to be perceived by others; personal taste; geographic – where customers close to the marketer may value especially attentive service. In business-to-business markets valid segmentation might relate to the size of the purchasing company – in employee numbers, or turnover, or output, or number of locations; to the precise nature of its operations (e.g. a large commercial printer may well have different needs in terms of printing plates and chemicals from an in-company print department even though the output of both is printed material); or to the inclinations of management – since some managements like to be in the forefront of new developments and are open to the value of innovation while others are distinctly conservative in approach and averse to risk-taking.

Market segments can be discerned in most markets by careful analysis of consumer needs: if the segment is large enough, sufficiently distinctive and discrete in terms of contact and communication and potentially profitable the marketer will do well to design all the elements of the marketing mix to fit as closely as possible the needs of the target segment and so gain competitive advantage.

Market segmentation can be a significant means by which product life cycles can be extended. It is in the nature of almost all markets that they grow from their initial point when the innovative product idea is launched through increasing familiarity characterized by a rapid growth towards maturity and saturation when growth rates fall and eventually the market goes into decline. The astute marketer will want to avoid the inevitable decline of his brand and extend the validity of the technology. He or she will be aware of changing needs among specific groups – or will become aware of groups with needs previously unsuspected – and will develop products or services specific to newly-emerging segments and so revive the fortunes of a flagging product range.

As societies develop from concern with the basic necessities of life – food, drink, temperature – to higher levels in the hierarchy of needs (as described by A. L. Maslow) such as ego needs and self-fulfilment so greater fragmentation appears to develop – a desire for individualization. So basic commodity markets fragment into multisegmented markets. The staple bread market divides up to meet the needs of a wide variety of tastes and fashions and fads; the multiple retailer will cater both for the bulk demand for the packaged sliced white loaf and for the customer seeking wholemeal, or malted or poppy-seeded or French style and so on.

Indeed, whereas there has been great concentration of retail distribution power in the hands of a few multiple grocers – as shown earlier – there has also been simultaneous development of retailer segmentation. While the great retail chains project their chosen images in order to gain the loyalty of the largest possible proportion of the local population the specialist retailers catering for specific interest segments – ethnic segments, taste and fashion segments – have grown in numbers and importance. Important retail groups have grown up basing their success on a carefully defined image meticulously projected to appeal to particular groups – Habitat, Next, Mothercare, Benetton are good examples. The more recent difficulties of the Storehouse Group in no way diminish the individual success of Habitat or Mothercare but illustrate rather the difficulty of combining retail images each distinct in its appeal to its own target segment.

The changing media scene

The theme of segmentation can be seen continuing into the media scene. This is important to the marketer in that it increases opportunities to communicate effectively with specific interest groups. It can be seen in television chiefly with the advent of Channel 4, the commercial channel with many programmes targetted at minority interests providing, thereby, segment audiences tailormade for some advertisers. The commercial viability of cable television and of satellite television will be dependent largely upon their ability to deliver market segment audiences which match the targets of advertisers.

In the field of printed media also segmentation has importance, particularly among magazines, both consumer and trade and technical. Increasingly beside a handful of major publications which fill the broad central ground of an interest area there will be a proliferation of smaller circulation journals catering for specific interest groups. The effect for the advertiser tends to be an increase in the cost of reaching a thousand readers but a significant reduction in wastage caused by reaching readers who fall outside the target segment. Journals of interest to computer users are a good case in point.

Another aspect of the changing media scene which needs our attention is brought about by the restriction on time available to the advertiser on commercial television. Supply and demand equations apply. Since it is recognized that television advertising carries considerable impact, advertisers have long aimed to use the medium if they can afford to. Falling audiences for the commercial channels might have been expected to reduce demand and therefore bring about cost stability at the least. Unfortunately for the fast-moving consumer goods advertisers who have traditionally used the medium they have been joined in recognizing its efficacy by many other advertisers commanding considerable budgets – privatization issues, corporate defence against would-be acquisition invaders, financial services companies happy at deregulation and competing mightily to handle our money, etc. The effect has been the lifting of television advertising costs well beyond inflation rates.

Many advertisers hoped that we might one day see limited advertising on BBC TV but that was not a recommendation of the Peacock Committee. There has been a slight increase in the amount of time allowed for commercial breaks in Independent TV programme output. But the chief hope for relief from the ever-upward pressure on the real cost of broadcasting commercials must come from the growing significance of cable and satellite television channels.

Another medium of increasing advertising significance must be commercial radio. Commercial radio on a local basis has been around for some years. Many of the stations outside the capital have found it difficult to make profits but commercial radio seems on its way to being strengthened on a planned national basis. That it is here to stay is not really in doubt. Advertisers and their agencies probably have to come to a better understanding of how to use the medium effectively. This should involve clearer understanding of the audiences delivered by commercial radio at different times of day/days of week and of their needs and of how to use the medium effectively to convey the advertising message. That has so far been mastered by relatively few – surprisingly so in the light of the excellence of so much British television advertising.

The changing agency scene

Changes in the world of advertising agencies and other marketing communications services companies have been more of emphasis than of basic kind. As more and more such companies have come into degrees of public ownership by way of the Unlisted Securities Market or the Stock Exchange so for many groups of agency senior managers new priorities have come to the fore. This has complicated their tasks even if it has brought them considerable paper wealth; in addition to the difficult problems associated with managing a creative 'people' business while satisfying demanding clients in an increasingly competitive world it has also brought the problems of satisfying the demands from the financial markets for a better and better return on their investment. Growth has had to come from a restless acquisition quest. Agencies such as Saatchi and Saatchi or WCRS have busily acquired other advertising agencies and have also built strengths by acquisition in other areas of marketing communications services – public relations, sales promotion, creative design, etc. They have aimed to increase their geographic coverage by acquisitions in the US and elsewhere.

Such acquisitiveness has had more logic in meeting the demands for growth from the financial markets with their agency equity holdings than, realistically, with the operating circumstances of a marketing communications conglomerate. Such organizations are not without their operating problems – client conflicts, coordination of the activities of disparate and geographically separated units, resolution of the conflict between financial performance targets and the demands of clients for service and creative output – these are just some examples. Another obvious difficulty, should there at any time be depression of the share price, is vulnerability to acquisition from other marauders. Further problems arise from the fact that the assets of advertising agencies are embodied very largely in their staff. Client loyalties are often to the particular team within the agency handling the account: should that team decide to move away and set up on their own the account might well move with them. If the large agency groups become too concerned with financial targets they may well be creating an atmosphere which fails to induce loyalty from talented employees seeking very special forms of job satisfaction.

Thus there are tensions in the agency scene which have grown up in recent years and which will probably continue to grow. In all likelihood we shall see large stock market-quoted agency groups increasing in number and importance but it is almost certain that independent advertising agencies set up by talented individuals wishing 'to do their own thing' will continue to proliferate. In that sense the lively variety of the advertising agency scene in this country will be constant.

A discernible trend of another kind in the agency scene is a reflection of the increasingly competitive marketing environment in which so many companies operate. Clients are being forced by competition to be cleverer in managing the development of marketing strategy in order to survive. We have seen that this means closer understanding of the benefits which consumers seek in order to build differential advantage into the marketing mix. Advertising agencies are having to reflect this closer understanding of the consumer marketplace. The best of them, with intelligent account planning functions, have been in the forefront of uncovering consumer motivations in order to develop highly effective communications strategies. In those many fast-moving consumer goods markets where the physical differences between products and product functions are minimal the whole onus for differentiation is likely to fall upon advertising and other communications activities. Tough competition in the marketplace brings such issues into ever-sharper focus and makes greater demands on agencies and other communications services providers. Those companies meeting those demands from their clients will be the ones deserving the marketer's support and loyalty in the coming decades.

BIBLIOGRAPHY

Davidson, Hugh. *Offensive Marketing.* (Penguin Business Library, 1987)
Hart, Norman A. *Practical Advertising and Publicity.* (McGraw-Hill, 1988)
Kotler, Philip. *Marketing Management; Analysis, Planning and Control*, 6th edn. (Prentice-Hall, 1988)
Porter, Michael E. *Competitive Strategy.* (The Free Press, 1980)
Wilmshurst, John. *The Fundamentals and Practice of Marketing*, 2nd edn. (Heinemann, 1984).

2

The advertiser

Kenneth Miles

All advertising begins with the advertiser – the company or individual with products or services offered to buyers. The advertiser may depend substantially on other people to turn his selling activities into effective advertisements but since it is his product and his money which starts the whole process, it seems sensible for this book to start with his point of view. This chapter concentrates on the operation and attitudes of the advertiser himself.

A look back into history will reveal many examples of products being offered for sale from the early days of the printing press; indeed, one can go back a great deal further to Roman, Greek and earlier times when messages or signs were placed outside shops to give some indication of the trade being carried on there. Of course, when society takes a simple form with small towns or communities, the need for this kind of advertising message is fairly limited; but even in simple rural societies the beginnings of a selling message can be apparent.

I do not know that a look back into history helps us very much to understand the nature of today's advertising, but those examples of nineteenth and early twentieth century advertising which still survive today are of more than academic interest, since they show clearly the messages and the visual devices which have been effective during the last hundred years – some of which still survive today. The message can only develop in step with the ability of the receiver to understand and respond to it; this is one of the reasons why advertising is a good indicator of the verbal and pictorial interest of ordinary people from one decade to another.

Why companies and individuals advertise

While we conventionally think of advertising as an announcement by a manufacturer of consumer goods, nevertheless advertising can take many different forms. The subject may be goods or services or jobs; it may be a public announcement by the Government or some other body, or it may be the 'small ads' by individuals. Overall, however, the objectives and motives of the advertiser are the same – he or she wants to inform possible customers of what is on offer, and persuade them to buy his goods or accept his point of view. We may summarize this by saying that he wishes to 'sell' to the public even though the subject of the sale may not be tangible and may not be immediate. The other aspect which is essential to understand is that the advertiser is using this form of selling as an alternative to face-to-face selling – probably because he wishes to sell on a substantial scale and to people he cannot meet individually.

Advertising, then, is an essential part of selling, provided we use that word in the broadest rather than in the narrow sense. It has two components, information and persuasion, and the mix of these is capable of infinite variety. Anyone who has ever framed an advertisement – even a classified ad in the local paper – will know how important it is to try and get inside the mind of the likely buyers to decide what form of information they will welcome, and what form of persuasion they will respond to.

A simple notice placed outside a house 'House for Sale – Immediate Possession' contains elements of persuasion but also factors which might deter a potential buyer. When we get on to company advertising for products or services, we can see several objectives operating in parallel and sometimes in conflict with each other.

The first objective may be to *inform* you of the qualities of the particular product so that you can bear it in mind when you are ready to make a purchase. The second objective may be to persuade you to *buy* soon; the third to convince you of the *quality* of the goods available so that you will know what to look for when you are approaching a purchase or discussing it with someone else. A fourth objective might be to persuade you of the long term quality and reliability of the *company* and its products, including the fact that they will still be there if you want to come back and make another purchase or get some after-sales service.

Sometimes these objectives are treated separately in different advertisements, sometimes they are all rolled up into one. That is why it is absolutely essential for the advertiser to be clear what he wants to achieve at any particular time. There are no set rules – it is impossible to say that only one objective should be pursued in any one advertisement because the human mind does not necessarily work so simply. Nevertheless, if the advertiser is confused about what he wants to say, then the probability is that his advertisement will also be confused and will be less effective.

And it is with the effectiveness of his advertisement that the advertiser is principally concerned. As I have said, this is a selling message used as an alternative to the other possible ways of making a sale. Advertising must be effective and productive in its selling – if it is not, then it is money wasted and the advertiser should find an alternative way of communicating his selling message. After all, these do exist as we can see from those companies who run effective operations without spending more than a very small amount of money on advertising.

How advertisers organize themselves

In a small or one-man company, advertising decisions, like all others, are taken by the individual at the top, who is responsible for everything. In most commercial operations, however, there is a degree of specialization and this is particularly true of advertising and marketing sections of the company. Let us be clear that there is no single right way of organizing the management structure responsible for advertising within a company – nevertheless, we can see some clear trends that have emerged over recent years and consider why they have taken place.

In the period up to the 1950s, most companies probably had an advertising department working in parallel with the sales department. These were days of relative stability when a company's place in the market and its product range were broadly familiar. To over-simplify a little, the production people produced the goods, the sales force went out and sold them and the advertising department was responsible for material that told customers about these products – advertising was, to a substantial extent, a support service to the sales force.

When in the 1950s more competitive marketing opportunities emerged and developed in the UK, the management pattern tended to change. Marketing departments were formed in which there were a number of energetic managers responsible for developing, launching and building products or brands that might be quite new to the market. These marketing people – brand managers or marketing managers – became responsible for all aspects of a range of products. They would analyse their markets, identify opportunities, organize the product development, the packaging, brief the sales force on how the product should be sold to distributors, and above all, decide upon the advertising message to the final customer. In these circumstances, advertising specialists or specialist departments tended to disappear and to be replaced by integrated marketing groups in which everyone was knowledgeable about advertising. They would not be advertising specialists but they would work closely with the Agency and others outside the company in order to turn the marketing and advertising objectives of the company into finished form.

On the whole, this process worked well for many years and is still to be found in a great many companies. For full effectiveness, however, it depends on thorough training and very good working relationships both within the company and outside the company. Where it may work least effectively is in companies where, because of size or other reasons, there is no great continuity in the individuals holding these advertising and marketing responsibilities, leading to a stop/start pattern of activity which is bad for the advertising content of the product.

Another development which affects this kind of management structure is that the advertising world has become increasingly complex in the last decade. The choice of advertising media available, and the rapid change in their rise and fall, together with the increasing competitiveness in most major markets – all these factors mean that companies do need expert knowledge and advice on developments within the advertising world that may affect them and their product in a crucial manner. A delay of a year or even a month in picking up a trend or development which one's competitors are following may be very costly to a company.

In consequence we now see an increasing number of advertisers aware once again of the need for specialists who can concentrate on certain areas of advertising activity in parallel with the work of brand managers and marketing managers. Many companies have, for years, had a market research specialist and possibly a promotions specialist we now see a return to the need for a media specialist. His role is not only to evaluate individual media plans, arrange block buying and group discounts etc; he will also be called upon to understand and analyse the changing media opportunities and requirements of the company and its competitors. With the advent of international media, direct broadcast satellites and the like, he may well need to look several years into the future as well as examining contemporary media. This role may be carried out by an advertising specialist within the company, or a specialist adviser from outside to supplement the work and understanding of company management. Whichever way it is handled, the need for advertising and media specialists is clearly growing.

The media and the message

One of the perennial questions in advertising is – where does the advertising plan start? Is it a decision that the advertising should carry a particular message or that it should appear in particular media? There is no clear answer to this question, but a little time spent on examination may help to explain the problems facing the advertiser.

The perception of a product or service which the potential customer holds will contain many elements. It will include the name of the product (and indeed of the company); some idea about its use or purpose; identification of some kind such as its packaging or a label; and of course a statement of the benefits which it offers the customers, usually presented in the form of advertising. All these factors we may summarize as 'The Message' and in many cases they are decided before the specific advertising decision is even approached. The question may then appear to be 'Do we advertise it on television, in the press, on posters, at exhibitions, etc.,' but in effect a part of that decision about the message will have already been made.

For some mass consumer products these will be integrated decisions so that the advertising approach to be followed at the launch stage may well determine the look of the pack and the claims made about the product outside the advertising itself. In general, however, a company will form a fairly close outline of the product, its performance and its benefits *before* the specific media are considered. In the advertiser company, therefore, we may say that probably the discussion about the message comes before the media decision. In an advertising agency, however, this may be the reverse – particularly with those packaged products which are likely to use television as the major part of their advertising communication.

There is thus an essential difference between the way advertisers and agencies approach the whole subject of communication. This is perhaps one of the sources of the differences between them which sometimes may lead to friction and to disagreement. It is all the more important therefore to examine how the advertiser views his agency, how he chooses the agency, how he briefs and works with the agency. In many cases the agency may have a very long-term relationship with the advertiser and be seen almost as an extension of his own department. This contains many advantages in terms of closely integrated thinking, but it may also lead to problems if the agency fails to take the objective attitude which the client really needs in assessing the market and the consumer.

Choosing, briefing and evaluating the agency

In the advertising world more time is spent on the subject of 'client/ agency relationships' than any other single area. The issue is reported frequently in the marketing and advertising press – usually in terms of a news report about an agency appointment or an agency sacking; and it is also regularly a subject on the agenda at programmes, seminars and training sessions. The choice of an agency is not the only major decision which an advertiser may make during the course of a year but it can certainly be the most far-reaching and it is essential that it is approached not only on subjective grounds, but also as a professional management decision. A good relationship between client and agency may be fundamental to the success, not only of the campaign, but of the product as a whole.

At its best, this is a working relationship in which professionals on the client side work closely with those in the advertising agency to produce communication which truly reflects the needs and aspirations of the client's marketing programmes. In many cases the agency staff know almost as much about the client's business as he does himself and may well be in a better position to make sound judgements on what is needed. A relationship of this kind can be truly effective to the advertiser and satisfying for all concerned.

One reason advertisers often fail to get the best out of their working relations with their agencies is lack of knowledge of just how the agency functions. An agency has only three things to sell its clients – its time, its talent and the way that it organizes them. A clear understanding of these basic elements will more often than not enable an advertiser to establish and maintain a fruitful working relationship, and thereby avoid the popular malaise of too frequently changing from one agency to another.

The roots of a profitable and enduring client/agency partnership lie in the early establishment of a set of working rules or disciplines, preferably set out in a clear, written agreement. But these, however well they may be constructed, cannot overcome the problems created by inefficiency on the part of either client or agency.

The seeds of a poor relation between advertiser and agency often stem from insufficient attention being given at the outset to finding the agency that can most nearly fill the advertiser's particular needs. Once the agency is selected, the first essential discipline to observe is to follow a clearly defined pattern in establishing the method of contact between the advertiser and his agent. Nothing is more harmful to the working relationship than ill-defined or ill-observed lines of communication. It is important for the agency to know who has responsibility for the eventual approval of the advertising. If it is the managing director, then the agency must know to what extent the advertising or brand manager, marketing manager or director has the authority to demand changes in the plans en route to the top.

Many a weak advertising campaign is the result of compromise between the agency's original proposals and the demands of the client as each rung of the ladder is climbed. One way round the problem of approval, a way that allows the advertiser the chance to comment at all levels and yet allows the agency the opportunity of sticking to its beliefs, is to lay down that any revisions demanded by brand management to the agency's creative proposals on their way up the ladder should not prevent the agency in their final presentation to the ultimate boss from submitting, alongside the amended proposals, the scheme they planned at the outset.

A clearly defined formal system of contact and approval, although essential, is not the whole answer to a fruitful relationship, but it is the right basis on which to build. To this foundation the advertiser must add, not once but continually, the spark of inspiration that will galvanize the actions of the agency. He must become, in effect a miniature,Diaghilev, repeatedly seeking ways and means of maintaining the creative team at a high level of performance, while at the same time preventing the erosion and disillusion that are born of relations which, with the passage of time, can become stale and sterile.

What are the major causes that create such a situation? Consider the following:

1 Incompatibility of personnel.
2 Falling sales – competitive growth.
3 Changes in agency staffing or ownership.
4 Financial instability of either party.
5 General dissatisfaction with the advertising campaigns.
6 Poor servicing of the account.
7 Client reorganization or acquisition.
8 Changes in the basic terms of contract.
9 Lateness in payment of bills.

Of these nine points, only 3, 4 and 7 provide problems that cannot be solved by discussion and amendment.

On point 2, which is often the basis for a parting of the ways, it must be accepted that many factors other than the advertising can contribute to this state of affairs, and it should be the concern of both client and agency to explore these in full before condemning the advertising as the guilty party.

It must be understood that the agency is in business on its own account. It exists, as does a manufacturer, by seeking to run its business profitably and by maintaining its margins and expanding its trade as best it can; and this course is not always clearly appreciated or accepted by advertisers, some of whom imagine that by bestowing their 'royal appointment' on the chosen agency, they have secured, if not a humble slave at least an accredited genie ready at the slightest rubbing of their 'brass' to carry out their instant demands. This sort of attitude on the part of the client may cause much bad advertising to see the light of day.

On the other hand, if we accept that the agency is in business on its own account, we realize that its aims coincide only up to a point with those of the advertiser. What is good for the advertiser is not necessarily good for the agency. Once this is accepted, the dual nature of the relationship comes into focus, and the basis for future harmony can be established; as in all marriages, it is the long haul that counts.

The early intimacies and confidences which, during the honeymoon period, are exchanged only too readily (less readily by some clients than others), need to be developed at a later stage into a formal working relation in which there is a free flow of information; at this stage the client must feel confident that in imparting knowledge of his business, which is often of high security, he can do so knowing that the agency will respect this fact, and act as though they were part of the company.

The discipline of a firm timetable in planning the advertising is an essential ingredient of good client/agency relations. Any advertiser who fails to start his marketing planning sufficiently far ahead to allow both himself and his agency adequate time for all likely eventualities is creating conditions that will bring last minute rush, frustration and results poorer than they should be. However, it is no good the advertiser establishing and observing an adequate timetable if the agency does not do likewise.

Strict procedures for checking and prompt payment of invoices are needed in order to avoid the constraint imposed on the relationship by late or suspended payment. Finally, let it be said that it does not automatically follow that the agency is to blame if the advertising is not producing the required results. There are many aspects of the marketing mix which, if incorrect, can nullify the effect of a good advertising campaign. So before firing the agency for this reason, check that your own house is in order.

What the agency has to offer

Firstly, let us consider why, if at all, one should contemplate using an advertising agency. Indeed, in some countries, a sizeable number of companies do not. In France, for example, it has been estimated that almost half of all advertisers place their space orders directly with the media and at the same time themselves carry out the production of advertisements, posters, films and print material. On closer examination, however, you will find that those companies who work with advertising agencies are usually the bigger and more proficient at running their businesses, while the companies who work direct are for the most part the more conservative and less dynamic in their approach to business. Some of them have such small budgets as not to justify the use of an agency.

So it would be true to say that the reason why the majority of companies use the services of an agency is that of efficiency. Better to buy out in the market the best facilities and advice available rather than become involved with the problem of trying to reproduce these onself. But there are other and more compelling reasons why companies should follow this course. It is said that 'a prophet is not without honour save in his own country'. This applies to the advertiser who seeks to prescribe and swallow his own medicine. However expert the professionals who staff the advertiser's department may be, they run the risk of being too close to the problem to judge the effectiveness of the advertising's appeal to the outside world. Better and easier for an outside agency to place its head on the creative chopping block in the cause of advertising effectiveness than for one's own staff to do so.

But what the agency has to offer the advertiser is more than know-how and technical or artistic competence. It can provide the means for an exchange between the exterior world and the company, between the outside and the inside, and in the process of this constant exchange of views the message that has to be communicated is stripped of any self-satisfied gloss that an advertiser might himself be tempted to give it, and achieves instead a reality and an effectiveness for the task it has to perform.

Selecting the right advertising agency

Let us assume that you are convinced of the wisdom of employing outside agency help, your next question might reasonably be, How do I set about doing this? The following steps are therefore suggested as a basis for a plan that can be tailored to individual needs:

Stage 1 – Define the need Write down on one page a summary of what you think you need by way of an agency, and broadly what tasks you want it to perform. This will obviously include any international needs.
Stage 2 – Desk research Contact by phone or letter relevant trade organizations in the base country such as The Incorporated Society of British

Advertisers (ISBA). Check the opinion of media and other service personnel whom you respect and then check their opinion with some of the clients serviced by the agencies they recommend. Repeat this process as far as possible in each of the countries in which you propose to advertise.

Stage 3 – Formulate a shortlist   Eliminate all agencies handling competitive business (unless yours is a very large account). Eliminate agencies that do not offer all the services you require. Eliminate agencies likely to be taken over or sold out, unless you know and approve of the 'new' situation.

Stage 4 – Evaluation   Decide the basis on which you will equally evaluate all agencies on your shortlist, e.g. by means of a checklist evaluation or by speculative presentation (doubtful) and then visit each of them. Check their terms of business.

Stage 5 – Narrowing the selection   Assess your evaluations, reduce the shortlist to two or three and then revisit, having informed the agencies that they are in the final listing. From your second (or third) impression correct where necessary your previous assessment and make your final choice.

Stage 6 – Final selection and appointment   Agree the terms of contract, and the date and method of announcement. Inform the other agencies you visited and thank them.

The basis on which you formally evaluate each agency can be varied to suit your own needs, but it should certainly be the same for each agency interviewed. Your checklist will probably include the following.

- Number of staff.
- Turnover and growth.
- Breakdown or turnover between major accounts.
- Financial backing/affiliations.
- Bankers.
- Terms of business – and profitability.
- Membership of professional organizations (e.g. IPA).
- Agency organization and leadership.
- Method of operation.
- Client list (with starting dates).
- Accounts lost in the past two years.
- Account team with whom you would be working (not always the same as the presentation team).

Alternatives to the full service agency

I have devoted a lot of time to the question of choosing and working with an advertising agency because it is at the heart of successful activities on the part of the advertiser. It is not that there is a 'correct' choice of agency awaiting each advertiser so that all his problems will be solved when he finds the perfect match, but it is certainly the case that the time and effort devoted to thinking carefully about one's own needs and objectives should enable the advertiser to exercise the necessary discipline of thought and planning to achieve a satisfactory result. Indeed it can be said in a sense that 'all agencies are good' – provided that the best is brought out of them by the client working well with them.

Nevertheless, the traditional picture of the 'full service agency', re-munerated on the traditional basis of 15 per cent of the gross media cost, is by no means the only way of producing successful advertising. In the 1970s there was a steady growth in specialist agencies – both those specializing in media selection and booking, and those specializing in creative work. It is estimated that these specialist agencies account for something like 20 per cent of all advertising expenditure and probably a higher proportion of the Manufacturers Consumer Advertising (MCA) or mainline advertising. With the formation of the Association of Media Independents, these specialist media companies have a structure which gives them a collective voice in the market. They have contributed towards a greater understanding of the need for close attention to media specialization, in a period (as we have already seen) in which media subjects deserve careful study.

There are many marketing companies now which give some or all of their business to these specialist agencies as an alternative to a full service agency. It is commonplace for one or several brands to be handled on what is known as the 'à la carte' basis – that is to say the advertiser chooses one specialist organization to handle the creative work, another to handle the media booking and perhaps a third to carry out the sales promotion or other activities which the brand may need. It is generally expected that, taking the cost of these activities together, the total com-mission or fee paid will be less than when they are all handled by a full service agency. It is impossible to be sure just how often these charges are genuinely less, because the client may be obliged to carry out, within his own company, some of the activities which would be handled by a conventional agency; but certainly this is the expectation, and many advertisers express themselves pleased and satisfied with the results they are getting from the 'à la carte' approach.

However, it is suggested that if this approach is taken only to reduce immediate costs, then there are dangers ahead. The most important thing is to obtain the highest level of ability and service from the agency handling the advertising, whether this amounts to one agency or a number working independently and if the saving of 1 per cent, 2 per cent or 3 per cent of expenditure is the principal target, then these 'savings' may result in corners being cut. It is of course possible also to save money by negotiating a lower level of commission, or a fee equivalent to a lower level from a full service agency. Some agencies, as a matter of principle, will not do so but in the majority of cases agencies will discuss the subject with a major client if there is a sound basis for a long term agreement. Advertisers who believe their account is 'different' from most others should consider carefully what activities by the full service agency they do not need and which activities they can genuinely expect to call for. On this basis, it is possible to put forward a proposition to an agency and then discuss a lower fee level which may be satisfactory to both sides.

In Britain, we are fortunate that this degree of flexibility exists and has been encouraged by the application of the Restrictive Trade Practices Act to services such as those provided by agencies. Until the late 1970s, tight control was kept on the commission paid by the media to an agency and the rules about 'rebating' this commission to the advertiser. Since this tight hold has been broken, it is now much easier for special arrangements to be freely negotiated. By contrast, in many other countries this flexibility does not exist and this has helped British agencies and media specialists to obtain an increasing amount of business from overseas clients who find London a very strong centre, both in terms of skills and also in terms of the remuneration arrangements which can be found. Advertisers should recognize the wealth of agency ability and choice that exists in Britain.

Budgets and plans

In any examination of the role of the advertiser and his problems, the setting of the budget figure and the making of plans for the advertising campaign must feature among the most difficult areas. Indeed the basis on which budgets are decided will vary so much from one company to another and from one marketing situation to another that it is difficult to generalize in any constructive way.

Let us look at a few possible marketing situations:

(a) Brand launch or major change.
(b) Mature market – holding/increasing your brand share.

(c)   Heavy competitive attack from other brands.

(d)   Declining market – maintaining profitability.

Clearly, the approach to the brand plan and the advertising plan in these different circumstances will require a totally different strategy towards the budget. For example, in launching or re-launching a brand the company will almost certainly set clear volume objectives for sales, for consumer trial, for repeat purchase and so on; and the budget allocated for advertising and promotion will be that which is felt to be necessary to achieve these objectives. The figure will of course not be plucked out of thin air. It will be based on the experience of other brands in other or similar markets in relevant circumstances.

Depending upon the size of the market and the nature of the products, it may be desirable to aim for an almost 100 per cent awareness by the target audience in all parts of the country, with a high requirement for product trial. Alternatively, if the product is directed at a specific minority market, again the objectives for awareness, trial, etc., in relation to competitive products are likely to call for substantial levels of budget spending, probably using a major medium such as television or colour magazines. If the product is an industrial one aimed at business buyers, then heavy coverage in the trade press, in key exhibitions and through direct mail may be called for. In all these circumstances the budget will be set in relation to the advertising objectives appropriate to the launch; at the same time a close watch will be kept on the relation of that spending to the volume expected and the profitability which the company looks for from the launch. It may be that in year one the advertising budget will be disproportionately high in relation to the gross profits of the brand with the expectation of the 'payback' being achieved in say the third year of the launch. However, while this approach was fairly appropriate in the 1960s and 1970s when markets were more stable than today, there are few companies in contemporary circumstances who can be confident that a brand launched will go on increasing or holding its volume and thus justify a long payback period. The majority of companies now look for a payback within a relatively short time from the launch date.

If the market is in a mature state and the advertising objective is to hold share in relation to other competitors, then it is probable that the advertising budget will be fixed in relation to share of total market expenditure. Rule of thumb figures may not be absolutely right but if your brand is holding 25 per cent of a particular market then it is probable that the share of your advertising will be around that figure also. If, to take extremes, you allocate only 10 per cent of total spending in that market, then you are clearly taking a great risk that you may be outspent and out-advertised by your competitors; if on the other hand you allocate 50 per cent of the total expenditure in the market then the probability is that some of your budget will be wasted. Even so, however, it is prudent to allocate a significant sum to a reserve which can be held until it is clear that competitive spending during the year is not going to change dramatically; a Board of Directors may agree to a substantial reserve while insisting that it should not be touched without formal approval.

In a market where competition is extremely heavy and other brands are spending in an attempt to take your market share – or you are aiming to take theirs – clearly it is not desirable to calculate the budget on a rule of thumb basis. In these circumstances it is probable that the total budget – both above and below the line – will be studied carefully in relation to a series of short term objectives, whether defensive or offensive. The effectiveness of every pound spent will be scrutinized closely and discounts given to major buyers, promotional incentives designed to find new customers etc. may be regarded as less cost-effective than a straight defence of the heartland of your market. It is particularly in these circumstances that the key question arises 'Do we want to reinforce our strength or patch up our weaknesses?'. In this situation the decision about the size and nature of the advertising and promotional budget may well be regarded as the key decision towards the brand. Is the company determined to maintain and defend that product – or is it prepared to take chances and let the competition win the battle?

A declining market also presents problems since the aim will probably be to maintain profitability while keeping the product visible in the market. In such circumstances it may well be that the budget decision will centre around an allocation of pounds per ton, or pence per case sold, so that in regions or television areas where sales are still strong, more is allocated to advertise the brand than in areas where the brand is weak. Allocating the advertising budget pro rata to current sales may seem to be a rather negative decision, but it may in fact be a thoroughly realistic manner of allocating scarce resources.

Under the heading of 'Budgets' we should also look at the question 'Is the advertising budget disproportionately high or low in relation to other costs within the responsibility of Marketing Managers?'. This is where market research will almost certainly help to evaluate alternative factors – for example, are the packaging costs justified in relation to the consumer's perception of what packaging contributes? Could savings be made on pack sizes, flavours, colours etc., and used to concentrate on the real strength of the brand through its advertising? Conversely, could a small reduction in the advertising budget bring about disproportionately large improvements in these factors; in distribution, in visibility through public relations activities? The point to remember is that advertising and promotional budgets cannot be seen in isolation from the other costs which are the responsibility of marketing management.

Finally I must mention the self discipline required to allocate a proportion of the budget to research. When funds are tight and budgets are but, it is easy to look at certain items in the overall budget and take them out – research is one of the items which is often most easily cut. I recommend that this decision is only to be taken in extreme circumstances, since research – into the product, the pack and above all the advertising – should be seen as the eyes and ears of marketing management, not as a soft option which can be eliminated. Research, when properly used, can be the way to measure the effectiveness of the day-to-day decisions being taken, particularly about the effectiveness of the advertising and of media decisions, even of the detailed media buying itself. In all budgets except the most savagely cut, a percentage allocated to research should be regarded as a real necessity and not a reluctant gesture.

Advertising and the overall company scheme

For most products, advertising is the most visible part of the product and the company itself. It is particularly important, therefore, that it is given its full value and understanding within the company and it is the job of the marketing and advertising specialist to ensure that this happens. Your first audience is your own colleagues – your sales force. It is not always easy to make them see that advertising is a cost-effective part of the company's total selling effort but that should be the aim.

Opportunities should be taken at sales conferences, in house magazines, and in general conversation to emphasize the objectives and achievements of the company's advertising. This should not be clothed with mystique and regarded as something which is only the concern of the marketing or advertising department, but presented as a major company activity which brings strength and opportunities to the company's products. Advertising should be presented as an investment, not just as a cost. This means, of course, that decisions about advertising investment must be capable of being defended logically and objectively, even though they may often depend on individual experience and flair.

The credit for decisions should be given to other people where appropriate, and you should not be afraid of explaining the role of the advertising agency. It is probable that when your colleagues really understand how an advertising agency works, and what its skills really are, they will be less scornful of the apparent 'waste of money' which many managers in production, accountancy, etc., assume will inevitably be associated with advertising. At the same time, however, always emphasize that the decisions about advertising are made within the company and that you are not the puppets of the advertising agency.

Marketing people sometimes forget that 'their advertising' is not their own property but the property of the company as a whole. It is a great asset of your colleagues, their wives and families are proud of the company's products and proud of its advertising.

Supporting activities in the marketing budget

Because this is a book about advertising, there is only a limited amount of space to devote to the other areas of the marketing budget which may be of great importance for many companies. Sponsorship, point of sale material, exhibitions, public relations, promotions – all of these may have an important part to play in the short-term or long-term objectives of the company or brand. It will always pay to take these activities seriously, even if the final decision is to allocate to them only a small or nil proportion of your total spending. Each year, when plans for the following year are being discussed and agreed, it is recommended that you list a number of subjects of this kind, examine your own practices and those of your competitors and consider whether some investment in these areas could make a contribution. This should not be a token question designed to satisfy yourself that last year's decisions were right and should be repeated again next year; but rather an honest and objective look at possible alternatives, possible support activities which can give an additional dimension to the main areas of your activity and spending.

The marketing manager in a company will have to remember that these decisions must be made by him and that he cannot necessarily expect more than a limited amount of help from his advertising agency. Agency specialists will no doubt honestly and sincerely believe that you will get the best return from your investment by placing it in media advertising. This is after all the area from which the agency draws by far the greatest part of its own revenue and profit. This advice may well be right, but the advertising executive – the client – must bear in mind that these recommendations are not the only ones possible and that other alternatives should be evaluated.

So – look critically at your own budgetary decisions, at your own media split, even at the content of your own advertising. Consider how it may be regarded by somebody standing outside your company and looking in. Consider whether you are putting too many eggs in one basket and whether some of the supporting activities mentioned above could give your customers a new way of looking at your product. You may end up returning to the same decisions with which you began, but at least you will know that you have done so after a full evaluation of the alternatives, not just an assumption that yesterday's decisions will be right tomorrow.

Special situations

Generalizations about advertising are usually made on the basis of fast moving, packaged consumer goods, but there are many other forms of advertising, many other markets which require a different look and some specialist knowledge. We only have the space to mention some of these briefly but they are of great importance for many companies.

International advertising requires a particular discipline and a particular concentration. It is not easy to obtain the necessary knowledge about the media in other countries nor to be sure how your advertising message will really 'translate' into a different country. This is true not only of consumer products but also of industrial ones. It is all the more necessary therefore to make sure that the message and the media which you choose are right for your target audience. The message must not be obscure, it should not involve a play on words, it should not make assumptions about your product or your company which cannot be supported in different markets where your selling may even be carried out by agents not by your own staff. At the same time, it must not also be so bland that it has no point.

Corporate advertising, which is now widely used in North America but is still the exception in Europe, also calls for a long-term approach. While brand advertising may have a promotional or short-term value and is capable of being varied to meet different market circumstances, it is extremely rare that corporate advertising, except around a single event, will achieve very much without a long-term plan.

A short-term approach may mean that money is wasted or merely that it is directed to the wrong objectives. The choice of target audiences, and realism about the achievements of the advertising or other communication, will be crucial if corporate advertising is to achieve the kind of results that you and your chief executive may be looking for.

Direct advertising or marketing – whether through direct mail or face to face communication of some kind – calls for specialist skills which are not always fully appreciated. It is often assumed that 'anyone can write a good letter' and from there that 'anyone can write a good direct mail letter'. Neither of these assumptions should be taken for granted and you only have to look at the quality of what arrives through your letterbox to realize that this is so.

The skills of direct marketing and direct advertising can certainly be taught and they can sometimes be learnt through experience but they should not be taken for granted. On the other hand, when they have been acquired they can serve a very valuable purpose, perhaps doubling or trebling the response rate when compared to a routine communication. The last few years have seen rapid growth in direct marketing expenditure and skills, and we can expect this to continue in the future as more people take the subject seriously and acquire the knowledge that is needed. After all, direct marketing well applied can be 'targeting' at its best, and most companies now use it as part of their activities.

The responsibility of the advertiser

No chapter on the role and the operation of the advertiser can be complete without a look at the wider responsibilities which he bears in addition to those within his own company. It is of course true that his first responsibility is to his company, his product and its long-term success. As I have pointed out, the role of the advertising is to sell in an efficient and cost-effective manner and that must always come first.

At the same time the manager with the responsibilities for advertising must, like the company itself, bear in mind other responsibilities – some of which are obvious, some less so. In the first case he must obey the law of the land, and he must make sure that his advertising does so as well. There are a great many statutes which contain some limitation or requirement where advertising is concerned – indeed in certain industries there is a substantial amount of legislation. Other laws have come into effect in recent years, sometimes as a result of EEC directives, and it is essential that the people with responsibility for advertising are well aware of these legal requirements and take them fully into account. It is rare, at the moment, for legal action to be taken against advertising, but it is not impossible in the future. The first requirement in following the codes of practice is that the advertising should be 'Legal, decent, honest and truthful'.

But of course the major way in which we control the content of advertising is through the self-regulatory system and the Codes of advertising standards and practice. These are covered fully in another chapter but the point to make here is that it is clearly the responsibility of the advertiser to be fully aware of the implications of the Codes, and of the advantages to industry generally of making sure that they are followed in spirit as well as in the letter. The self-regulatory system is not perfect and occasionally a company may feel that its own interests are not being fully taken care of; but it is important to realize that if genuine and continuous support to the self-regulatory system is not given by advertisers, then a new legal system will undoubtedly be imposed, which would result in many more constraints and a much less satisfactory end result.

Above all, advertising and advertisers must recognize an overriding responsibility to the customers. Quite apart from its being against the Codes of practice and (probably) against the law, to deceive or mislead customers through your advertising is just plain bad business. As we all know, it is possible to make a sale once or find a customer once through a misleading claim – the street salesman of shoddy goods trades on this ability – but it is not really possible to stay in business for any period of time if you behave in that way. Emphasis on environmental issues, for example, should not lead a company to overclaim in a way which may mislead its customers. Being truthful, therefore, being informative, being likeable, presenting your company as the kind of people with the kind of products that your customers will want to do business with – this is plain commonsense.

This chapter draws substantially on the one written for an earlier edition by Mr Alastair Sedgwick, formerly a director of Gillette with wide experience of advertising, sponsorship and public affairs. Our thanks are due to Mr Sedgwick for agreeing that his text may be used in this way.

3

The advertising agency

John Josling

The origin of the advertising agency

Early advertising agents were exactly that: they were selling agents for newspapers, receiving commission from those newspapers on the amount of advertising space they could sell to advertisers. Often they would act as media brokers by buying space in quantity and then retailing it to advertisers in smaller portions: the main point to grasp is that their income came from the media, much as it does today – despite the number of changes which we shall discuss later in this chapter.

These early agents soon discovered that it was easier to sell the space if they offered to show the advertiser how the space could be filled – i.e., to design the advertisement and to write the copy. This rapidly grew to a stage in which the agent, from being a one man all-rounder, started to employ specialist writers, designers, and at a later stage, media buyers and production executives.

As the early agencies built up their client lists, clients became more important to them than the media. Thus, although the income of agencies continued to be derived from the media, it was the advertiser that guaranteed their continued use of any particular medium and therefore the commission from it.

The first acknowledged advertising agency was William Taylor, in 1786. The name of Jem White, who started up in Fleet Street in 1800, still exists today in the context of White Bull Holmes, a well known recruitment advertising agency in London.

As advertising developed during the 1920s and 1930s some famous advertising themes emerged: they became famous for two reasons, first originality, and second the fact that they were used consistently for a long period of time. The examples which even today may be remembered are 'Guinness is good for you', 'What we want is Watney's', 'Virol for growing babies', 'Bovril prevents that sinking feeling', 'Players please', 'Craven A does not affect the throat' and many others.

It is interesting to observe that some of these famous slogans would not be admitted today under the series of laws and self-imposed controls which now exist. This former freedom of advertising is particularly noticeable in some of the medical advertisements which ran in the earlier part of the century, making outrageous claims to cure a whole assortment of afflictions.

The changing character of the advertising agency

The period between the two wars was largely one of creative advertising, an era in which flamboyant personalities who ran their agencies in an autocratic manner generated campaigns of great originality, style, panache, and memorability. In this sense they were right for their times, and some of the great entrepreneurs of that period included people like Sir William Crawford, Sir Charles Higham, and Stuart Menzies, and noted writers such as G. H. Saxon Mills.

The advertising agency business has always been one in which individuals have been able to strike out and start up new companies: after the Second World War a number of such individual companies were to be found in London, including companies like Cecil Notley, Everetts, C. R. Casson, Napper Stinton and Woolley, T. Booth Waddicor, Colman Prentis and Varley and many more. But more significant developments were underway in the emergence of larger agencies, heavily influenced by America; there was a general move towards research in assessment of tasks to be done and measuring advertising performance. Big agencies like Young & Rubicam, The London Press Exchange, J. Walter Thompson, McCann Erickson, Erwin Wasey and others built up substantial marketing and research departments (the forerunners of today's planning departments). These departments not only conducted research into what the advertising task was, but also started to become closely involved with clients' own plans for developing and marketing new products. Side by side with this development was the growth of research companies and more sophisticated measurement systems. During the 1950s companies like A. C. Neilsen, Attwoods, and – a little later on – AGB were able to provide highly detailed pictures of consumers' daily activities in purchasing goods, and in the effect advertising had in influencing their choice.

In the early part of the 1950s colour in magazine production gradually improved. It was not at that stage a dominant force on a large scale, apart from a small number of mass-circulation magazines. The newspaper world was comparatively untouched: nevertheless printing techniques were improving all the time, leading to the skills of production buying becoming much more accepted in advertising agencies. Production departments gradually assumed an importance far beyond that which had applied in the 1920s and 1930s, and began to have influence on campaign planning.

Then, in 1955, on 22 September, came an event which was to change the face of advertising – and therefore of agencies. This was the launch of commercial television, largely in black and white in the early days. Until that time most large-scale campaigns had sought to begin with a half page in the old broadsheet *Daily Express* (the leading circulation newspaper at that time); now campaigns were launched with mass television coverage, and the exploitation of this to the appropriate trade distributors of the product concerned. Advertising began to permeate the life of the nation to an extent hitherto unknown, and helped to lead to the acceptance in society of advertising as a commercial weapon. More and more it became an essential part of the market planning of large manufacturers.

Equally, advertising began to attract a more critical eye from the nation. Such was the mushrooming of the advertising industry that the law was amended on a number of occasions to cope with new situations as they arose. One of the most significant measures was the Merchandise Marks Act of 1956, later replaced by the Trade Descriptions Act of 1968, providing a strong legal framework in which advertising has been required to operate.

Side by side with the strengthening of the law, a *voluntary* code emerged, sponsored and supported by the Advertising Association – the body which represents all sides of the advertising business. The Code of Advertising Practice was formed originally in 1961, and was followed in 1963 by the Advertising Standards Authority which carried the status of a semi-official body. This provided a source through which consumers could complain about advertisements: details of complaints were published, with not only the name of the advertiser, but the name of the agency concerned. Thus the agency had over the course of twenty or thirty years become a more professional organization: relying more on professional research and market techniques, carrying a greater sense of ethical and moral responsibility, but at the same time almost exploding with new bursts of creativity as the new medium of television changed the whole scene. Radio advertising started to offer commercial opportunities but its real progress was to come later in the 1980s. Cinema advertising also provided agencies with immense creative opportunities during the 1950s, but its audiences were rapidly affected by the advent of television. But however much cinema audiences changed, creativity in the cinema remained of a very high standard, and does to this day. The late 1980s in fact saw a considerable revival of this important medium.

As the 1960s drew to a close a fresh spark of creativity seemed to light up the London agency scene: what many regarded as the deadening hand of marketing and research techniques was lifted by a new generation of young creative advertising people seeking more exciting ways of communicating in a very competitive world.

Companies like Saatchi and Saatchi and Kirkwoods were formed with the beacon of creativity shining forth. In the late 1970s this rebirth of the creative influence found an important new way of giving expression to itself. The development of 'media brokers' (companies who performed all the media planning, buying and checking work previously done by an advertising agency) enabled bright young creative people to start their own agencies much more easily. The media buying responsibilities and financial risks were passed through to media brokers, who received part of the commission. The fledgling agency was then able to concentrate its energies on the true and final product of any advertising agency – the advertisements themselves. Many agencies which started on this basis are today famous names – companies like WCRS, Gold Greenlees Trott, Bartle Bogle and Hegarty, and many others.

With the competitive business atmosphere emerging everywhere during the early 1980s, a number of monopoly procedures were broken down. Amongst these was the rigid commission system, by which advertising agencies were not allowed to pass back any commission received from the media to their clients. Once this practice was officially deregulated, deals between agencies and clients about the level of commission to be retained by an agency became common. In general terms however, the rule that 'You get what you pay for' applies as much in agency life as in other spheres of business. And gradually it emerged that 15 per cent of the billing often represented roughly the right sort of fee for which an agency could supply a full agency service. It certainly represented a good starting point for negotiation. In some cases this had to be supplemented by an additional fee, since even a full 15 per cent commission did not cover the amount of work an agency did. On other occasions the agency has been satisfied with a commission below the 15 per cent norm: a typical example would be a multimillion campaign using three or four television commercials repeated over the year. An industrial advertising campaign involving dozens of low unit cost trade or technical publications is a very different kettle of fish.

The structure of a modern advertising agency

Account handling

Today's advertising agency is a complete service organization. The point of contact for a client is the account handler, ranging from the board director in charge of an account to account supervisors, account managers and account executives. It is the job of the account handler to maintain contact with his client, building up a full understanding of that client's marketing and advertising situation, so that he or she may brief the agency on what needs to be done. The account handler then plays his role as a member of the agency team in analysing the advertising problem and devising the appropriate solutions. Next, he has the task of

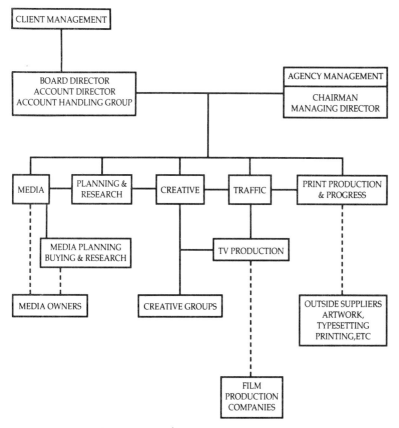

Figure 3.1 *A typical advertising agency*

presenting the agency solution in a clear and articulate manner to client personnel, who could range from middle management level right up to the chairman of the board. Finally, once a campaign has been approved by the client, the account handler is responsible for ensuring that it is implemented. This means supervising the whole process of producing press and poster advertisements in their final form, preparing artwork, proofs, etc., making television films and ensuring that the whole programme of printing and production is completed on time.

The account handler, therefore, has to be a jack of all trades: he needs to be a good all rounder who understands all facets of the business, he must be a clear thinker who can get to the nub of the situation and brief his team accordingly, and he needs some of the skills of a showman in presenting work to a client. Finally he has to be a highly efficient executive to ensure that all parts of the machine are working effectively – and of course, to make sure that the agency gets paid properly and punctually for its work!

To perform this apparently superhuman task, the account handler relies on a number of departments within the agency.

Creative department

The most important department is the creative department, since it produces the product for which an advertising agency exists. Creative departments, headed by an experienced creative director, usually consist of pairs of creative people (one art director and one writer) to work on a series of accounts. Although there is usually a pairing of separate skills, often either the 'visual' or the 'written' content might come from the other partner, so closely do such teams work. The creative team sits in on the original briefing from the account handling group, and is supplied with a steady stream of facts and information about the client concerned. Frequently the creative team produce questions which go beyond the pure process of creativity, since they, like other senior people in the agency, are part of the marketing team. The creative team then produces preliminary creative ideas and roughs, gradually working up to more finished material to show to the client. All creative suggestions must stem from an agreed *plan*: the first task therefore is to ensure that there is an appropriate campaign *strategy*, so that ideas and suggestions for individual advertisements meet a well-defined and relevant overall plan.

Nowadays, the creative department works very closely with *the planning department*.

Planning

Today's planners are the kind of people who would in earlier days have been in either the 'marketing' or research department of an agency. The skills of a planner are to understand a client market thoroughly, to be familiar with the trends in that market, and to be in tune with appropriate marketing strategies which will hold and increase that client's share of the market. At the same time, the planner must be sufficiently flexible in his thinking to be able to sit down with a creative team and evaluate the broad campaign strategy which is most likely to bring the best results for the client. This process comes long before the creation of effective headlines and individual advertising themes.

The planners' tools are all forms of existing market research, often the commissioning of special surveys, and particularly the use of research to evaluate different advertising strategies.

Media

The department in an agency which effectively spends the money is the media department. This department is responsible for being totally familiar with all available advertising media, with particular reference to the rapidly changing patterns of individual readership or viewership. The increasing sophistication of the media scene means that media departments now consist of media researchers, media planners and media buyers. An immense amount of backroom thinking goes on determining the correct media strategy, which has to be established in tandem with the planning and creative departments. The 'thinking' departments are therefore creative, planning and media, guided by the account handler and sharing his contribution. Once media strategy is established, the media department is responsible for drawing up schedules indicating which media will be used, the cost of such media, and recommended dates, size or length of advertising space or time, etc. This will involve considerable discussion and personal contact with media owners, and at this stage the beginning of the buying process is started. Eventually the media department is responsible for buying media, which is more of a marketplace activity than ever before. Television time particularly is bought with considerable variation in costs for different time sections. Quite apart from the rate of commission that an agency might have agreed with its client, there is also a considerable saving to be made for the client by the agency against the media owners' published rate card costs. It is not uncommon for an agency to achieve 20 per cent or more saving by shrewd buying. The media department should still be judged, however, on the quality of its buying as well as its cost saving.

Production

The main department for the account handler to use in implementing an agreed advertising campaign is the production services department. This is sometimes called creative services, but basically it is the department that takes agreed advertisement designs, and turns them into material ready to be used in the press, or on the hoardings, or for mailings. (Television production needs rather different skills with which we shall deal later.) The production department, in conjunction with the creative department, establishes what kind of artwork, typefaces, photography etc., are required, and then commissions appropriate outside suppliers to carry out work. In the case of basic production artwork such as typesetting, simple line illustrations and so on, a number of outside suppliers and studios would be used by the production department. In the case of more specialized and more expensive artwork, such as fashion photography or drawn artwork by well-known artists, the creative department will specify which is to be the supplier. The production department is responsible for negotiating the right fee, making sure the work is delivered on time, seeing that the account handler gets the work agreed by the client, then seeing that appropriate printed material is delivered to media owners on time. The skills required in this kind of department are the ability to handle a mass of detail with speed and precision, to integrate the practical threads of a campaign, and to keep one's patience at all times. Being at the end of the line it is the production department that suffers from any delays from client liaison, writing, designing, and agreeing strategies and treatments. Press dates and air times wait for no man, not even the finest of creative talents!

Television

The television production department is responsible for maintaining a detailed knowledge of the television production companies available, for selecting appropriate companies and obtaining estimates for client approval. Television production is rarely a case of choosing the cheapest company, since different kinds of film require different kinds of television production skills. Normally a production department would produce three estimates, with a very strong recommendation for a particular company – which may not be the cheapest. There is a creative evolution which continues during the making of a television commercial, and often subtle amendments to scripts or scenes are made during the shooting of a film. Nevertheless, the TV producer is responsible for advance briefing of the agency team and the client on the details of casting, props, background, timing, etc., so that little is left to chance during the actual shot. It is usually wise to ensure that the client is represented in some way at the TV shoot so that last-minute problems of details or the way in which a product is shown may be amicably agreed. The producer is responsible for the production timetable allowing time for various stages such as rushes, rough cuts, double heads and answer prints up to final grading and finished copies for transmission.

Client/agency relationship

The relationship between a client and its agency is that between two principals, despite the word 'agency'. Although an agency buys media on behalf of its clients, it acts in its own right in law and is therefore responsible for its own debts. This makes it particularly important for an agency to recover its expenditure from its clients as soon as possible. The media from whom the agency derives its commission (its bread and butter) insist on payment of their invoices in a matter of weeks after appearance. It is not unusual on the other hand for clients to delay paying their agencies for up to three months or more. Sometimes this happens through inefficiency, sometimes through carelessness and sometimes through deliberate manipulation of funds. An important part of an agency's commercial life is therefore to chase up its customers to pay the bills. This in turn becomes an important part of the account handler's life, often conflicting with his prime task of winning client confidence, persuading clients to accept new campaigns, and above all to keep the account with the agency.

A business partner

To sum up, the modern advertising agency is a complete business marketing partner, whose role is to help analyse the marketing problem, find the advertising solutions which will improve the marketing process, conceive the creative approach to the right advertising campaign and then use a whole series of outside suppliers – ranging from media owners to suppliers of typesetting – to bring campaigns into effect. Guiding it all, with highly talented people to assist him, is the account handler.

How a modern agency works

Systems

In the structure outlined above, a modern advertising agency lays down a number of systems, accompanied by suitable paperwork, to make sure that events proceed as smoothly as possible.

Every piece of work initiated within the agency is normally allocated a job number, which provides a vehicle for logging all time spent and expenses incurred on that job. Normally, work will not be undertaken in an agency until an official job number has been opened, and a formal

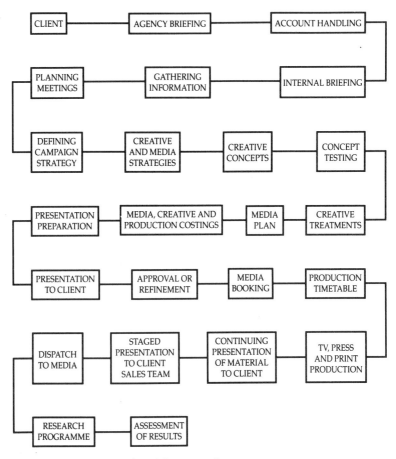

Figure 3.2 *Preparing an advertising campaign*

brief has been put into the agency system. It is the job of the account handler to prepare a formal briefing document, listing the purpose of the exercise, the target audience, the virtues and disadvantages of the product, the competition the product is up against, and so on. It may well be some days after a client meeting before a formal brief can be issued, and depending on the time available an informal briefing may be held by the account handler. He will, however, be committed to putting on paper a formal analysis of the situation. The brief will not necessarily be accepted in this form by other departments, since they will wish to question some of the assumptions in the brief, but finally an agreed brief will be cemented within the agency. This brief will then be agreed with the client, so that unnecessary expense is not incurred by beginning work which is on the wrong track. Outline strategies, as described above, may also be presented to a client in the early stages of preparation, and the agency may also wish to carry out 'dipstick' research into its early ideas. This can be done in several ways, but the normal method is to carry out a series of group discussions, each discussion containing about twelve typical consumers in a discussion led by a trained research pyschologist. After a general discussion on the product field concerned, the subject moves round to the client product and then rough advertising ideas are exposed for evaluation. While such methods are invaluable in assessing consumer understanding of new communications ideas, care should be taken not to overvalue such results unless a more substantial quantified survey is undertaken at a later stage.

Reaching the audience

Defining the target audience and the advertising message is not always as easy as it may appear: the traditional methods of deciding whether a product was aimed at the top, middle or lower end of the socioeconomic scale are no longer quite as reliable as they were. More credence is being given to 'lifestyle' research, and the levelling up which has taken place in society (or levelling down, as some people would put it!) also makes the task of defining a target audience more difficult. There are still strong geographical differences in lifestyles which are of assistance where a product is not marketed nationally, but the influence of modern media is constantly eroding the regional pattern.

There are a number of methods by which one may tackle different sectors of the audience – geographical or otherwise. The fourteen area television contractors provide a means of carrying different advertising approaches or product messages in different regions: regional editions may also be bought in a number of national magazines such as *TV Times* or *Radio Times*. Some national newspapers also have regional variations. Direct marketing, originating from direct mail but now encompassing direct telemarketing and other techniques, is providing a much more sophisticated method of 'niche marketing', i.e., reaching specified layers of the audience.

Production costs

The cost of production can be staggering, especially with smaller advertising schedules: the old formula of allowing 10 per cent of a schedule for production is no longer safe. Television production is particularly frightening, where a thirty-second commercial can cost anything from £50,000 to £250,000 at today's prices, depending on the techniques involved. So heavy are the costs that television production companies and therefore agencies, normally ask for 50 per cent of the estimated cost in advance from clients. There are also considerable post-production costs to be considered in the finalizing of prints and distributing copies to television stations, payment of artist repeat fees, etc. Often costs on a television budget continue to come into a client for up to a year afterwards.

Buying

The agency's role includes buying as well as thinking and planning: it is therefore expected by its client to buy economically and well on all fronts. Savings on media costs, production costs, time costs and delivery costs are all looked for. The best claim that any agency can make to its client is 'We make your advertising pound go further' – and this has to be in terms of quality of advertising as well as skill in buying.

New technology

Agencies have been considerably helped by the pace of new technology. In addition to the new equipment employed by any modern company, such as word processors, personal computers, fax machines, etc., a number of other new developments have speeded up work. Desktop publishing means that the wide number of marketing and advertising planning reports produced by an agency can be produced more quickly and economically on the premises; information technology means that systems such as 'Harvest' can provide immediate detailed assessments of the marketplace, with the kind of detailed information that used to take many days to collect; the audio/video world has developed in a way which has considerably improved the quality of film or tape (both are used for television commercials); printing techniques in national press media are vastly improved, with acceptable newsprint colour now the norm; the provision of artwork for media having superseded printing blocks almost everywhere. Computer graphics have also helped to create some astonishing visual effects.

Personal relationships

The most important single factor in running a successful advertising agency is establishing the right 'chemistry' between the people in the agency, and between the agency and its client. Like an ill-assorted football team full of superstars, whatever the talents you have the goals will not be scored without the right teamwork. A great deal of top agency management time is spent in ensuring that staff are kept informed of client developments and of agency progress. This calls for continuing personal contact with staff in the agency both on an individual basis and through staff meetings. In few environments are the processes of staff communication and staff welfare as important: agency teams consist of volatile and talented people – all of them highly individualistic. Status is comparatively unimportant: talent is what people respect.

On the client side good relationships need to be established at all levels. The day-to-day working contact between agency and client is usually at account manager/brand manager level, possibly with monthly reviews between the teams at a slightly higher level (account director/ marketing director). It is important that the top management in an agency see the top client management (chairman/managing director) from time to time – part of this contact may be at a social level. It is productive for both sides to engender a warm, understanding, loyal and frank relationship, so that both parties may speak to each other in language that the other clearly understands. Much time may be saved by such a close understanding, and it is also much easier to spot the occasions when things start to go wrong. It is also important from time to time for an agency to take a stand on a campaign which it has produced, and believes to be right, but which the client will not accept. It would be a sad thing if the agency, by speaking frankly, were to prejudice its business with any particular client, thus the importance of the under-standing between the two companies. If an agency has met the brief, albeit with creative ideas which the client finds unexpected, the agency should stand its ground. If it is to do this, it is important that the leader of the presentation team is himself convinced that the agency has the right solution before he goes into battle. Should the battle be lost, i.e. the client elects to overrule the agency, then of course the client has the right at the end of the day to spend his own money as he wishes. The agency must then decide whether it is willing to be overruled, or whether its professional reputation may be injured by producing the wrong kind of advertising. This is a decision made on the merits of each case, but the rule of Mammon normally applies in that the agency takes its cue from the size of the account.

Most clients hold an agency responsible for the moral and legal standards of its advertising, and would expect that the agency met the needs of the law, of the Advertising Standards Authority and of the Code of Advertising Practice. There is also the intangible element of 'good taste', which a successful advertising campaign never infringes. Poor corporate behaviour usually rebounds commercially.

The agency as a business

Remember that although the advertising agency is concerned with exciting elements such as art, design, writing, television, radio and cinema, it is at the end of the day a business, and is in business to yield a profit – without the profit, no business, no staff, and no exciting advertising campaigns.

We have touched earlier on the ways in which new agencies start up and may be financed: it is safe to assume that an agency needs financial resources of the equivalent of at least three months' forward turnover under its belt, to allow for the time taken between the spending of money on behalf of clients and regaining that money from clients. Normal business practices must be closely observed. Estimates should be given in writing to clients, clients should approve such estimates in writing, bills should be sent out promptly and chased for prompt payment. Considerable care must be exercised to ensure that budgets for large items like television films or the printing of large quantities of posters do not exceed the figures given to clients. While 'above-the-line' work, i.e. for media, is done as part of the commission arrangement with clients, 'below-the-line' work, i.e. for printing, merchandising material, promotion schemes and so on is separately estimated and charged to clients on a fee basis. Again care must be taken to ensure that all contingencies are provided for so that the agency is not caught short by sudden unexpected additions.

Special care must be taken with experimental creative work. Often a creative director will wish to prepare some advertisements along a particular line which has not yet been authorized by the client for expenditure. Such work is frequently finished outside an agency and a weekend's work can often result in thousands of pounds worth of costs to the agency which are not necessarily recoverable from the client. The agency must decide whether or not it wishes to take this risk, and if it does it must ensure the costs are kept under control.

Some clients are not as profitable as others, and indeed in some cases 'live off' other clients. It is often difficult in agencies to assess how profitable smaller labour-intensive clients are, since they tend to be fitted in to a busy workload however much it stretches the individual's man-hours. The more advanced agencies now run their own profitability assessment schemes by which everybody in the agency completes regular time sheets. In this way the true costs of handling a client may be assessed against the revenue obtained from that client. By means of regular monthly reviews the client may be apprized of the situation, and should the agency not be making required profit levels the client may be asked for additional fees. Good clients, given the right information, will normally agree to such suggestions, but the agency may have to decide in the long run whether or not to part company with an unprofitable client. This is always difficult, because such a parting does not necessarily result immediately in any reduction in the agency's costs. However, a comprehensive view of the agency's clients could result in savings in costs outweighing the comparative loss in revenue. Again, a typical business situation.

Correspondingly there are times when a tempting new account should be declined if it genuinely does not look as though it will yield a profit. The temptation is always to take on anything that comes along, but a business-like agency must set itself certain financial standards either in minimum levels of revenue or of profit. The average net profit an agency makes on its billing is usually estimated to be around 2 per cent, although a more desirable target should perhaps be in the area of 3 per cent. In other words, about a fifth of the agency's revenue (the income it receives in commissions from its turnover) should end up as net profit.

New business

Searching for new business is a permanent activity of every agency. Professional regulations about the vigour of approaches to other agencies' clients are now considerably relaxed, and most business acquisition is done by personal contact between senior client personnel and senior agency personnel. There are ways of promoting an agency, mainly by direct mail, advertising in the trade press or through special companies such as the Advertising Agency Register. The latter arrange to show clients about ten video tapes of selected agencies' work in return for a fee from both client and agency. The considerable coverage given to agencies in the trade press, and the good quality of reference material available, not to mention the public nature of advertising, means that most clients have already in their minds a pretty good idea of the ten agencies they would consider looking at should they decide to make a change. The usual form is to visit half a dozen agencies, to draw up a list of three for a 'pitch' and then to ask the selected three agencies to present all on the same day at different times. A respectable advertiser will usually pay some kind of nominal fee, although this inevitably does not cover the true costs of the agency's work. A typical pitch will last for an hour and a half, including about a quarter of an hour for questions. It will usually be a slide/video presentation, led by an account handler, followed by a planner, followed by a creative director, followed by a media director. In this it follows the normal sequence of preparation of the campaign within the agency. A great deal depends on the 'chemistry' and the personality of the presentation team. Are these the sort of people we want to work with? The chances are that the actual skills and work put forward by competing agencies will be very similar, so the personality factor can make the final difference.

Future trends

The advent of the media broker, described earlier, has opened the way for lower commissions paid to agencies, and the establishment of a number of 'new-wave' agencies. Reference has been made to 'third', 'fourth', and 'fifth' waves of creative hot-shops. These agencies buy à la carte, often with a fairly small staff in-house. In this sense they revert to the origins of advertising agencies, but as success comes, normally develop into the more traditional pattern. Signs of 'establishment' are the addition of a formal media department, a complete in-house creative department and membership of the IPA (the Institute of Practitioners in Advertising, the agency's professional body).

Is it not only agencies who buy à la carte, as clients also use this method in some cases. Where a client has personnel who are experienced in the advertising business, they will find it possible to buy media from the media brokers, creative work from a studio, and handle their own production. While this approach has many temptations in apparent cost savings, experience has shown – and IPA statistics confirm – that the majority of advertisers come back to a full-service agency in the long run. It is usually because the exercise takes far more time and makes far more demands than ever envisaged, and because lack of coordination of the promotional effort creeps in. Moreover, control at the client end is often in the hands of executives not properly qualified in the advertising business.

While, on the one hand, recent years have seen the emergence of many new smaller creative agencies, there have equally been rapid international developments at the top of the tree. By means of merger and acquisition, the big international groups have become even bigger, urged on by the greater internationalization of world advertising, and in particular of course the increasing and integrated marketing strength of Europe. Most agencies (whether or not they belong to an international group) have now formed strong international affiliations or associations so that they have the facility to place advertising worldwide. At the end of the day, whether it is one big international group under one name, or an association, the client is very much in the hands of the agency on the spot. It is usually staffed by nationals of that country, and the end-product will still be the result of the relationship between that agency and client management personnel in that same country.

For decades now the medium-sized agency has been threatened, since it was deemed back in the 1950s to be on the point of extinction, squashed between the big multinational groups and the small emergent creative hot-shops. A look at the current list of agencies (660) indicates that life has gone on, although names and ownerships are constantly changing.

International advertising, something of a poor relation in the past, is likely to become a much more powerful element in the industry. Apart from the factors described above, the emergence of Third World countries enjoying more sophisticated techniques will lead to further internationalization of communication, and the spread of satellite broadcasting will further influence the scene. International brand marks and slogans and the spread of the English language are both key factors in this development. Other factors likely to affect the future are continued technological development in the home sector: for example, direct marketing in the form of letters through the door being replaced by personal fax messages, personal messages on your vision screen and through your telephone viewer.

Society's attitude to advertising is also important. As the pendulum swings to and from materialism/consumer care, different governments may ban different categories of advertising. In some countries there is strong opposition to advertising per se. In Sweden, advertising for tobacco and alcohol is banned: in the UK we have seen gradual restrictions imposed. Cigarette advertising is no longer allowed on UK television, and has had to resort to the cinema and the outdoor poster medium; alcohol advertising is restricted and has been the subject of fierce public debate; other environmental factors such as lead-free petrol versus ordinary petrol may also find themselves subject to advertisement control.

All of this illustrates a very important point: advertising is married to the society in which it lives, and to be successful has to reflect that society.

Training and application

Getting a job in an advertising agency is still as difficult as it has always been. There is no proper industry training scheme for entry into the agency business. There are bodies who will provide knowledge and information abut the industry: the IPA (see above) provides training courses; students can enrol for the CAM diploma which is set up by the Communications Advertising and Marketing Education Foundation, and professional organizations such as the Chartered Institute of Marketing, The Institute of Public Relations and others, all run seminars, courses and lectures. With or without training or qualifications from these bodies, getting a job is still a matter of applying diligently to as many advertising agencies as possible, and using as many personal contacts as possible. The more people you know in the business the more likely you are to get in. A few of the larger agencies run their own training schemes, but the appeal of the business has been such that agencies are able to pick from the cream of graduates, choosing those with first class degrees from the major universities. Creative entry is usually drawn from those who have either been to art school or have read an appropriate subject at university, such as English or Law.

However, new entrants are always needed, so candidates with the enthusiasm and tenacity to keep searching, keep reading, and keep learning will eventually find themselves in an agency.

What are the qualities required? A lively interest in everything going on around you, particularly on the business scene; an interest in other people and the way they live and work; the ability to get on with other people both in times of friction as well as in times of success; the ability to work in a team so that the sum of the whole is greater than the sum of the parts; a sense of imagination; the ability to express yourself well in spoken or written form; and an interest in everything new. By and large, there is no other business organization quite like an advertising agency.

BIBLIOGRAPHY

Douglas, T. *Complete Guide to Advertising.* (Macmillan, 1984)
Fletcher, W. *Advertising: How Does it Work?* (Teach Yourself Books, 1978)
Jefkins, F. *Advertising Made Simple*, 5th edn. (Heinemann, 1990)
Jefkins, F. *Advertising Today*, 4th edn. (Blackie, 1990)
Lawson, R. G. *Advertising Law.* (Macdonald and Evans, 1978)
White, R. *Advertising: What It Is and How to Do It*, 2nd edn. (McGraw-Hill/Advertising Association, 1988)

4

Media

Mike de Vere

Background

The 1980s have seen dramatic changes to the UK media marketplace –
near 24-hour television broadcasting, satellite broadcast, a national
commercial radio network and a revolution within Fleet Street. These
events occurred against a background of greatly increased advertising
expenditure versus the retail price index (Figure 4.1).

The importance of media expenditure cannot be overstated. To many
companies, it now represents the largest item of capital expenditure after
the cost of raw materials.

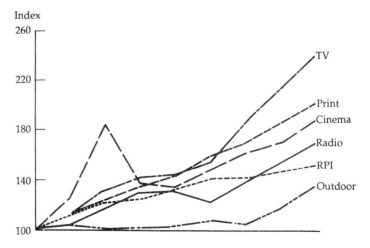

Figure 4.1 *Media inflation versus the retail price index 1980–88*
Source: SSA/AA

Introduction

We can consider the contribution media makes to advertising in three ways:

1 Size and classification, i.e. their relative importance in terms of advertising revenue and their classification in terms of audiences.
2 Contributions made by media owners to help advertisers.
3 What the advertiser can get out of the inherent characteristics of each medium.

We will examine each in turn.

Size and classification

The first point to make about UK media is that its variety and excellence is unsurpassed. The availablity of good quality media is unbeatable even if our television system and radio network lacks the competition found in the USA, if our magazines lack the choice of the Germans or our posters the cluttered ubiquity of the French. This was not always appreciated by British advertisers until foreigners showed them the way. Our motor industry shunned television until its selling power was revealed by the Europeans and the Japanese. Our furniture manufacturers largely ignored press competition from Italy, Germany and the States until it was too late. More recently, financial advertisers have shown increasing interest in television's ability to brand products and services and this sector now accounts for approximately 10 per cent of total advertising revenue. The simplest classification of media in terms of their global importance to advertisers is shown in Table 4.1 and Figure 4.2.

In terms of display advertising, television has increased its share of total revenue and this is shown in Figure 4.2. This also illustrates the emergence of radio. If, however, we include press advertising expenditure from all sources including classified, the proportion represented by television is considerably reduced as shown in Figure 4.3.

Press

Despite the increasing share taken by television, press has maintained its dominance, though if we only count those press media used mainly by national advertisers, i.e. national newspapers and magazines, the 1988 total at £1,199 million is less than the figure for television.

The expenditure shown in Table 4.1 and Figure 4.2 only counts display advertising. Classified advertising is an increasingly important source of

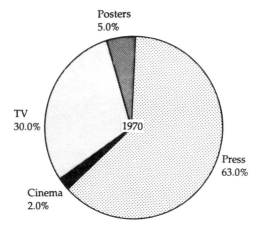

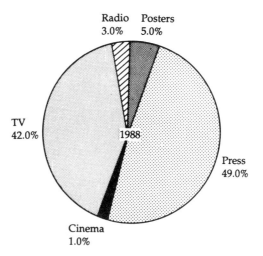

Figure 4.2 *Proportion of display advertising expenditure 1970–88*
Source: AA Yearbook

revenue to the press if subject to the winds of economic change, particularly where recruitment and property are affected. Table 4.2 details the
importance of classified advertising to the press in general.

Classified advertising has, therefore, increased its share of the total
and now accounts for approximately 40 per cent of all press advertising
expenditure. It also differs in importance depending on the type of
publication. To publications such as *The Guardian, The Telegraph* and

Table 4.1   Total display advertising expenditure (£ million)

	1952	1960	1970	1980	1988
Press	72	151	268	1099	2454
Television	0	72	125	692	2127
Posters	10	16	22	107	244
Radio	1	1	1	54	139
Cinema	3	5	6	18	27
	86	245	422	1970	4991

Source: Advertising Association (including production)

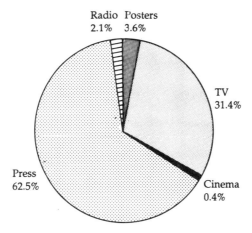

Figure 4.3   *Advertising expenditure by medium (1988)*
Source: AA Yearbook

Sunday Times, classified advertising revenue represents a share in excess of 40 per cent of their advertising income; while the popular press, i.e. *Sun/Mirror*, are much less reliant upon it as a revenue source.

   National newspapers can be categorized as follows:

1   National dailies
2   National Sundays

   These categories can be broken down even further:

1   Popular (e.g. *The Sun*)
2   Mid-market (e.g. *Daily Mail*)
3   Quality (e.g. *Financial Times*)

Table 4.2 Total press advertising expenditure (£ million)

| | 1970 | | 1988 | |
	Display	Classified	Display	Classified
National newspapers	84	25	860	239
Regional newspapers	59	83	563	981
Magazines	47	4	339	31
Business and professional	44	9	336	173
	234	121 (34%)	2098	1424 (40%)

Source: Advertising Association (including production)

While Figures 4.4 and 4.5 deserve substantial commentary they do illustrate that nationals are good discriminators by class. They are, however, progressively less so by age and sex as Tables 4.3 and 4.4 show. For ease of reference, I have limited the amount of information shown and extracted just three ranges of age.

National newspapers are, by definition, ideal for national advertising. Most publications are able to offer regional editions, i.e. North and South. Some, however, provide still finer regional targeting. These regional facilities, while useful to advertisers, are relatively expensive versus the proportion of circulation represented. Further, the popular

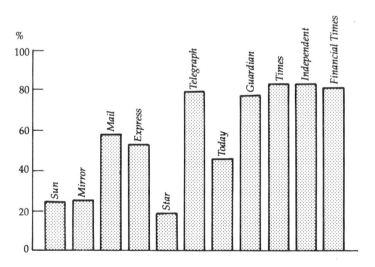

Figure 4.4 *Percentage of readers who are ABC1 – national dailies*
Source: National Readership Survey January–December 1988

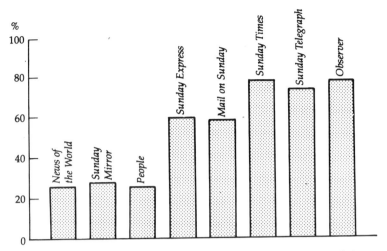

Figure 4.5 *Percentage of readers who are ABC1 – national Sundays*
Source: *National Readership Survey January–December 1988*

Table 4.3 Percentage of readers by age

Publication	15–24 (%)	25–34 (%)	45–54 (%)
The Sun	26	19	13
Daily Mirror	21	17	15
Daily Mail	16	14	16
Daily Express	13	13	16
Daily Star	28	23	13
Daily Telegraph	12	12	17
Today	26	41	12
The Guardian	20	25	13
The Times	19	18	17
The Independent	25	25	12
Financial Times	19	22	18
News of the World	25	20	14
Sunday Mirror	22	18	15
The People	18	18	15
Sunday Express	14	12	17
Mail on Sunday	22	20	15
Sunday Times	20	20	15
Sunday Telegraph	14	15	16
The Observer	21	23	15

Source: *National Readership Survey January–December 1988*

Table 4.4   Readership profiles

Publication	Men (%)	Women (%)
The Sun	53	47
Daily Mirror	55	45
Daily Mail	49	51
Daily Express	49	51
Daily Star	60	40
Daily Telegraph	55	45
Today	56	44
The Guardian	58	42
The Times	57	43
The Independent	63	37
Financial Times	72	28
News of the World	50	50
Sunday Mirror	51	49
The People	52	48
Sunday Express	48	52
Mail on Sunday	49	51
Sunday Times	52	48
Sunday Telegraph	54	46
Observer	55	45

Source: National Readership Survey January–December 1988

press especially has limited distribution within Scotland. This region, therefore, requires upweighting in order to equalize coverage by the use of Scottish papers such as *The Daily Record* or *Sunday Post*. In summary, regional facilities offered by the national press lack the scope, flexibility and economy of other non-press media.

We have historically thought of newspapers as black print on white paper; pre-print colour was available in very few papers and was extremely expensive at up to double the cost. The process used was a heat-set system which requires heat to dry the ink; consequently, those sections containing colour had to be printed separately or pre-printed, hence the term. New technology allows colour to be printed on-the-run (at the same time as the rest of the paper) without the need for heat and is termed a cold-set system. Papers utilizing this process are able to make use of colour on all pages if required and to use this facility for up to the minute photographs or topical advertisements. During the past couple of years, the availability, price and quality of colour has changed dramatically due to the growth of on-the-run colour. Many advertisers, previously deterred by the price of glossy pre-printed sections, have now been attracted by the economy and quality of the colour which is currently costed at a surcharge of between 50 and 70 per cent of the price of the equivalent mono size.

Regional newspapers

Daily newspapers

Regional daily papers are normally published from Monday to Saturday, either morning or evening, and are centred around towns and cities with large populations.

Substantially lower advertisement rates than national newspapers allow regional dailies to offer precise coverage of a relatively small area at a reasonable cost. In addition, some regional dailies produce editions which cover only a portion of their total circulation area.

Classified advertising – the 'small ads' – normally to be found towards the back of daily newspapers, are useful customer sources as they tend to be reasonably priced and avidly read. Whether taking space in the classified section or placing a display advertisement, most regional dailies will offer discounts for long-term bookings or for an annual commitment.

The daily regional newspaper is likely to have a reading life of only a day or two so, while it is possible to plot the immediate effectiveness of an ad, it will only have a short time of exposure. However, the ad will have the advantage of appearing in a well-regarded publication and will benefit from the goodwill that a regional newspaper generates.

Weekly paid-for newspapers

Weekly regional newspapers usually published on Thursday or Friday (some of them have a mid-week edition) tend to have smaller circulations than the dailies.

Ad rates are usually lower than daily regional papers and allow an even more precise way of reaching the public. They are also closely allied to the communities in which they circulate and are often an important part of local life.

Weekly papers often have a reading life of a week or more, so ads appearing in them have more chance of being seen. Weeklies also carry regular features – usually on home-related topics – which are useful for reaching a specific audience. Since a weekly paper's circulation may cover only part of an advertiser's area, it is best to experiment with a number of different editions to gauge which ones work best.

Free newspapers

Free newspapers are delivered once a week to homes in most areas of the country. Although they are free to recipients, advertisers have to pay for space bought in them.

For reaching almost every home in a defined area, free newspapers frequently achieve researched readership levels of 90 per cent. They offer a cost per thousand to advertisers which is typically half that of competing paid-fors.

Free newspapers generally tend to be less regarded by readers than bought newspapers, although many advertisers find the 'frees' attract exactly the right kind of customer. Free newspapers exist solely on their advertising revenue and can vary widely in their standards of quality.

In many cases, readers seeking a product or service rely on a free newspaper containing a large proportion of advertising. Advertisers should not automatically dismiss their local free publication simply because it contains a large amount of advertising. Advertisers should first examine their requirements and objectives and choose the type of newspaper that suits them best.

Ad managers of all local newspapers will be able to advise on the best way to go about advertising in their publications. Apart from the advice you receive from the ad managers, spend some time doing a little research yourself. Collect copies of all local papers – weekly, daily, free – and read them thoroughly. This way you will discover who they are aimed at, what area they cover, whether they will appeal to the type of person you wish to promote your business to and lastly where you would like your ad to appear – many papers regularly carry specialist sections on, say, entertainment or DIY, which may suit advertisers perfectly.

Historically, regional newspapers have been used by national advertisers on a tactical basis, e.g. new store openings. A cost per thousand premium around three times the price of national newspapers have made it uneconomic to utilize either paid-fors or frees.

Magazines

Magazines offer a different environment for the advertiser. They can be extremely selective in terms of sex, age and class and offer a range of colour ranging from the just acceptable to a match for almost anything available. Most are published on a weekly or monthly basis.

They can be categorized into four areas – general interest, special interest, trade and technical and supplements.

General interest magazines can be further broken down as follows:

1 Women's e.g. *Woman, Bella, Cosmopolitan, Elle*
2 Men's e.g. *Penthouse, Men Only*
3 Juvenile e.g. *Beano, Judy, Eagle, Thundercats*
4 Teenage e.g. *Smash Hits, Just Seventeen, 19*
5 Programme listings e.g. *TV Times, Radio Times, Time Out*
6 Home interest e.g. *Homes and Garden, Ideal Home*
7 General e.g. *Punch, Readers Digest*

The publications, while relatively general in their coverage, offer advertisers some efficiency of scale. Circulations in excess of 3 million are available via the programme journals and approximately 1 million for some of the women's weeklies and *Readers Digest*, while a high proportion of publications offer weekly or monthly circulations of between 100,000 to 300,000 copies.

The past three years has witnessed a greatly increased number of magazine launches, especially publications targeted at women.

During the early 1980s, falling circulations and readership within this market sector suggested that saturation point had been reached. In 1986, the German publishing house, Gruner and Jahr, launched a general interest women's monthly, *Prima*, with the editorial accent on the practical side of things. The publication's circulation grew quickly to achieve a figure in excess of 1 million, more than many women's weeklies and more than twice the circulation of most of its competitors. This gave ample proof that, providing the product was good and innovative, the consumer would expand her repertoire of magazine purchase!

Cross-frontier publishing is now becoming increasingly common. Gruner and Jahr followed the success of *Prima* with a weekly, *Best*, while the German house of Bauer has also launched a women's weekly, *Bella*. In response to this threat to their domain, IPC has launched *Essentials* into mainland Europe following a highly successful launch in the UK.

Special-interest magazines concentrate their editorial on a particular occupation or interest – music/hi-fi, motoring/motorcycling, gardening, sport, photography, boating, angling. The category of publication is of most interest to advertisers with a relevant product, e.g. cameras or hi-fi, etc. appearing within, say, *Amateur Photographer* or *What Hi-Fi?* On a strict comparison with general interest magazines and supplements (usually commanding a significant circulation advantage), these magazines are less cost efficient. They do, however, target the enthusiast with very little wastage or those consumers looking for advice prior to purchase.

Trade and technical magazines are aimed at specific groups such as grocers, builders, newsagents, doctors, farmers, architects, engineers and wine merchants, etc.

Titles vary enormously, even within a particular field. Some are philosophical, some practical, some buyers' guides. Some are general, some highly technical. Most are national, although a small number of regional publications exist, especially within Scotland and Northern Ireland. Their selection requires a close knowledge of their editorial content. For a number of advertisers, this category is an essential communications device to the appropriate outlets.

An increasingly important category is that of the financial/business press. The range of publications covers all press from the *Financial Times*, *Sunday Times Business Section* and business pages within most of the popular and quality press to glossy magazines such as *The Director* and *Management Today*. Other publications include directories and year-books, ranging from British Telecom's *Yellow Pages* and *Thompson Local Directories* to *Glasses Guide to Used Car Values*, *The Baby Book* and *Benn's Press Directory*. A further category is that of the free magazine. The circulation and readership of these publications has grown dramatically during the past ten years. Funding for these publications comes jointly from the sponsor and the advertiser, e.g. the American Express publication, *Expressions*. Distribution is via a mailshot against a pre-agreed mailing list, e.g. Green/Gold cardholders or by specifying a type of urban area. In the case of the latter, property advertising is key to funding. Further, many publications are given away within retail shops, hotels and London railway and underground stations.

Advertisers will evaluate critically the claims made for such publications since it is natural to question the reader's involvement with something that he has neither asked nor paid for. The fact remains that many free publications are of excellent quality and proven advertising efficiency. Each must be judged on its merits.

Colour supplements are given away with the parent newspaper. The reason for their existence is two-fold:

1 They provide the publisher with a method of enhancing the perceived value of the publication and help maintain reader loyalty.
2 They are a valuable source of additional advertising revenue and in many cases enable the newspaper to attract advertisers that would never entertain the idea of appearing within the predominantly black and white environment of the accompanying paper.

Many Saturday and Sunday publications provide a supplement. These tend to reflect the tone of the parent paper. This represents a highly competitive market and the sales departments constantly battle to attract advertising from the many paid-for publications which exist.

The economics of publishing

For the press proprietor, it is important to get the right balance between cover price and advertisement revenue. If one is too high, readers may be lost; if the other is too high, he may lose advertisers. Equally, publishers are able to restrict the available pagination as a method of sustaining a pre-determined rate per page. Again, a general reduction in pages may result in readers perceiving the publication to represent inferior value and thus change loyalties. Lost readers make it extremely difficult to maintain or increase advertisement rates.

The past five years has seen a revolution in Fleet Street and newspapers now represent a profit-making industry rather than a means to a knight-hood for the relevant proprietor, coupled with a substantial loss.

New technology and the abolition of many restrictive union practices, together with a severe cut in staff, has allowed newspapers to enter the 1980s and they now resemble the hi-tech world of many city financial institutions, with, in many cases, journalists inputting their stories direct into the system while the computer takes care of the print and typeface.

This transformation of the industry has caused papers to become larger with many of the quality papers running upwards of two sections. New newspapers are now also a viable proposition. Recent launches include *Today*, now selling close to 700,000 copies, *The Independent*, 400,000 copies, and *The Sunday Correspondent*. One thing that has not changed is distribution. All papers are distributed around the country via road and rail. The density of our population and an efficient communications network is one of the reasons for the UK's range of national newspapers.

Not all publications carry both editorial and advertising. Paperback books hardly ever carry advertising. *Exchange and Mart* carries no editor-ial but is packed with classifieds and some display.

Direct mail

Direct mail has grown rapidly since the 1970s aided by developments in technology, utilizing powerful computers to capture, store and manip-ulate huge amounts of information. This medium now accounts for approximately 8 per cent of UK advertising expenditure (source Royal Mail/Advertising Association) and, with an expenditure of £483 million, is significantly greater than outdoor, radio or cinema.

While mass media are by definition fairly indiscriminate in who they reach, direct mail can be addressed to selected individuals and as such is the most selective of all media. Furthermore, its strength lies in a letter addressed personally to an individual about an opportunity likely to be relevant to him or her. A personal approach of this kind is hard to ignore and has been proved by many advertisers to be far more effective than mass media advertising, despite its apparently higher cost.

Direct mail has traditionally been used by mail-order companies, pool promoters, holiday advertisers and publishers. Lately, however, direct mail has enjoyed the patronage of blue-chip names and the legal profession as well as increasing activity from the political parties. It is also substantially used as an alternative to the business press by industrial and services advertisers and particularly by local businesses.

Direct mail has the particular virtue that it is nearly always attempting to solicit direct response. As such, it is capable of direct evaluation in a way not usually possible with other media.

The Post Office naturally has a direct interest in the development of the medium and provides a commercially-orientated marketing service to advertisers and agencies.

Modern technology is improving the flexibility of direct mail rapidly. A primary requirement of direct mail is a list of names and addresses of potential customers. Whether advertising through direct mail to consumer or business markets, there are four main types of list source in addition to a company's own marketing database:

1 Response lists: lists of people who have responded to direct marketing offers.
2 Inquirer lists: people who have inquired about a product or service, but who have not completed the purchase.
3 Subscription lists: names and addresses of readers of magazines and journals. They are usually updated on a regular basis and often contain fuller and more contemporary information than compiled lists.
4 Compiled lists: lists derived from published services ranging from professional/trade and technical directories to the electoral roll.

Further, there is now the opportunity to select addresses within small geographical areas using systems such as ACORN, PIN, Super Profile or Mosaic. These methods of consumer selection enable the advertiser to be quite specific in terms of the recipient of their mail-out. For instance, ACORN classifies neighbourhoods into thirty-eight residential types of housing and, therefore, of the kinds of people living in them, varying from *very high mansions* status, at one end of the scale, to *Glasgow tenements* at the other. TGI measures households' consumption of a wide range of goods. Thus it is possible to mail to lists of individuals living in housing types that are heaviest potential consumers of a given product field.

This fine selectivity available is matched by improvements in computer storage, analysis systems and printing processes so that messages can be varied to make them more personal.

Television

ITV (Independent Television) is controlled by the Independent Broadcasting Authority which contracts programme companies (hence often called contractors) to serve fourteen geographical areas ranging from London, the biggest, to Channel, the smallest. This service has traditionally included the selling of advertising time within their areas.

Television viewing is largely a family activity, certainly in peak hours (roughly 7.00–10.30 p.m.). In consequence, it delivers a mass audience and lacks the ultimate selectivity of press (especially magazines). Viewing is biased downmarket and to older viewers. Its main weakness, therefore, lies in reaching upmarket and young people as Figures 4.6 and 4.7 demonstrate.

Viewing is also affected by the seasons and weather. Figure 4.8 illustrates that a good summer reduces the average hours of television viewed. This tendency for people to watch less television is compounded

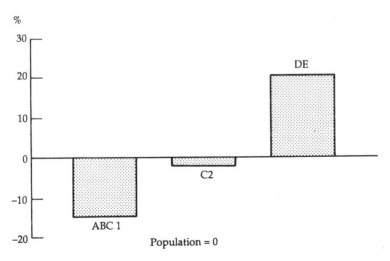

Figure 4.6   *All television – class profile*

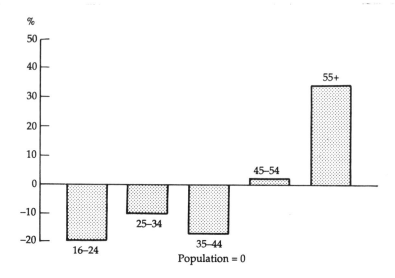

Figure 4.7   *All television – age profile*

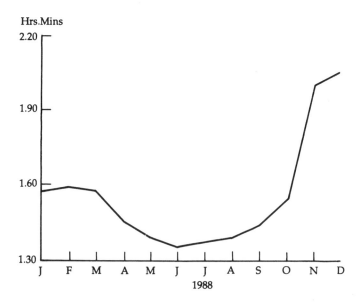

Figure 4.8   *Average daily viewing – all individuals*
Source: AGB

by the summer programme schedule which, because of the reduced potential audience, is the least strong of the year.

Typically, ITV achieves 42 per cent of the total viewing and Channel 4 9 per cent, while BBC1 and BBC2 achieve 38 per cent and 11 per cent respectively.

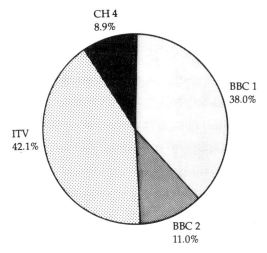

Percentage of viewing all individuals

Figure 4.9 *Share of television viewing – 1988*

Because of the very high levels of coverage available, television is an expensive medium in terms of capital cost. Nevertheless, it has proven its branding and sales ability for a very wide range of products and services. Further, different times of day achieve a markedly different type of audience composition. For instance, morning time television contains a high proportion of young housewives; not surprisingly, weekday television between 4 p.m. and 5 p.m. contains a very high proportion of children; while late night night television (11 p.m. onwards) is extremely popular with young adults. These differences are due to availability to view, which the programme schedulers then allow for when constructing the programming schedule.

Advertisers can take advantage of these differences and media buyers bias the construction of their schedules according to the viewing group required. It must be stressed, however, that television is a mass market medium and targeting via timebands or programming reduces wastage but does not eliminate it.

Television is sold regionally. This facilitates single or multiple region tests; also the ability to achieve greater or lesser weights of advertising by region and to test different pieces of advertising copy by region.

The economics of the airtime market are simple but the process of negotiation and sales is complex. Airtime is a commodity of fixed supply since commercial minutage is limited to an average of seven minutes per hour with seven and a half minutes in peak time. The price of airtime, therefore, depends on the level of demand. Thus, providing the audience remains constant, revenue growth of 10 per cent will result in costs per thousand increasing by the same proportion. Demand fluctuates by time of day and season. Figures 4.10 and 4.11 illustrate how costs vary across a year and by television region.

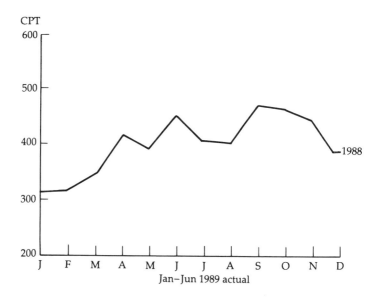

Figure 4.10 *Television costs – thirty second adults costs per thousand*

The mechanism used by most contractors to regulate price to demand is known as the pre-empt rate card. In principle, this allows a spot priced at, say, £5,000 to be pre-empted by the next rate up on the card – say, £6,000. Thus, if the buyer responsible for the initial purchase wishes to repurchase the spot, then he would have to pay the next rate up on the card beyond £6,000. The buyer is, therefore, constantly trying to assess the likely rate for a spot, together with the audience, allowing for variations such as BBC programming, weather and recent viewing trends.

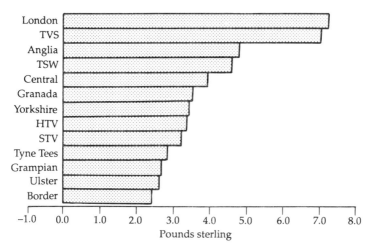

London
TVS
Anglia
TSW
Central
Granada
Yorkshire
HTV
STV
Tyne Tees
Grampian
Ulster
Border

-1.0 0.0 1.0 2.0 3.0 4.0 5.0 6.0 7.0 8.0
Pounds sterling

Figure 4.11 *Average adult cost per thousand – 1988*

C4 currently achieves approximately 8–9 per cent of the total television audience. Its attraction to advertisers is the wide range of specialist programmes allowing better targeting. The channel maintains a marginally more upmarket and young profile compared to ITV especially during peak viewing times. Sales are handled by the same department that sells ITV and agencies generally purchase a combination of the two in order to optimize the coverage of a particular campaign.

TV-AM and the recently launched C4 breakfast service, C4 Daily, offer shorter, sharper programmes and are more in tune with the lifestyle most people lead at this time of the day. Advertisement sales are via TV-AM's own sales operation and the weight of advertising purchased is usually negotiated in advance and not subject to the prevailing market – thus no pre-emption.

Posters

The poster medium is highly diverse and embraces many different sizes and sites. The most obvious feature of the poster industry is the roadside site. These come in a variety of standard related sizes and are illustrated below in Table 4.5.

The most common poster size is the 4 sheet, often located in purpose-built bus shelters and the 48 sheet generally located on major traffic routes either free-standing or mounted on gable walls of buildings. There has been little change in the size of poster panels over the years, apart from the development by More O'Farrell/Ashdel of the Superlite.

Table 4.5

	Size
4 sheet	40″ × 60″
16 sheet	6′8″ × 10′
32 sheet	13′4″ × 10′
48 sheet	20′ × 10′
9 panel	27′ × 10′
12 panel	36′ × 10′
96 sheet	40′ × 10′

These panels are around one-third larger in area than 4 sheets and are backlit – a distinct advantage during the long winter evenings.

For many years, posters were largely monopolized by a limited number of advertisers (mainly brewers and cigarette companies) who held long-term contracts on the best sites. This system of contract was known as T/C – i.e. the site was retained until countermanded by an advertiser. This deterred other advertisers who wished to make short-term use of the medium.

The poster industry has undergone a series of dramatic changes during the past decade. Involvement of the Monopolies and Mergers Commission has caused a number of structural changes within the industry. The major poster holding companies had each built up a franchise on a particular size. The past four years has seen a redistribution of sites with each company now holding a more representative cross-section of sites. Currently, seven major companies own approximately 90 per cent of the total number of UK poster sites.

Despite this redistribution of site ownership, contractors increasingly concentrate their marketing efforts on particular sizes and this is a trend which has gathered pace in the past year or so.

There have been changes in the various methods of purchase and sale. Line by line is still, however, the most popular method of buying posters. This is true of all sizes apart from 96 sheets and 12 sheets where an estimated 60 per cent and 90 per cent of panels respectively are sold in pre-selected packages. Perhaps the most important event to have happened within the industry is that of OSCAR (Outdoor Site Classification and Audience Research). This is the most credible piece of research to have been commissioned in the history of the medium. Basically, it attempted to quantify coverage and frequency against broad target groups on the basis of traffic, etc. The final development occurred in January 1989 which fine-tuned the original research and was conducted around 6,000 plotted poster sites. The net result of this survey was to allow media planners to look at poster passages on a regional and national basis, and to do so for sub-groups of the population – within the limits of the sample size.

Posters are more of a subjective medium than any other in terms of awareness and impact. They are flexible in terms of geographical location and advertisers are able to change copy on a weekly basis if necessary. They may even be used on a solus site basis, e.g. Valentine's Day messages, etc.

Radio

Radio is a comparatively new medium to UK advertisers. It has not yet secured either the status or the advertising investment achieved in other countries, notably Australia and the US, or even Ireland. The reason is that, unlike in many other countries, commercial radio has not been around for as long as television. Consequently, companies and brands have not been born with radio as an integral part of the advertising mix.

While Radio Luxembourg has been broadcasting an evening service in English to the UK since before the Second World War, its audience is heavily concentrated among teenagers and young adults. Patchy reception also contributed to its comparatively poor use by UK advertisers with appropriate products.

Commercial radio made a significant breakthrough in the UK in 1973 when the London Broadcasting Company (LBC) and then Capital Radio went on air in London. By 1989 in excess of fifty radio stations (many operating a separate AM and FM service) were transmitting to a potential audience representing about 92 per cent of the UK adult population.

Radio derives approximately half of its total revenue from local advertisers, although this figure may vary according to the region covered. Generally, it is lower within major urban areas and higher elsewhere.

Airtime is sold via packages which then slot the spots into breaks appropriate to the nominated audience. Most radio stations subcontract national sales to one of five sales houses which then group sell radio stations by region to national advertisers. Capital Radio and LBC are notable exceptions, however.

The audience is, generally speaking, skewed slightly downmarket and towards males. This can differ, however, according to the content of the radio station. The two stations serving London, for instance, offer the advertisers two different types of audience composition. Not surprisingly, radio is most effective in reaching young adults especially those aged 15–24.

The radio audience peaks during the morning and evening shows, i.e. drivetime. Figure 4.12 demonstrates the extent of these peaks compared to the audience available across the rest of the day.

All adults 15+ (0000's)

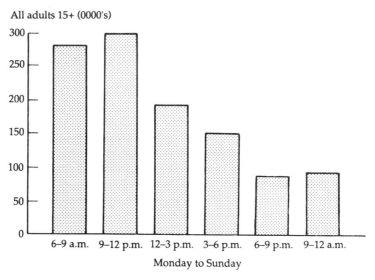

Figure 4.12   *Independent radio audience by segment – January–December 1988*
Source: JICNARS

We are still on a steep learning curve on how to use radio most effectively. Experience suggests that radio can prolong the life of a television campaign at a much reduced cost. Further, a number of recent commercials have utilized much longer timelengths, sometimes in excess of one minute. This may allow the listener to draw his or her own mental picture of the product and create their own imagery. The Guinness advertising would appear to represent a good example of this genre.

Cinema

Many factors contributed to the decline of the cinema audience across the 1970s and early 1980s. These include a high proportion of films containing explicit scenes of sex and violence and hence only of interest to a limited proportion of the population, high unemployment and the closure of cinemas. The number of screens has fallen from 4,600 in 1951 to approximately 1,350 in June 1989. The industry has, however, recently invested in many new screens created from the conversion of much larger halls into smaller multi-screen auditoriums; also flagship developments such as the UCI ten-screen complexes which include other attractions such as restaurants. Credit card bookings also help alleviate the queues. The quality and variety of films has also had a marked effect upon audience levels through the 1980s, as Figure 4.13 demonstrates.

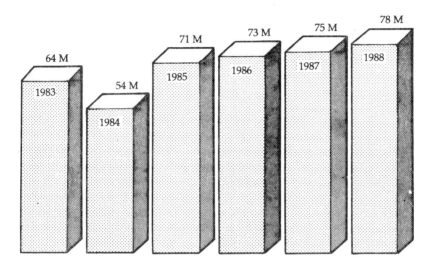

Figure 4.13   *Cinema admissions – 1983–88*
Source: CAA/Marplan

Not surprisingly, cinema is a young medium and is used heavily by advertisers of alcohol, jeans and banks, etc. who target at a young audience. Figure 4.14 demonstrates the importance of the 15–24-year-old population to the cinema.

In terms of class and sex, the bias is progressively less dramatic with 51 per cent of the audience comprising of ABC1s versus 41 per cent of the population, and 51 per cent being male versus 48 per cent of the population (JICNARS January–December 1988).

Advertising can be bought in individual cinemas as exemplified by the local curry house, by town, by television region or nationally. Alternatively, packages can be bought into specific films such as Walt Disney cartoons. This enables advertisers to be specific in terms of targeting, e.g. mothers with young children. Advertising is sold by two companies: Rank Screens Ltd and Pearl and Dean. Rank is currently responsible for about 80 per cent of all admissions.

Cinema invokes much greater audience involvement than any other media. The auditorium is dark, the screen dominates, and distractions

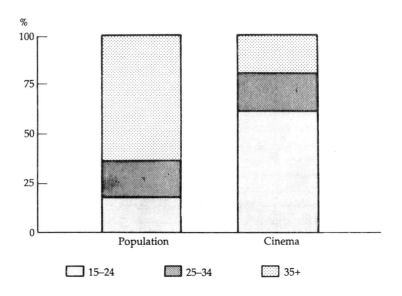

Figure 4.14   *Cinema audience profile – age*
Source: JICNARS January–December 1988

are minimal. Much of the advertising is entertaining and audience participation can be extremely positive.

The audience is heavily biased to under 35s with a core of 15–24-year-old and is, therefore, an ideal medium for banks, hair care, jeans and alcohol.

While there are many positive attributes, there exist a number of drawbacks which temper demand. These include high production costs (one print per cinema screen), high production values to make the best use of the medium and limited coverage. It takes approximately 20 weeks of continuous advertising to achieve c.50 per cent coverage of the core audience – adults 15–24 – and versus the broader target group of adults aged 16–34 coverage is further restricted to c.40 per cent. A television campaign would achieve coverage levels of about 70–80 per cent within a 3–4 week period but at a significant cost per thousand premium and with much less impact and ambience.

What the media owner puts in

It is important to recognize the nature of the triangular relationship between advertisers, agencies and media owners. The advertiser wants to buy the largest relevant audience for the cheapest price and appoints an agency or media buying specialist to do this for him. The media owner wants to maximize his revenue and profit, like any other company. Advertising is the sole or the most significant source of revenue for most media. The main exceptions are large circulation popular newspapers and cinema.

The advertiser expects impartial advice from his agency because the latter has no direct interest in any medium. The media owner on the other hand is pleading a special case. Media owners sell the merits of 'their' medium and those of their specific region or publication to both agencies and advertisers; and why shouldn't they? After all, they regard advertisers as their clients as well.

All major UK media are sold on the basis of published rate cards but substantial deals can be offered to allow for seasonal variations in demand, and to attract particularly worthwhile business or new product test activity. This has resulted in highly specialized and competitive media buying. Buyers of television airtime and press space are continually negotiating in order to obtain the most competitive costs per thousand. In the case of television, a buyer's achievement is tracked against the average cost per thousand achieved by individual contractors by month. The buyer's ability to beat predetermined criteria is regularly monitored by the client. There is a tendency, therefore, for media owners to regard media departments as being mainly concerned with beating down the price and having a conservative nature that precludes risk-taking on the imaginative exploration of new media opportunities that cannot be quantified in the normal way. As a result, media owners approach advertisers direct particularly when selling new media or publicity methods outside the norm, such as sponsorship.

The picture painted is rather extreme and it should be stressed that successful media placement depends not only on getting good value for money but also on close involvement with the media and an under-standing of how their varied characteristics can help the profitable sales of our brands. The endeavour will work best when advertiser, agency and media owner can operate together. This requires a degree of trust which has to be earned.

Having covered this general point, we shall examine the specific contributions that media owners make to the advertising business.

The advertisement sales organization

Historically, major media have been responsible for their own sales departments. Specialized, or low capital cost, media may be sold through specialized sales organizations or independent media representatives. Radio, ORACLE, and overseas media are good examples of categories represented by the former.

Large organizations have in the past been responsible for their own product, e.g. IPC or Thames Television. Departments operate on the group principle, with individuals responsible for agencies; these then report through a group head to an advertisement director (or sales controller). The latter has overall responsibility to the board for advertisement revenue, forecasting and pricing. Together with the managers, the head of sales is responsible for recruitment, training and staff morale.

Recently, however, the formation of TSMS would appear to be challenging the old order. This independent sales house sells airtime for Central, Anglia and Border television, and is also responsible for upwards of 20 per cent of total television advertising revenue. This new concept has embarked upon a policy to represent media covering the full spectrum of available opportunity – from posters to print to broadcast – on both a regional and national basis.

Motivation is the key to the success of any sales force. The sales rep must be able to call upon an effective research and marketing back-up and utilize the available data to support the case for (a) the medium in general and (b) their own specific product.

Agreements can be made between buyer and seller within pre-agreed limits of tolerance. Increasingly, however, agreements become more and more formal. Contracts relating to share of revenue, pre-agreed commitment levels, proportion of advertising by day and time of day, distribution and volume of expenditure are now included within a television contract; while press agreements can encompass just as many issues. Agreements are confirmed in writing and both buyer and seller then spend much time ensuring the finer points of each contract are delivered.

Successful sales departments are well-run team operations. Regular agency contact, comprehensive computer back-up, and a complete package of market research are all essential in persuading the agency to invest money on behalf of their client.

Market research

Until the mid-1960s, media owners had no direct access to market research. They recognized that this severely limited their ability to make effective sales arguments and in consequence started to finance major market surveys, e.g.:

- Television companies in the Television Consumer Audit (TCA), a pantry-check panel covering a wide range of grocery fields operated by Audits of Great Britain (AGB).

- Publishers in the Target Group Index (TGI), a diary panel covering not only grocer and chemist lines but long-term purchases such as durables and finance, operated by the British Market Research Bureau (BMRB). Recipients of the questionnaire are also asked questions relating to their use of media in terms of average hours of television viewed or publications read.

In addition to this research, available on an industry-wide basis, a number of media owners have initiated their own tailor-made schemes. For example, Central Television maintains a significant panel of homes. The panel monitors consumption of a wide range of consumer products and media. Thus one is able to track the media consumption of, say, users of baked beans, and target airtime accordingly. The *TV Times* conducted a survey examining the way consumers read. Recipients of the questionnaire were asked a series of questions relating to their leisure time and how much was spent reading, both generally and specifically.

Thus media owners are able to build a solid case for their particular media, e.g.:

- Television salespeople, data on product consumption by area.
- Press reps, data on consumption both demographically and by readers of individual publications.

Additionally, media owners are increasingly looking at means of providing a unique sales proposition for their particular area or publication etc.

Media owners now have at their command market research often superior to that held by advertisers or agencies. This represents a very solid contribution to the advertising business.

Media research

Media owners have always recognized that they have a prime responsibility to invest in research showing the size and composition of their audiences. These surveys are discussed in a future chapter.

It is worth pointing out that the bulk of television, press and cinema and all radio and poster research costs are borne by media owners.

Agencies and media specialists are, however, now extremely well equipped and hold copies of all major media research surveys, e.g. TGI, NRS, and all major client-orientated research. Media buyers utilize these surveys to determine the optimum press schedule, the ideal weight of regional advertising and the suitability of a region for a new product. Ultimately, the media buyer must balance the information given by a nominated research source against the rate negotiated.

Merchandising

Media provide a very wide range of merchandising services, e.g.:

- Cooperative manufacturer/retailer advertising (press, cinema, radio).
- Dedicated sales forces to gain distribution and in-store display. These are run by the television companies and their use is dependent upon a television campaign running within the appropriate region.
- Information bulletins and newsheets to retailers about forthcoming advertising campaigns (television, radio).
- Presentations to retailers' and advertisers' sales forces in conjunction with advertisers (television, cinema).
- Guaranteed product distribution via specified retail outlets (television).
- Pre- and post-campaign research facilities (television).

Production cooperation

All media owners regard agencies as being totally responsible for advertisement production. It is worth remembering, however, that the radio sales companies offer studio facilities and other help, and that television companies and cinema contractors have low-cost production facilities. In many instances, the availability of studio time enables the media owner to maximize usage and thus reduce overheads.

The advent of colour within the national press has caused a great deal of trial as agencies and advertisers become used to the facilities available and the limitations in terms of colour reproduction. Most newspapers offering on-the-run colour now give agencies the chance to examine the advertisement in situ prior to a full commitment. Mirror Group Newspapers have taken many notable initiatives within this field and have many case histories available to substantiate the use of colour (and the additional cost).

Editorial relevance

Editorial independence is a cardinal feature of the British press. Editors have the right to reject advertisements they consider unsuitable for their readers and advertisers have the right not to use media with whose views (usually about their brands) they disagree. Anyone interpreting the latter as an attempt to influence editorial simply does not understand how the system works.

While there is a tendency for editors and broadcasters to show no involvement with advertising, the more enlightened recognize their mutuality of interest in providing the best all-round service for their readers and viewers. Thus, publishers run features with appropriate advertising that is a genuine convenience for the reader. Features constructed solely with the intention of pulling in advertising revenue are unlikely to gain reader respect and will fail.

All media make a great effort to present and sell their editorial, programmes and films to advertisers and agencies with varying success.

Sponsorship

UK media have gained relatively little financial benefit from sponsorship and are much less knowledgeable than their counterparts in America. While there has been recognition of the potential, legislation has prevented more of the ideas achieving fruition; this is especially true in the case of broadcast media.

Magazines have been loosely involved within this area as companies or brands are able to sponsor appropriate supplements or sections. Magazines have also allowed one or a number of products to feature prominently within editorial sections designed to be 'in keeping' with the feel of the publication. The products each contribute towards the cost of producing the feature, which is termed an advertorial.

Newspapers have, however, generally steered well clear of any form of sponsorship and will certainly not allow any product or service to be associated with news stories because of the all too obvious hazards attached.

Television companies and, to a lesser extent, radio are beginning to recognize programme sponsorship as a potential source of significant advertising revenue.

Advertisers are allowed front and end credits, together with a credit during the programme promotions. The art lies in merchandising the sponsorship. Slotting commercials for the company or service into the sponsored programme should give the advertisement more credibility, and back-up promotions such as books or leaflets all enable the advertiser to maximize the investment.

Current examples to be seen on ITV are Powergen's sponsorship of the national weather forecast and National Power's sponsorship of the 1990 World Cup. Both packages cost the advertiser in the order of £2 million.

In summary, therefore, this is an area set to expand rapidly through the 1990s and may well account for c.5 per cent of all television revenue (say £100 million) by the middle of the decade.

What the advertiser gets out of each medium

We have already discussed the way media differs in the audiences they reach. This provides a start point for deciding which medium to use for a campaign. Further, for our advertisements to work to best effect, we must understand how people read, view or listen to each medium and how we can best exploit the characteristics to get our message across. What makes all of this particularly interesting is that we are in the middle of a media 'revolution'. So, after looking at each medium in turn, we will examine the way the future could change things.

Television

Television has and is undergoing a period of significant change. The penetration of video recorders, now approaching 60 per cent; C4; 24-hour broadcasting; and satellite all contribute to make the advertisers' task more difficult and challenging. Fundamentally, however, the fourteen existing terrestrial-based TV stations do and will continue to dominate commercial television audiences and commercial revenue through until at least the middle 1990s.

Television is unquestionably our pre-eminent branding medium. Its physical qualities of sound and moving pictures and its universal popularity make it the most effective medium for selling brands and services. On top of all this, commercials are generally popular and achieve standards of commercial production that are often far better (and considerably more expensive per minute) than the surrounding programmes. Proof of the entertainment value and interest in television advertising was the *Today*-sponsored commercial awards, first televised in early 1989. Readers of the newspaper voted for their favourite advertisements under different categories. For the record, Saatchi & Saatchi won the outright award for their British Rail commercial.

While the attributes of television have been well-documented, its popularity has had an adverse effect upon the price. The cost of achieving national coverage of, say 80 per cent of all UK adults has increased since 1980 by 240 per cent and now requires an investment of approximately £800,000 excluding production.

Advertisers, however, are still able to utilize many of television's unique benefits. It is still possible to mount a national campaign with just a few days' notice (or a few hours in the case of some contractors). There is the option to test or restrict advertising to one of the fourteen ITV regions and if special targeting is required, one can isolate those programmes or timebands containing a disproportionate number of the appropriate target audience.

The benefits mentioned above can be coupled with television's undoubted ability to brand and sell products. Campaigns can generate national interest especially, those which adopt a soap opera style of format, e.g. recent work for Cointreau and Nescafé. This demonstration of its strength makes it the number one choice for the majority of national advertisers.

Cinema

Cinema, while sharing all the attributes of television, has a much higher level of audience involvement. The large screen, darkened auditorium and quality sound system add a considerable impact to the commercials shown. Further, the advertising, especially those ads made for cinema, tend to be a great deal more entertaining than a similar cross-section on television.

As discussed, the core audience is aged 15–24 although people tend to drop the habit of cinema once the first baby arrives. It also takes many months to arrive at conventionally accepted levels of coverage. Campaigns are generally bought on an alternate week basis; this allows the advertiser to produce one print per screen as opposed to the two required for consecutive weeks.

Cinema provides a quality of reproduction and an ambience that is unique and many advertisers such as Levis, Holsten Pils and National Westminster invest year after year in the medium.

Press

To generalize about so varied a medium is not easy but let us isolate the key characteristics of reading.

Press is a static medium – words and still pictures. It is, therefore, the prime medium for communicating information in detail – essential for many advertisers, e.g. performance and luxury cars, financial, products and pricing in direct response advertising.

Being printed, the advertisements can be kept and referred to later, unlike those on television. They can be cut and mailed off with a facility not yet possible with any other medium. All these attributes also apply to direct mail which is, in this context, an extension of press.

Press advertising can be used to fulfil many different needs. The impact of a full-page advertisement in the national press can provide information directly prior to many purchases. High coverage can be rapidly achieved. One insertion within the full range of available dailies would achieve coverage against all adults of approximately 60 per cent and approximately 80 per cent if Sundays were to be included.

Conversely, we can hone in on very specific target groups utilizing many of the specialist titles available. An added bonus for advertisers is that one is able to appear within sympathetic editorial or to create advertising appealing directly to the readers of the specialist publications.

Given the variety of weekly and monthly titles available, advertisers can select the quality of reproduction they require. Once the title is selected, one can choose the site within the publication, the editorial ambience required, and whether or not it is important to have the first car or building society advertisement – different sites hold differing levels of reader traffic. Horoscopes and letters pages command a very high level of reader traffic while a feature on motoring within a woman's monthly or weekly may narrow the level of consumer interest. Food advertising, especially those containing recipes, can be sited with the food section; it looks good and it will be read by consumers specifically interested in food.

Magazines are read at whatever speed we choose, we can flick pages or miss complete sections.

There is a great deal of advertising (many publications devote half each issue to advertising) and thus competition for a reader's attention. It is up to the media buyer to position the ad within the most appropriate publication, and then select the best environment. But the creative skill lies in surprising us so we stop, look and read.

Posters

Although some press ads look like posters, the poster is, in the way it is seen, very different from a newspaper or magazine. Reading is usually a solus activity. Magazines are able to carry advertisements for products which could embarrass if they appeared on family television. The poster is a highly public medium, seen by crowds. This can give a brand credibility with 'the people'. This is further helped by the size of the dominant sites, the 48 sheets, the supersites, the bright lights of Piccadilly, airships – the biggest advertisements to be seen.

By definition, posters can be seen by one and all. Targeting would appear to be impracticable. A level of fine-tuning is, however, possible according to the type of site selected:

Roadside sites:	High coverage of the population. This is especially true of the more mobile.
4 sheets:	Can be sited close to outlets appropriate to the brand being advertised, i.e. supermarkets or off-licences. They are used more often than not by housewife-orientated advertisers.
Taxi advertising:	High concentration within city centres and a high reach against UK business people, overseas tourists and London ABs.
Underground systems:	Cross track and escalator panels are an excellent

means of reaching young people and are consequently used for alcohol, jeans, etc.

These represent the high proportion of all sites. Further selection can be made via railway stations and airports.

Of the hundreds we pass, few are looked at. In the main, therefore, designs comprise a picture and few words. Good design, strong graphics, the drama of surprise and frequent changes of design help to grab attention.

Radio

The nature of radio listening will cause campaigns to maximize frequency and not coverage. This is beneficial to advertisers as conventional wisdom believes that consumers require more exposure to radio advertisements than for an equivalent television campaign. Radio costs per thousand are around a third of the cost of a television campaign. Advertising budgets, therefore, achieve greater exposure per advertising pound. Radio's main strength is its bias to young adults, particularly men. In this respect, it provides a complementary advertising vehicle to television which is biased up-age and female.

Radio is a 'friendly' medium and although in many instances offers a background to other activities it can and does build a rapport with the listener.

Our ability to use our imagination to create a scene and picture characters requires a mental effort lacking in other media, and this is surely halfway to making a sale?

The future

The 1990s will see the media landscape transformed. We will discuss the likely changes media by media.

Television

The past decade has seen dramatic changes: notably video recorders which have achieved a household penetration in excess of 50 per cent; nearly half of all households own two or more television sets and many have a remote control facility. Additionally, teletext is available in nearly a quarter of homes.

Looking ahead, satellite broadcast is set to dramatically increase the number of available channels. Currently, SKY offers four channels and

BSB a further five channels. Other direct broadcast satellite channels have yet to be allocated to the UK.

Due for launch in 1993 is the planned fifth terrestrial channel covering 60–70 per cent of the country, while the possibility of a sixth channel is also under consideration. A further significant development is that of local services broadcasting via cable and microwave transmissions (MMDS). Finally, the night-time hours of the BBC channels may be allocated to the newly founded ITC as a separate commercial franchise.

Each of these developments presents the viewer with an alternative to watching a commercial break. In this respect, agencies must respond with advertising that is increasingly interesting, that involves the viewer to an even greater extent and is remembered by the viewer after a strictly limited number few exposures.

Press

The Fleet Street Revolution has now all but taken place. Newspapers are making record profits, colour is being rapidly introduced to an increasing number of publications and new sections and supplements seem to appear almost monthly. Further, since 1985, we have seen the arrival of *Today*, *The Sport* and *The Independent*; 1989 saw the launch of the new Sunday newspaper, *The Sunday Correspondent*, which prompted *The Independent* to follow suit in 1990.

It would appear, therefore, that further developments will be few and far between. Unlike magazines, it is doubtful that UK papers will become Pan European for the British public requires UK news and *our* perspective of world events. Developments should, however, increase the choice and flexibility to the advertiser. More colour and more regionalization, together with a facility to provide inserts will all help generate greater advertising revenue and, therefore, profit.

Magazines are likely to adopt a more European approach in the future. Cross-frontier publishing enables the proprietor to amortize costs and establish a business base in other countries prior to 1992. In addition, more advertising will be negotiated on a Pan European and worldwide basis.

In the summer of 1989, G & J announced a joint rate card with a rate incentive for negotiations embracing all countries of publication. As advertisers take a more European view and standardize brands and advertising strategy, the G & J initiative should be followed by similar schemes.

Cinema

A great worry for this particular medium must be the declining 15–24-year-old population. This has represented the core audience for the medium and is responsible for much of the advertising revenue.

The strength and attractiveness of the medium should prevent any significant change. Despite the ever-increasing number of video hire outlets, the cinema audience continues to grow. The American film industry (the main supplier to the UK) continues to produce blockbuster after blockbuster. Films now produced appeal to a very broad target group. This fact, coupled with the investment made in the industry and the increasing amount of leisure time, should ensure that cinema enjoys a very prosperous period.

Radio

During late 1988 and 1989, many radio stations commenced split transmission services which gave an alternate choice of listening on both AM and FM frequencies. At a stroke, this doubled the commercial stations, improved choice and enabled existing stations to achieve a larger and more defined audience. The future will see immense change. Short term, the establishment of a further 20–30 incremental radio stations will enhance listeners' choice and complement the existing stations.

This incremental service is a forerunner of the type of service that will be provided by the 'several hundred' small radio stations to which the forthcoming broadcasting legislation will give the green light. These radio stations will serve strictly local communities, often with a transmission area covering a few square miles. The IBA (Independent Broadcasting Authority) has also authorized a further three national radio stations (one AM and two FM).

Thus, there is every opportunity for the industry to show significant revenue gain as each station appeals to more potential listeners, enhances the commercial audience and, in turn, attracts more advertisers into the medium.

Posters

Much restructuring has recently taken place. The new decade should see the poster industry in much better shape and organized to offer a much more competitive service; while new inspection services and a better general presentation of the plant will also help to improve the attractiveness of outdoor against other media.

Change will be evolutionary, not revolutionary. Developments within the medium will consist of more illumination and a greater number of multifaceted sites, while increasingly flexible advertising packages should at least enable the industry to hold its own in terms of advertising revenue share.

Research

This has recently emerged from near obscurity to dominate the trade press as the industry undergoes a complete transformation.

How do you accurately measure the audience to any one of the thirteen commercial radio services soon to be available in London? Advertisers need to know who and how many consumers read each one of the ever-increasing newspaper sections and also how much time is devoted to reading. A rapidly expanding number of homes can receive the four established television services plus those channels available from Sky and BSB. With thirteen channels to view and maybe three televisions in a household, how will we measure the attention level and profile of the audience?

The advertising industry is developing data systems fusing general audience information together with purchase habits. This will enable advertisers of, say, catfood to isolate programmes of specific interest to cat owners rather than the more general socioeconomic figures previously available.

These issues (and others) I am sure represent the tip of what will emerge as a sizeable iceberg.

The future

The 1990s will see the business of media flourish. The changes which will inevitably occur will allow great opportunity for those with foresight and flair. Whether you are buying, selling or planning, one thing can be guaranteed – that the business will continue to grow in stature and profile and certainly won't be dull.

BIBLIOGRAPHY

Periodicals

Admap (monthly)
Media Week (weekly)
Campaign (weekly)
British Rate and Data (BRAD) (monthly)

Advertising Association Year Book
Marketing Week (weekly)
Marketing (weekly)
Viewpoint (ITCA)
Magazine Marketplace
What's New in Marketing (monthly)
BBC Annual Report and Handbook

Books

Broadbent, S. and Jacobs, B. *Spending Advertising Money.* (Business Books, 1987)

Cowley, D. *How to Plan Advertising.* (Cassell, 1989)

Davis, M. *The Effective Use of Advertising.* (Hutchinson, 1988)

Henry, B. *British Television Advertising – The First 30 Years.* (Century, 1986)

Institute of Practitioners in Advertising. *Advertising Works.* (Cassell, 1987)

Nevitt, T. R. *Advertising in Britain – A History.* (Heinemann, 1982)

Rees, R. D. *Advertising Budgeting and Appraisal in Practice.* (Advertising Assocation, 1984)

Thompson, Lord of Fleet. *After I Was Sixty.* (Hamish Hamilton, 1975)

Torin, D. *The Complete Guide to Advertising.* (Macmillan, 1985)

Windlesham, Lord. *Broadcasting in a Free Society.* (Basil Blackwell, 1981)

5

Sales promotion in marketing

Peter Simmons

Sales promotion and merchandising are not the products of a marketing age. The first recorded sales promotion was when Eve gave Adam that apple, and, depending on how she offered it to him, it could also have been the first recorded merchandising campaign.

Selling and persuasion are as old as mankind, and it is only during the last 100 years that mass coverage media – press, television, and radio – have dominated the field. The baker's dozen was around centuries before the commercial break; look at old prints of street markets and you will see some magnificent merchandising.

What is sales promotion?

In the general sense everything that is done to sell a product is sales promotion, i.e. it is intended to promote sales. In the particular field of activity we are considering we define sales promotion as:

> A range of marketing techniques designed within a strategic marketing framework to add value to a product or service in order to achieve specific sales and marketing objectives.

The growth of an organized industry

Within the advertising and marketing function sales promotion has traditionally been handled as a by-product of some other activity, perhaps advertising, or even by the salesforce on a local and occasional basis. In the 1930s the first of the major national schemes was created with the promotion departments of newspapers well in the fore.

The specialized agencies became established during the 1970s. In the early stages, like advertising agencies, they were acting as sales agents earning their living by offering merchandise or services in connection with sales promotion.

The whole field of sales promotion or below-the-line has now become bigger than above-the-line or media in many companies. The agencies that service the big spending companies have grown in size and experience, are often working continuously with their clients, and are appointed in the same way as advertising agents to work on specified brands or product groups.

A flexible tool

The many techniques available in sales promotion offer marketing management an enormous armoury with which to attack his problems. There are techniques which have broad appeal to all sectors of the market and all categories of operators concerned with it – salesmen, retailers, wholesalers, agents, regular users, occasional users, non-users. At the other end of the scale we have precise techniques which are capable of being directed to and confined to a tightly defined target group.

This quality is increasingly valuable in many consumer product and service markets where there is no longer a single identified market but a number of different segments with differing user characteristics.

Hotels direct different appeals and promotion propositions to business users and conference organizers from those used to appeal to tourists, family holidaymakers and weekend break users.

Yoghurt used to be natural yoghurt, then came fruit yoghurt. Now there are very low fat yoghurts, children's yoghurts, set yoghurts, active yoghurts, whipped yoghurts as well as the original types.

This situation has produced the need for precise promotion communication that can deliver an appropriate offer to a specific target audience. Sales promotion has, therefore, become closely aligned to database marketing using tightly specified and controlled direct mail or door-to-door distribution to communicate to the desired audience – whether they are existing users or, more likely, known competitive brand users.

Objective setting

With a wide range of precise devices available and the accuracy of delivery which has come with the use of computerized databases and records, it will be evident that one of the most important functions of the marketing manager in sales promotion planning is to define accurately the target audience and the objectives of the initiative.

Before the means of solving a problem are determined, it is necessary to define precisely the characteristics of the problem and the proposed method of solving it. On the surface, people choose a product or service for the simple reason that it offers them the best proposition. When we look at what constitutes the best proposition, we find a wide range of interacting factors. It is a well-known fact that when the petrol gauge is on E, your favourite brand of petrol is the next one you can find. In a less pressing situation your brand decision may be far more complex. The convenience of the garage will remain high on the list, but it will be moderated by such other considerations as price; what you feel about the brand or the service given; whether they take credit cards or give trading stamps, drinking glasses or football badges; whether they have an automatic car wash; or whether the attendant plays football for the local team or knows your name. Undoubtedly the most spectacular and significant sales promotion device is advertising. We must, therefore, consider all the others in this light.

Products and services have personalities or brand images, and these can be their most valuable properties. It can cost millions of pounds to create this personality, and everything that happens to the brand affects it. This is particularly true of promotion activities. Promotion devices tend to be strident and highly conspicuous; they therefore have a considerable effect on the personality of the product, and if used inconsiderately, not only make no contribution to the personality but can work in direct opposition to it. Thus it is possible for an advertiser to spend half his promotion fund in the press to emphasize the high quality of his product, and the other half in various promotion devices that cheapen it, debasing the impression of quality.

We have now covered the two great commandments of sales promotion – it must relate accurately to the objectives, and it must be compatible with the total brand proposition. Basic and self-evident as this may seem, it is a fact that promotion schemes are peddled from company to company and sometimes bought because they are bright, amusing, clever, funny, original, will get this month's sales target, or have worked for someone else, somewhere else, without any considered regard to the fundamentals of the problem of the brand or the intended method of solving it.

The setting of the objectives is essential to promotion success; if you can get the objectives accurately defined, you are well on the way to a successful promotion. Some promotion agencies have their own systems of objective analysis. Some agencies have their own briefing procedures, which are often regarded as confidential property as they make the difference between one promotion house and the next. A checklist is set out below covering the main aspects of a promotion. No system can be complete in this respect. At a certain point science gives way to art, and here the skill, experience, intuition and sixth sense of the promotion consultant becomes the key advantage you buy when you hire him.

Good operators will want quantifiable objectives and will press until they get them. Modern data analysis and research facilities make it possible to provide accurate information in respect of all the important aspects of the main product and service markets and there is no activity in which this is more usable than sales promotion.

Producing a brief

The following checklist covers the main aspects of a promotion brief:

1 Define products to be covered:
   (a) Product.
   (b) Sizes.
2 Define promotion target audience and quantify.
3 Set date of promotion:
   (a) Trade or consumer.
   (b) Date of sales briefing.
4 Define area of promotion.
5 Examine basic market, product information and trends.
   (a) Total market sales.
   (b) Company brand sales.
   (c) Brand shares.
   (d) Market segmentation data.
   (e) Distribution.
   (f) Consumer profile information.
   (g) Promotional history last twelve months.
   (h) Advertising pattern last twelve months.

The information in this section must take account of regional, seasonal, and other local variations, including the listing of major dealers or non-dealers if necessary or major users and non-users of a service product.

Promotion briefing

The brief should define the objectives to be achieved precisely. These usually occur in any of the following terms. (Target should be related to promotion period and follow-up periods in such detail as necessary, including size, ratios, etc.) Requirements should be given on a quantified and specific basis covering the necessary points, for example:

1 Distribution.
2 Stock cover.
3 Consumer trial/level to be achieved.
4 Purchase frequency.
5 Sales volume – compare normal level and post-promotion targets.

Promotion budgets

Sales promotion budgets are normally pre-set as part of the annual marketing budget. Some organizations include a dynamic pound per case or percentage of turnover element. In the case of the dynamic budget a promotion which is a runaway success can be highly desirable, if it is a fixed budget promotion outstandingly high participation can be a serious financial embarrassment.

The response to the techniques available vary from market to market but there is now a considerable database available from which to develop forecasts and an experienced operator should be able to predict response levels and costs accurately.

Setting the budget

The budget should be related to the objectives and be complete. Some sales promotion techniques carry a number of additional costs and these should all be taken into account. The following should be covered by the budget plus any special items which arise in the particular circumstances of the product or service to be promoted.

1 Sales force incentive.
2 Trade bonus.
3 Consumer promotion.
4 Material production costs.
5 Special packing costs.
6 Supporting media costs.
7 Supporting display costs.
8 Additional labour costs.
9 Pre and post research costs.

Target audiences and techniques

A detailed analysis of the range of promotional devices is beyond the scope of a single chapter. We can examine the main promotional audiences, however, and consider the effects of various promotions on them. There are three main audiences – company staff (usually salesmen), the retailer or agent, and the consumer.

Employee promotions

The use of promotions to motivate company employees must be considered in the light of the fact that the employee is already being paid to do a job to the best of his or her ability. For this reason, and because most promotion devices have their maximum appeal at their launch and gradually become taken for granted, employee promotions are generally of limited duration and designed to produce a special effort. If an employee promotion is mounted on a continuing basis it can become regarded as part of the salary and it loses its special effect.

There are various ways of structuring an employee incentive. It may be awarded on an individual basis, which would appear to offer the maximum incentive for the person to go out and do their best; but in some situations a team award is more effective. It is easier to set accurate targets for a team, and most people will be very reluctant to be seen to be letting down their colleagues, whereas what they do for themselves is their own business. A team incentive also provides the team manager with an opportunity to bond together and lead the team. Incentives directed towards the family can encourage a person to do better than they would for themselves.

Trade promotions

Dealer or retailer promotions are designed to motivate the middle-man to act on behalf of the promoter. This does not preclude his acting on his own behalf or that of the employer simultaneously, but it does not necessarily follow that this is the case. The promotion should therefore take account of the interests of the dealer as well as those of the promotions sponsor if it is going to gain maximum acceptance.

The trade incentive or buyer incentive grew up very quickly at one stage, to the point where many companies, both receiving and giving incentives, felt that they had got out of hand and in some cases amounted to little better than bribery. The result has been a sharp falling off in this type of activity and some leading organizations have specifically forbidden their staff to offer or participate in incentive schemes.

An important part of a promotion company's work is cooperating with its clients to spend the dealer promotion money available as cost-effectively as possible. A company must always bear in mind that retailer and dealer promotions are usually at the expense of consumer promotions, and the more that is spent with the dealer, the weaker becomes the consumer franchise. There are some markets, particularly industrial markets, in which the dealer has a predominant influence over the sale, and in these cases dealer aids and promotional devices assume a special importance.

Consumer promotions

By far the most conspicuous promotional activities are in the mass consumer markets. They do not absorb as much money as trade promotions, but they are far more evident, and most promotion companies concentrate on these activities. As we saw earlier, the consumer promotion is a marketing tool; it is a means to an end and not an end in itself, except for companies who are in business to sell and run promotions.

A consumer promotion is obviously a complex, expensive and major marketing consideration. It needs to be planned well in advance, as part of the total annual programme for the brand.

The type of promotion to use, and the form it should take to achieve the agreed objectives is, in part, a technical and factual consideration and in part a judgement. Pre-testing can resolve some points of doubt, but security, time, economics, and the practical difficulties of testing certain types of promotion, make the final decision one of judgement, which is usually taken at the most senior marketing level.

As a broad guide, some of the principal characteristics of the four main promotion categories are set out in Figure 5.1.

	Display	Trial/ awareness	Loyalty	Raise trade stocks	Widen trade distribution
Contests/ games	×	×			
Reduced price	×	×	×	×	×
Extra/ other product	×	×	×	×	×
Premiums/ refunds	×	×	×		

Figure 5.1   *The four main promotion categories and their effect*

Figure 5.1 is only a guide, and the form of implementation of a promotion can affect its characteristics. For example, the average contest attracts a minute entry compared with the normal number of product users or buyers. It does not, therefore, normally rate as an inducement to the trade to increase stocks.

However, if the contest is sufficiently powerful – for example, every entrant gets a prize, the main prize fund is particularly lavish, the contest is to be promoted by a leaflet put through every letterbox and by television advertising, and there is a supporting trade promotion – retailers might well consider increasing stocks to meet the demand the contest will produce.

Types of sales promotion

Sales promotion techniques are very varied depending on their method of communication or nature. However, they can be grouped into two categories – 'immediate' or 'delayed' according to when the promotional benefit is available. In the delayed situation the consumer is likely to have to mail-in to obtain the offer item or benefit. The main types of techniques in each of these categories are:

Immediate	Delayed
Price promotions (money off)	Free mail-in offers
Free with pack	Self-liquidating
Free extra product	Premiums
Reusable container packs	Competitions
In-store demonstrations	Prize draws
Money-off coupons	Coupon valid against next purchase
(door to door or magazine	Phone-ins
distributed).	Shareouts
	Refunds

Promotion research

As Lord Leverhulme said: 'Half my advertising is wasted but I don't know which half.' In sales promotion work it is usually possible to know accurately, quickly and even in advance which part is working and which is wasted.

Pre-research of promotion concepts is now an essential element in the promotion planning of many marketing operators. In combination with good historical data, pre-testing can give a precise indication of the consumer appeal and comprehension of an offer and the level of response likely to be achieved at various levels of proof of purchase or other participation requirement.

The planning of the pre-test and the post-evaluation should be carried out in advance. The pre-test panel may be required for post-test analysis. The post-test database may need to be established in advance as the promotion activity could destroy the starting position and certain factors required for comparative analysis will be unknown and irretrievable.

The emphasis placed on evaluation can provide a revealing insight into the motivation of a promotion consultant.

Creativity – the magic ingredient

Intangible and, to a considerable degree, defying definition creativity is the element that can turn a straightforward promotion offer into an exciting, motivating and attention-gaining campaign. The creative element is second to none not only in the nationally-advertised promotion but also the small day-to-day workhouse promotions.

A £1 cash refund offer is powerful but rather mundane. Rephrased as a '£1 Cash Dash' with the full reward only being available if applications are received by a set date and excitement as well as an additional cutting edge to the promotion has been added.

Creativity can also be the means of picking up and exploiting the brand's advertising strategy and theme. This may not always be feasible as the variance in media and the techniques used in advertising and sales promotion can provide a constraint.

The skilful practitioner will achieve a balance between creativity and effective communication. Because an offer is simple it is no reason to dress it up so that its consumer communication and impact is diluted or obscured. The test of creativity in sales promotion lies in sales not awards.

The management challenge

The essence of good sales promotion management is accurate briefing and total marketing coordination.

In theory, an 'on-pack' can be operated and a consumer response generated without the other parties – the salesforce and the trade – being involved. However, for a promotion to achieve its maximum potential these other parties need to be communicated with and motivated to sell more/buy more.

The communication of the proposition to all concerned is an essential element in its success. This may involve nothing more than a sheet in the standard A4 sales presenter, it may require a desktop video presentation or justify a presentation in Paris. It is in the harnessing of the enthusiasm of all involved that the good promotion can be made great.

In sales promotion the marketing manager has at his disposal a flexible device that can be used regionally, or in certain types of retail outlet, or in an individual store. The immediacy and direct effect of many promotion techniques offers a quality that is particularly attractive in a tight marketing situation.

It is possible, by means of a well-planned and controlled promotion programme, to influence sales so that the effect of the promotion can be achieved within the sales canvas and the cost of the promotion can be recovered immediately. This is rarely possible by the use of traditional advertising media.

The ability to direct promotional effort at a target group of consumers or retailers provides a means of tackling specific aspects of the marketing problem without wasted expenditure. If a weakness is detected in cooperative societies, for example, a promotion can be aimed at and confined to this category of retailer. It can be confined to co-ops in the Greater London area and even individual stores within the society. The promotion can appeal to men only (free cigar), women only (50p off this month's *Good Housekeeping* magazine), children only (free badges), or to everyone (10p off). It provides then a practical means of 'precision marketing'.

BIBLIOGRAPHY

Britt, S. H. and Boyd, H. W. *Marketing Management and Administrative Action.* (McGraw-Hill, 1973)
Lawson, Richard. *Sales Promotion Law.* (Blackwell Scientific, 1987)
Petersen, C. *Sales Promotion in Action.* (ABP, 1979)
Williams, John. *The Manual of Sales Promotion.* (Innovation, 1983)

6

Creativity

Maurice Drake

The creative area of advertising is one on which most words have been written and yet is by far the hardest to write about. But let us remember one thing. Every branch of advertising and marketing can be creative. The men who took an old-established sweet such as mint cream and chocolate, produced a new shape, a new pack, a new name and a new positioning as the after-dinner mint, created a whole new and highly successful product. The first media buyer to suggest half pages across in women's magazines created a whole new media pattern.

Way back in the past, the first space broker who had the idea of selling more space by offering to write and design the client's advertisement created the advertising agency. But here we are dealing with the more traditionally thought-of creative area of advertising, the actual creation of ideas and advertisements.

Now the physical and mental processes of creativity cannot be described. This is a moment of magic that not all are capable of, and even those that are would be hard put to it to write down how it happened. What can be described, however, are the disciplines of creativity; and there must be disciplines, for no good creative idea ever came out of the ether without pre-decided strategies and guidelines, whether formal or otherwise.

The need for disciplines means one important fact. Creative people in advertising have also to be business people. They must know what they are doing, why they are doing it and at whom they are directing it. All these facts should be distilled in a creative strategy.

The creative strategy

Let one thing be clear. The discipline of a creative strategy is not a straitjacket to creative thinking. A good strategy – and there are many useless and unexecutable ones – allows the creative person to direct his thinking into the correct channels instead of just trying to pluck an idea out of the air.

It is important that the strategy should be agreed by the creative people, naturally in consultation with the client contact and marketing departments. There is a good reason for this; the strategy is the means by which the creative team understands the product and the marketing environment in which it must compete and the potential consumer. In addition, a strategy agreed by the creative department can be executed in an advertisement. That may seem a strange point, but many strategies produced outside the creative department are simply tidy documents that contain far too many elements and could never be executed within the confines of anything other than a documentary film or a leading article!

So what should the strategy contain? In the main the contents fall under the following headings:

Why we are advertising

This sums up, as succinctly as possible, why the client is advertising at all. It may be to launch a new product. It could be to change the positioning of a well established product, or to take advantage of a seasonal sales peak or extra use of the product in an area that varies from the national norm, or perhaps to achieve a fast rate of trial and sampling. In other words, that situation or circumstance upon which advertising can act and achieve results must be evident.

What the advertising must achieve

This is not a rephrased reiteration of the above, but a statement of what end result the advertising must have on the consumer. There lies the key difference between the general objective and the advertising objective. The latter is a means of achieving the former.

For instance, a general objective to raise brand share may be accomplished by an advertising objective to change a consumer attitude or misconception. The former is to sell more, and the latter is to convince consumers to desire more.

Prospect definition

This is the key to any good strategy. No product can be all things to all people. It is far more profitable to have a motivating effect on a specific group of consumers than to give a blunt-edged promise to an indifferent mass. This principle of consumer segmentation, which is so much part of modern advertising and marketing, throws great responsibility on the correctness and clearness of the prospect definition.

For that important reason it must be so much more than just a bald statement of the prospect's socioeconomic grouping. This is part of it, but by no means all of it. Socioeconomic grouping gives you some traditional guide to the prospect's habits, attitudes and disposable income. But imagine if you were asked to go out in the street and find a man in the C2-DE socioeconomic group. You might find dozens with that description. But which one would you choose?

This is why the prospect definition must be so much more. It must be like a police Identikit picture and description, so that the advertising can pinpoint the most potential consumer.

Another factor is age, and in clearly defined limits – not something vague like '16–45', for the strata of appeal between those ages are infinite. Obviously the sex of the consumer is important, and whether married or single, and number in family. As far as possible the prospect definition should also cover consumers' aspirations, hates, loves, habits, anything that can help the creative people not only to identify them but to *understand* them.

Promise

This is the 'reason for being' of the product, which singles it out from competition in the teeming market place. This is 'why to buy'. Remember the famous Charles Atlas advertising; this did not just sell a body-building course on bigger muscles. All the others said that. It was the one that offered weak people the chance to be strong people, and in that promise reposed the seeds of its success.

Above all, the promise must be consumer-orientated not product-orientated. In one example an underarm spray that was a powder in an aerosol stated, 'It's surprising what a little powder does for an underarm spray'. That was product-oriented. It was changed to 'Now you don't have to get wet to be dry'. See the difference – that's a consumer promise. And research proved it right to change it.

Reason why

Obviously evidence as to why a promise is possible will strengthen the promise. It is not always possible to have an exclusive product difference, in formula, engineering, speed of experience. But one reason why, for instance, can be the number of people who have tried the product and found it to be all it promised.

In any case, the consumer must be given some firm basis for believing that the product will keep its promise. If the strategy is properly written and based on known facts, in whatever form a particular agency may choose, and if it contains this kind of information, it can only lead to better, more effective advertising.

Creating the advertising

As already stated, the 'inspiration' element in creating advertising cannot, in all truth, be described. But the 'perspiration' element can.

By that is meant what a good, professional creative man, or woman, looks for in an idea, the criterion they set themselves and how they organize their thinking. One important thing to bear in mind is that good advertising is true advertising. Apart from all the self-imposed regulations and laws that govern advertising, in big long-term business lies, however subtle, will only sell a product once. When it is in use, a product can only survive on its performance.

So the creative task can be described as gift-packaging the truth. We have to make the product news interesting enough to stand out and be seen among all its competitors.

Working from the strategy, it is the creative person's aim to find new language, both in words and visuals to present the product and its benefits to the consumer. For it is saying something that may not be unique, but in a unique manner, that marks the great campaigns.

Let's take some classic examples.

'Palmolive makes skin look young again!' A good promise, but hardly a new thought. But the creative person said, 'Palmolive brings back that schoolgirl complexion' – a visual imagination-provoking set of words, and a campaign that made history. 'More people eat Heinz Beans than any other'. This could just have sounded like a successful manufacturer patting his own back. But 'Beanz Meanz Heinz' said exactly the same thing, but so memorably that it went into the language, and the new spelling of 'beanz' is now used more often than the standard dictionary version. 'We make our flour finer by taking all the lumps out'. Sounds as if you are about to see a picture of the factory, until a creative person invents the brilliant little 'flour grader' for Spillers Homepride.

Notice one striking thing about these three campaigns. Out of all the teeming messages in print, television and posters, we all see and hear it is possible to remember that advertising and the major selling points of the product. And yet none is in a very interesting category or is saying anything very startlingly different in terms of promise.

That's what makes them great campaigns.

Therein lies the task that faces every creative person – turning information into communication.

Methods of working vary from person to person. Some prefer to work alone, but more often it is a team – writer and art director. The most productive method is that of free association. That is rather like a group of people telling stories.One might have a story about a salesman in which there is a barmaid, this reminds the next man of a story about the barmaid and the sailor, and someone else is immediately brought to mind of a story about a sailor, and so on. What is happening is that each is 'sparking' the mind of others – a kind of chain reaction.

Thus a creative idea is suggested, evolved, going through change after change in the chain reaction until that inner gut feeling all creative people know emerges and says, 'This is it!'. Then comes the polishing, the crafting that turns it into media-filling sales-building advertising.

Creating for the media

Naturally the advertising is governed by the strategy. So, in fact, is the choice of media. The basic message remains the same whether you are in TV, press, posters or radio, but each different medium calls for differing techniques and offers its own advantages and opportunities.

Television

Of course, television offers you more of your consumer's senses than any other medium. You have at your command both sound and sight with the bonus of movement. This is what makes TV so powerful in one particular area – that of demonstration.

With the coming of commercial television in 1955, we had, for the first time in Britain, the ability in advertising to go right into the homes of our consumers and demonstrate our products with all the persuasion of door-to-door salesmen.

This makes for one commandment in advertising (amazingly so often transgressed) which should be chipped in stone. If your product can be demonstrated and you are in TV, then demonstrate it! If your product is any good, then nothing, no persuasive words or catchy jingle, will sell it like it can sell itself. But remember, a demonstration is not an idea.

Not all products lend themselves to demonstration however. This is when you need to examine all the other techniques available to you. But please think of the creative idea first, then the techniques that can best serve it, not the other way round. There are too many instances where a technique is thought of first and then people look for an idea that will fit it.

Let us look at some of those techniques.

The playlet

Called by some unkind people the 'tele charade', this is where a small happening in the lives of people representing the prospect definition is centred round the use of, need for, or conversion to the product. It is not unlike the way Christ used the parable to make a particular point to his listeners. The TV playlet can be humorous, serious or even sad. With the use of children it can bring a warm tear to the eye. But be careful. Make sure that in its confines you can tell your necessary product story. The typical commercial length today is 30 seconds. Remember that in TV, you get less sound time than visual time, so that you have 29 seconds in which people have to speak in at least a good imitation of real life and a situation has to be set up and resolved. All that calls for really expert writing. There are more bad playlet commercials on the air than any other kind.

The voice-over

This is perhaps the simplest kind of commercial. You could call it the press-ad on TV. The vision shows the demonstration, the situation, the view, or the problem and the end result, and the voice track guides the viewer through, explaining and persuading. There are pitfalls. Too many VO commercials are like children's reading books. In these there could be, for instance, a picture of a cat sitting on a mat and the words below saying 'a cat on a mat' – very necessary of course when teaching a child to read. But, in commercials, we are dealing with people who do not need this kind of picture–word combination. If the picture needs that close an interpretation, there is something wrong with the picture. The words and pictures should work in harmony, even counterpoint, but never simple note-for-note unison. If that happens, you are wasting one or the other. Examine your piece of work again and pinpoint the weakness.

Music

This falls into two categories: the jingle and mood or background music. The latter hardly needs any explanation, as it is part of our daily lives in television, films and radio. Of course, music can create or heighten a mood. Notice how, on the main line railway stations, they play marches in the morning to move along the rush hour traffic and soft music in the evening to relax the tired commuter!

The jingle, which is a folk art form, has made immense progress in recent years, with more and more young talent coming into the business. A jingle has the advantages of constantly reiterating a sales point in a way that imprints it on the memory, can give a commercial a longer life-span without a growing irritation factor. Just a few words on the creation of a jingle. The words can be written by the copywriter but the music calls for a professional. Of course, there has to be a large measure of collaboration as the words will need to be tailored to music, and vice versa. Another point to remember is that the jingle is designed to carry a simple message. Do not load it with sales points.

Personalities

This is a subject that is relevant to all the media of advertising but, possibly because television is very much a personality medium, seems to occur more often in the TV commercial. A relevant personality can be invaluable to the sale of a product. A cookery expert for a food, a racing driver for motoring accessories, a model for a beauty product – these are all relevant personalities.

Sometimes people such as actors or comedians are used just because they are personalities. Although they are just borrowed interest, and even a replacement for an idea (which is irreplaceable), there have been many instances where their use has been very successful. But watch out for possible problems; often they turn out to be 'video vampires', and later research shows they are all that is remembered. Very often, too, expensive comedians are contracted and then used in a straightforward serious way. When you think about it, this is a side of their personalities that is of very little interest to the viewer, and you are not getting the very talent that made them famous in the first place.

Testimonial

There are two types of testimonial advertising – that by well known personalities, as covered above, and that by ordinary people who have tried the product and are willing to testify to their satisfaction. This is, of course, a very good technique, as it is word-of-mouth advertising be-tween peer groups. The key phrase there is 'word-of-mouth', for to be really successful it is always best to use their actual words and phrases instead of trying to influence their style. And very often housewives express themselves much better, and more freshly, than copywriters write.

These are only some of the techniques available to the creative person. There are many others, and certainly new ones waiting to be invented. After all, the present ones did not exist until someone, somewhere, thought of them.

Posters

Here really is the distillation of all advertising. A poster, 16 sheet, 48 sheet or 4 sheet, cannot have many words. Some maintain an outside maximum of six, and therein must be contained a complete, compelling message to the prospect.

In no other form of advertising do the picture and the words have to be so happily married. There are many theories and suggested rules. It is said that if some liquid such as ketchup or milk is being poured, it should never reach its destination but leave the viewer to complete the picture in his mind's eye. Where a product has a continual showing on posters, some art directors believe that a 'colour palette' should be decided for the product so that all its posters have a colour relationship.

Creative groups working on a campaign that has no posters in its schedule have been known to create a poster anyway, just to distil in their minds the key selling idea they have created. Perhaps there is nothing more satisfying in all advertising than creating a good poster. It is a sure sign you know your craft.

Radio

This is a relatively new medium in the UK and there is more ignorance in this area than possibly any other.

Radio gives you the command of only one sense – hearing. But it does give you the complete freedom of your consumer's imagination, some-thing television makes very little demand on.

Just to use the music tracks of your TV commercials, or simply VO tracks of product information, is a criminal waste of the most immediate imagination-exercising medium we have at our disposal. With radio you can create the Battle of Waterloo in a room 10 ft × 10 ft, take people below the earth or to the stars, and so on.

In a famous recording made for the radio media of America there is a completely acceptable sequence where bombers load up with enormous chocolate meringues and drop them in a vast lake of chocolate. Then TV is asked to 'follow that!' The moral is made.

Press

It is almost impossible here to detail all the techniques available in press advertising. Photography, illustration, typography, even the humble but always successful strip cartoon, are all here to use. Each different sphere – spreads, pages, slim column ads or even earpieces – offer a different challenge. Today's press, particularly the magazines, offer many selected market segments. By age, sex, interests, class, there is a magazine somewhere that can pinpoint your potential consumer. You need all your skill to make your advertisement the one the reader stops at, reads and is persuaded by. The press may not hold for some the creative glamour of television, but it can be the most rewarding medium of all to work in.

Think creative

No textbook can make you creative if your talents lie in other directions. But we can all, in advertising, learn to think creatively about our business.

Next time you read a magazine, watch television, or see a poster, start to look at it differently from the ordinary consumer. Stop and analyse it. Decide what the strategy is, what the ad is trying to accomplish. Make up your mind if it is succeeding. If you believe it is not, decide where the fault lies – then produce your solution. This process is invaluable in forming and honing your advertising judgement, and will stand you in good stead in one of the most frustrating, exciting, rewarding professions in the world.

7

Production processes

Roy Topp

Press and print production

Introduction

In the advertising agency the production department can cover a very wide spectrum of operations, particularly when applied to press and print. The object of this chapter is to explain the functions and responsibilities of press and print production staff and also to look at the technical requirements of production personnel as well as other areas directly concerned with production, such as control (or progress or traffic, as it is sometimes called).

Since advertising agencies vary enormously in their size, make-up and philosophy, no hard and fast rules can apply to the organization of their various departments. Different agencies operate in different ways. Indeed, the type of work they handle will demand that they structure their departments to suit particular needs. It may be that one agency favours combining traffic and production duties as one function, while another prefers separate departments. Some agencies combine print buying with press production, whereas others separate these responsibilities. However, a basic system must apply for an agency as a whole, even though individual departmental responsibilities may vary. Therefore this section will deal with the functions and responsibilities of production, together with the other areas directly concerned, in their basic forms.

The printing industry

Before looking at the advertising agency and its production staff, let us first glance at the printing industry. Printing as an industry has grown over many centuries, for many years being firmly entrenched as a craft. It started when the Chinese invented paper in the second century, and took a big step forward when they began printing from woodcuts in the eighth century. Throughout the ages the craft of printing travelled eastwards in the hands, hearts and minds of returning explorers, slowly spreading throughout Europe and evolving into the highly technical and complex industry we know today.

The printing industry has historically been a craft-based industry, and this still applies today to a large degree. However, the last two decades or so have seen a tremendous technological explosion in printing, and, like many other industries, printing has moved, and continues to move, away from its craft-based origins into the world of technology and computer controls.

As in any industry subjected to great change, the people working in it have also had to face new challenges. The challenges posed by new techniques in printing have been no less for those in advertising most concerned with the printed image – the production executives. On the flood tide of these new advances has come a greatly increased volume of colour printing in the advertising and promotion fields. The craft attitude and skills are being supplemented by electronics, densitometry, standardization of film development, automatic plate-making and cylinder manufacture, and a host of ancillary controls, all directed at allowing the printer to produce a greatly increased volume of printing, particularly colour, more quickly, more economically and more consistently. Therefore production personnel have had to respond accordingly, and indeed must continue to respond, so that agency and advertiser alike may maximize the benefits of this relatively new era in graphic reproduction and printing.

The production executive

The printing industry as a whole covers a very wide spectrum of processes and allied operations. Much of their use in advertising is channelled through the agency production executive, who must be very familiar with the most common printing processes, such as lithography, gravure and flexography, together with relevant platemaking and cylinder-manufacturing techniques. A solid working knowledge of other processes, particularly screen process printing, is also required. He must put his knowledge to use in ensuring that the printer produces an acceptable result within the disciplines imposed by a particular process or printing situation. He should be the person whose advice the agency seeks, be it creative, account management or media, on all matters concerned with the printed image. He should, in fact, be the agency's graphic reproduction consultant, particularly in relation to the creative staff, for it is in the creative area that the train of events leading to a printed result begin. It is also the area where, through lack of proper advice and knowledge, many impractical ideas start on the slippery, downward path that leads to inevitable disappointment in the printed result.

This in turn demands, in addition to a knowledge of printing and graphic reproduction, a working knowledge of photography, film stocks and lens performance, colour laboratory work, and retouching techniques for both colour and black and white, as well as artwork preparation techniques, so that artwork prepared is reproduceable by the various processes when printed on a wide variety of substrates. A pretty picture may be aesthetically appealing but in an advertising context it is next to useless if it cannot be reproduced in a manner which shows the creative concept to its best advantage. Therefore the technical disciplines of printing must be catered for very strongly in the artwork preparation stage. This cannot happen unless the correct advice is given and this advice will only be forthcoming from knowledgeable production staff. In short the production executive, in addition to his other duties, should be the funnel through which all artwork must pass on its way to the printer. Then he can ensure that the material produced by his agency is printable and will, in fact, maximize creativity in terms of first-class reproduction.

The foregoing outlines the technical knowledge and background required for the ideal production executive. However, technical knowledge and know-how are not enough. The successful production executive must administer his group of accounts efficiently. In simple terms he must organize matters to ensure that the right material reaches the right publication at the right time.

Working in close liaison with the control or administration system and account management personnel, the production executive must ensure that artwork is supplied to him in time for the production of the necessary printing material, be it litho separations or gravure artwork. He will have to coordinate the services of his team of suppliers to meet the required timetable, thus enabling him to supply printing material to publishers by the time specified.

Before this, however, the production executive will have gathered together the necessary information to allow him to proceed. Normally working from a schedule of bookings supplied by his media department, he will have obtained such necessary mechanical information from each publication as size requirements and copy dates (the dates by which publications require material), together with the relevant technical data- printing process, material required (litho separations or artwork), screen rulings and angles for half-tone work and so on. In the case of four-colour advertisements for litho-printed publications he will need to know such things as printing process, mode of printing (whether a single colour, two colour, or four-colour press is being used), details of ink and paper to be used, printing sequence and other technical data, which must be passed to his supplier to enable him to produce the correct type of printing material. With all this information to hand, the production executive can then plan the progress of work through its various stages of artwork preparation, reproduction and proofing and agency to client approval, at which time material is released to the publication with specific instructions regarding dates of insertions.

Quality control

With the increasing complexities of the printing industry, the necessity for first class artwork, and the demands from agencies and advertisers alike for improved quality of the printed result, there is a great need for the intelligent application of effective quality control and careful production planning from development of the original concept through to the final printed result. Production staff concentrate not only on assessing the visual result of various types of proofs or printed copy but also on artwork preparation, thus ensuring that the reproduction quality of the artwork, as well as the creative content, is catered for. It is also important that quality control is applied to the technical areas of printing.

A sound technical knowledge allows the production executive to assess a creative concept for reproduction value. This is a very important aspect of quality control. Intelligent clients do not take kindly to being told after the event that while the concept was brilliant creatively, it really could not work when printed due to the limitations of the printing processes. The creative process does not stop when the work moves to the repro supplier and on to the printer. The teamwork should continue throughout the production process so that the final result is as envisaged and expected by all concerned.

When assessing photography, for instance, it is necessary to be able to define the ideal characteristics of transparency such as colour balance, localized colour distortion, colour saturation, tonal gradation and separation, sharpness and definition, granular structure and density range.

The production executive should also be able to advise on various retouching techniques or the degree of retouching needed for the different printing processes, particularly for national and provincial press advertisements. This should include advice on whether retouching or composition could be better or more economically done on a computerized workstation. He should be conversant with colour laboratory work. This includes the production of duplicate transparencies (made from the original transparency) and copy transparencies (transparency copies of flat artwork such as wash drawings). His technical knowledge in this area can be extremely useful to the art director in the preparation of artwork. Any help and advice the production executive can give to improve the origination can only lead to improved printing standards.

The same considerations apply to the printed image. No intelligent technical comment can be made about a printer's effort without a firm knowledge of the printing processes used. For example, the widely different characteristics of lithography, gravure printing or flexography must be understood when assessing the artwork being prepared and the printed result, both at proof and print stage. Unless the production executive understands the relative problems and characteristics, then he can make no expert judgement. In consequence, the printer will inevitably be allowed to produce lower quality work.

It cannot be emphasized too strongly that the production executive needs a deep knowledge of the swiftly developing and improving technology in graphic reproduction and printing. Only then will he be able to make his very important contribution in the chain of events that takes place in printed advertising messages, from the initial concept to the final printed product.

Control

Control (or administration, progress, traffic, whatever title is given) is a function in an advertising agency allied to production in that it is part of the whole process of moving the original creative idea from thought to deed. Many different systems exist, with varying degrees of responsibility being placed upon them and their personnel. In some agencies there is a separate control department, and in others a dual function of production and control. However, in all cases the control department or traffic function has a firm responsibility.

Ideally their responsibility should be to plan, coordinate, administer and expedite the workflow through the creative department so that a campaign progresses through its various stages to a predetermined time and cost plan. This should be done in such a way as to maintain the best possible creative standards while controlling all the internal and external costs incurred on each job. This requires the controller to work very closely with creative, management control, media, production, accounts and outside suppliers and publications. The controller's responsibilities are therefore considerable.

An important function of traffic can also be budget control. Most advertising agencies now cost out all aspects of creative and mechanical production material that pertains to a campaign before going into production. These costs cover photography, models, artwork and so on together with the mechanical production costs from the production house or printer. These, together with the known media costs give clients a complete breakdown of the total campaign costs, in advance of any financial commitment.

On the question of TV traffic, systems and methods are again varied. Larger agencies have very professional TV and radio production departments. However, a reasonable situation is for the traffic department to control the campaign up to the approval of the storyboard and script, and then to hand over to the TV or radio production department or production company.

The print department

In any agency system someone is responsible for buying the point-of-sale material and posters that back up the main advertising campaign. Point-of-sale material can take many forms, from simple, single sheet leaflets to complex display items dependent on cardboard engineering. A substantial knowledge of the processes behind this work is therefore essential for the personnel working in this area. Poster printing is also a very specialist area and has a very strict timing discipline involving deliveries to contractors and distributors.

In common with the production executive working with media, the print buyer must have a thorough grounding in platemaking and all the printing processes including screen printing, flexography and thermography, and have a broad understanding of bindery and warehouse techniques.

Again in common with the production executive, he needs to be able to advise on the best methods of achieving a creative requirement, and this means that a constant study of printing substrates and their receptivity to various printing processes is necessary. The substrate mostly used is, of course, paper, but there are many types of paper and their printing qualities vary enormously. Other substances in common usage are boards, plastics and metals. Also the print buyer should advise on creative design for posters to ensure the most economical use of sheetage.

Apart from having a deep understanding of both printing processes and substrates, the professional print buyer must also know his market and his printers. The professional will construct a panel of regular printers capable of printing the type of work he handles at the quality level demanded by the work and/or the agency's clients.

As leaflets, brochures, point of sale material, calendars and so on come in a wide variety of sizes and paginations, the problem of economical printing is as important as quality. Printing presses vary enormously in size and mode of printing, from small, single-colour presses capable of printing a sheet 460 mm × 640 mm up to the very large, four- or even six-colour presses capable of printing a sheet 1000 mm × 1400 mm. In addition there are many web-fed presses of different sizes and configurations.

Therefore, in constructing his panel of printers the professional print buyer will ensure that a suitable spectrum of press sizes will be available to him which is suitable for the work in which he is involved. This will enable him to plan print jobs to press and paper sizes, thereby ensuring the most economical use of materials and machinery.

The print department is therefore an integral part of a sales campaign. Its contribution must be built into lead times in any campaign launch.

Sales promotion

An increasing function within some agencies, particularly those with large consumer accounts, is the conception of a total sales promotion package for specific sales objectives. In some agencies also the amount of promotional support given to certain accounts warrants the setting up of a separate department to deal with this type of work, for which the staff would consist of a mixture of executives and print buyers. In addition to having a knowledge of sources for supplying giveaway items, or specially adapted or manufactured goods, this type of department must have a working knowledge of each of their client's sales and merchandising patterns, salesmen's journey cycles, warehousing and pre-selling requirements to meet crucial delivery dates.

Film and TV production

Since the start of television advertising in this country in 1955 a whole new branch of the film industry has emerged. Today it is an important and influental arm of that industry not only in the effect that its product has on the day-to-day lives of people but also in the contribution it has made to the art and techniques of film-making.

In the early days advertising agencies sought assistance from their colleagues in the United States, from documentary film-makers and from the lower echelons of the feature film industry. The two or three companies then engaged in cinema advertising, and one or two major documentary producers, became large and successful in a very short time. The first 15 years of the business saw many changes, some dictated by fashion but most by business failure. Today the advertising film director is just as likely to have emerged from an advertising agency where he started life as a writer, art director or producer, as he is to come from television or the cinema.

In the same way as the production companies have developed a knowledge and expertise in their particular branch of film-making, so the agencies have learned how to control and utilize the screen, large or small, for the benefit of their clients. Most advertising agencies with television clients operate their own television department, with an administrator and a number of producers working either as part of a creative group in the agency or on a range of accounts handled by different executives.

Some small agencies do not, of course, run television departments, and to provide this service to them a number of freelance individuals or companies have been set up. These companies, often offering creative work, production supervision and the necessary administrative follow-up, are also used by larger agencies, from time to time, to relieve pressure on their own personnel.

The first basic decision by the agency is whether to recommend cinema, television or both. The cinema tends to be more influential in the younger age groups – from teenage to mid-thirties – and it also has less restrictions placed on it in terms of the products it may advertise. Television is, of course, much more expensive but extremely powerful, and claims a much wider audience in virtually every respect. This means that in the majority of cases television will be selected unless there is a positive case for the cinema, in which event the same commercial with very slight technical changes can be shown on both media.

Assuming an agency is going to recommend the production of a commercial, a series of decisions have to be made before the producer is given a script or storyboard and asked to find out how much it will cost and how long it will take to produce. These decisions are usually made without reference to the television department, though systems vary to some degree in every agency, particularly in respect of the amount of control exercised by each department. An experienced producer can often point out basic faults in a proposed script or offer alternative suggestions to reduce costs.

The second production decision may well be what technique should be used. There are three basic filming techniques – live action, model animation, and cartoon including computer graphics – and to each of these can be added a wide range of optical processes or special effects provided by laboratories and specialist optical houses. The use of video-tape may also be considered at this stage, particularly if complicated optical effects have to be produced in a short space of time, but let us for the moment assume we are to produce a commercial on film.

Cartoon as a technique is used frequently to establish or promote a character that has become a trademark. It is also used to amuse and draw attention to demonstrations that would otherwise be dull, and of course it is used to attract the younger generation, although current legislation is likely to restrict this aspect of its use.

Model animation is the moving of otherwise inanimate objects in such a way that they appear to control themselves, and can indeed be given characters if required. Certain types of puppet come under this heading, where objects are moved physically in between the exposure of each frame of the film.

Live action is the major technique employed by commercial film producers, and it is perhaps obvious that it should be so, since the vast majority of advertisers wish to show their products or the effect that their products have in the most favourable but realistic manner. Imagine trying to demonstrate the effect of a shampoo in a cartoon!

Concurrently with some of the foregoing decisions, the choice of artiste or artistes appearing in the commercial may have been discussed in terms of whether or not to use a personality. It is probably true to say that such a decision is usually taken early in the creative stages, as scripts to be used by a well known personality are usually written with them in mind. The alternative, of course, is that a well known actor or personality can be used to lend authority to a commercial that is quite possibly lacking in other ways.

When all or most of these problems have been sorted out, the producer will contact one or more production companies, sometimes asking to see a demonstration reel of a particular director's work, sometimes asking immediately for a quotation for the production of the film. The period before the filming starts is the most important part of the production schedule.

It is during this period that the decision affecting the transformation of the script into a piece of film will be taken, and the team and facilities required to execute the script discussed and assembled. There will always be an argument for retaining an element of flexibility when filming. Situations arising may offer the opportunity to achieve a varying effect or improve upon a structure, just as some planned shots may prove impossible because of the disciplines of commercial timing. A director must constantly be prepared to review the film in the light of any enforced changes, and it is the job of the advertising agency producer to guide the director into creating the film that best achieves the client's aims.

A film can, of course, be shot indoors or out, and if it is indoors it can be on a set built in a studio or in an actual location. With the development of the new lightweight lighting sources, silent generators, faster lenses and generally smaller, more mobile equipment that has taken place over the past twenty years, the use of locations has grown enormously. A studio still gives the better controlled environment and the ability to remove walls or ceilings for the benefit of the camera, but to build an average detailed set comprising kitchen and living room will take two days and a labour force of approximately ten. In addition, every item of furniture, fittings and contents must be bought or hired by the art director and his buyer, transported to the studio, unpacked and checked, and the reverse procedure followed after filming. In order to achieve one day's filming the studio has to be hired for four days – two for building, one for filming and one for clearing the set away. If an existing location that does not require too much dressing can be found, the cost is likely to be less and the realism improved.

There are specialist companies with large numbers of locations on file cross-referenced, and many production companies keep their own location files. Sooner or later someone, probably an assistant director specializing in location work, will have to be sent to photograph all possibilities before the agency producer and director make a final selection.

Exterior location work, of course, speaks for itself. It is possible to build exterior scenes in studios, but there would have to be special reasons to make it worth while – for example, the shooting of a small section of jungle, with the accompanying effects of light and heat, could be achieved more cheaply in a studio than by going abroad or trying to recreate it outdoors in an English winter.

An advertiser may well wish to promote a product during a summer campaign with films shot under summer conditions – audiences are to some extent preconditioned into expecting summer scenes on the screen advertising summer products – and in order to have a commercial ready for screening it will have to be originated during the winter months or to have been made the previous year. This leads to a proportion of commercials being made abroad in warmer climates than ours, sometimes a considerable effort being exerted to make the locations appear English.

The economics of this situation may seem baffling, but in simple terms it is very unlikely that any advertiser can commit the money to produce films a year ahead. Even if he can guarantee there will be no developments or changes in his product, he certainly cannot control the market situation, which may exert pressures in various directions. The extra cost of sending a film unit abroad is often offset to some extent by the production company getting together two or more clients to share the crew's air fares, and, of course, the more or less guaranteed sunshine enables contingencies or insurance premiums to be reduced substantially. These factors combine to bring the cost down in real terms to a level that clients find acceptable when the alternative may be to run a far less effective campaign, and run the risk of wasting large sums of money on airtime or face the even higher production costs of delays through bad weather in this country.

At the end of each day the exposed film is sent to the laboratory, processed, printed and returned. This first print of all the takes selected by the director is called 'rushes', and from this print a rough selection of all the takes likely to be used in the final film is made. At this stage the film is the responsibility of the editor, working closely with the director and agency producer. The first assembly of the film may well be over-length and the sound track incomplete, and it is unlikely to be shown to the client before a considerable amount of work has been done on it, and the agency is satisfied that it has a production that fulfils its brief.

The film laboratory or optical house will be employed to duplicate those scenes of a film where effects have to be created – these are basically printed on a special machine frame by frame, together with other elements in order to reach a combined end result. It is a technical process that can produce simple white superimposed lettering on a scene, transitions in various forms from one scene to another, multi-picture scenes and an almost unlimited range of effects beyond that. The producer of a commercial has to decide whether the cost and the time taken in perfecting a complicated optical process are likely to be in his client's best interest.

Optical processes are instantly available with the use of computer graphics and videotape, and a substantial number of effects that will take a week to achieve on film can be created in minutes. The arguments for and against tape or film have been raging for years, and will go on for many more. There are advantages to both systems, and one should carefully select which one to employ. Tape has speed, and it is possible to shoot a commercial in the morning and transmit it by landline to the stations, which can record it for screening later that night. Film remains the more sophisticated in creative terms, and is more manoeuvrable in its ability to reach difficult locations, owing to its independence of the truck loads of sophisticated electronics needed to service a videotape production.

In most cases the production company and agency will have little difficulty in deciding whether to use tape or film, but perhaps one further point is worth mentioning. Tape imposes stricter disciplines than film, and a decision by the agency or client to make changes after the tape commercial is edited is likely to prove very costly. If a client has a reputation for requiring alterations or making small changes, and is not prepared to attend on the day of production and editing, or to accept the work of those who do, film is likely to prove considerably less costly.

In the two remaining areas of film technique – model animation and cartoon – film is now competing with computer generated graphics. Quite apart from technical considerations, model or 'stop frame' filming requires hours of patient work under controlled conditions, by just one or two people. Cartoon production necessitates much of the detailed preparation that goes into the planning of any commercial. The film technique comprises the photographing on a bench camera of a series of drawings which are keyed into a fixed position and which vary in detail to the extent necessary to create movement when photographed in sequence and projected at normal film speed. Computer generated graphics (also requiring few people) are composed on editing suites which can move, distort, mix, overlay and retouch images onto video tape, producing top-quality broadcasting material.

Once the final shape of the picture has been assembled by the editor and approved by the client, the sound will be added – commentaries recorded, effects and music laid to the correct position relative to the picture. If using film the soundtrack is then converted to a photographic track whose negative will be printed on to the final film alongside the picture, which is itself printed from the original negative (carefully stored since the day of filming).

TV administration

This section, within the Television Department, is responsible for submitting scripts and finished film or tape to the ITVA for approval, calculating and authorizing the payment of artists' repeat fees, and budgetary control. They also ensure that the productions evolve to time, in order to meet the playout dates to stations as dictated by the media schedules and the instructions for the rotation or showing of the commercials.

It should be remembered that the screening of a commercial is a powerful weapon in the advertising armoury, but it can be costly and wasteful if not used correctly. Sufficient time should be allowed in the planning stages, and ideally the creative people concerned with writing the script should have an understanding of production or should not be afraid to call in their producer for advice. Proper planning and setting up of a production will always save money. There are opposing schools of thought as to whether or not writers should be aware of the client's budget problems, as these may inhibit their thinking.

The argument for some control over creativity relative to cost at a stage before presentation of the idea to client is very strong. On far too many occasions scripts have been submitted to clients before being costed, and if the client falls in love with the idea, the agency is stuck with trying to produce it, very often on an inadequate budget. The inevitable result is a compromise, which at best may be accepted by a client who is disappointed, and at worst may lose the agency the account. Honesty when dealing with one's client is always the best policy, just as it is when presenting your client's case to the public.

BIBLIOGRAPHY

Daily Telegraph Magazine Guide to Gravure Printing. (Daily Telegraph, 1968)
Ingman, Dan. *Television Advertising.* (Business Publications, 1965)
Practical Printing and Binding. (Odhams Press, 1965)
Printing Reproduction Pocket Pal. (Creative Services Association, 1987)

This chapter draws substantially on the one written for an earlier edition by Terry Squires and James Garrett. Our thanks are due to Mr Squires and Mr Garrett for agreeing that their text may be used in this way.

8

Consumer research

Mark Lovell

Scope

A large number of different kinds of operation can be conducted by way
of consumer research, to the benefit of advertising. These include both
large-scale investigations and small-scale intensive studies among a few
carefully selected respondents.

The large-scale work may include the following:

1 Usage and attitude surveys.
2 Opinion research.
3 Research linking media exposure data with consumer data.
4 Advertising research studies:
   (a) concept tests
   (b) advertising pre-tests
   (c) tests of finished advertisements in natural conditions
   (d) tracking, or campaign evaluation studies
5 Product tests.
6 Packaging tests.
7 Surveys of observed behaviour – in particular situations, e.g. a
   supermarket.
8 Consumer audits (checking purchase of selected products over time).

A lot of this work may overlap: an advertising concept test, for
example, may be included at the end of a usage and attitude study. But
the main categories of research study are listed above.

Often a study is organized for purposes that are separate from the
development and monitoring of advertising, but every study may yield,
or be organized in such a way as to yield important data for some stage of
the advertising process. Let us consider them in turn.

Usage and attitude studies

These help determine how many people are purchasers or users of a brand, and of competitive brands or substitutes. By comparing these people with the population as a whole in terms of their demographic characteristics (age, social class, etc.) it is possible to construct a profile of the actual and the potential market.

This information might be further refined by reference to the attitudinal section: e.g. the target for a new brand might be users of a particular product who are not brand loyal, in the sense that they do not care particularly which brand they buy. Another way of looking at the attitudinal data is to build a picture of the target's needs and requirements of particular brands in the product field. This kind of research could show that the users of a product are becoming more price-conscious, or conscious of differences in quality; and this could be important for indicating the kind of features of one's own brand that are the most relevant to advertising that is likely to persuade the consumer.

Some usage and attitude studies are called 'once-off'. This means that information is gathered among a sample of people at one point in time. Other work may involve repeated waves of interviewing, among samples of people recruited by identical sampling methods. The data from the waves are then combined. Alternatively, data from a continuous panel may be used, which relate to a longer period of time.

Always providing that the sampling is satisfactory, results that have been obtained from more than one wave, or panel data, are more likely to provide accurate information. A once-off study may be liable to temporary market influences. Where seasonality is a known factor in a particular market, this point has to be considered very carefully. Another advantage of the panel approach to usage and attitude data is that brand switching can be measured. The extent of brand switching suggests market sensitivity to pricing and to new brands.

Opinion research

The principles of organizing opinion research are similar to those for usage and attitude surveys. The difference lies in the area of interest. Some advertising benefits particularly from foreknowledge of consumer opinions, and indeed some advertising is calculated purely and simply to influence those opinions. Research on the corporate image of a company falls into this category. The relative standing in the consumer's mind of two competitive giants may vary according to underlying trends in belief about the threat to the environment represented by each of their activities. When one is devising a campaign that has a provocative angle – e.g. humour at the expense of trade unions or the civil service, etc. – it is as well to take the trouble to find out whether these gestures are acceptable to the section of the population at which you are aiming.

Opinion research is usually concerned with awareness of certain issues, the importance of those issues to the informants, their beliefs about those issues, the attitudes they have developed on the basis of those beliefs, the strength with which these attitudes are held, and the order of importance of those attitudes to the informant. It is also concerned with finding out what kinds of group within a population think alike, and to what extent they think alike. It is useful to distinguish between the term 'belief' (usually used to indicate an opinion that need not have any sense of evaluation) and an 'attitude' (in which a kind of value judgement is implicit). For example, *I believe* that St Martin's is built of white stone and that it dates from the eighteenth century; my *attitude* towards white stone churches built in the eighteenth century is positive, so that I am anxious they should be preserved. Much opinion research is nowadays repeated at regular intervals – this allows the monitoring of trends in opinion, so that advertisers can observe and explore whichever brands are on the rise among given segments.

Research linking media exposure data with consumer data

Some standard media research surveys (e.g. the National Readership Survey) provide a link between details of consumer behaviour (e.g. car ownership) and readership data (e.g. readers of specialist motoring magazines). But there are situations in which it is useful to organize ad hoc surveys, or panels, in order to establish, for the same sample of consumers, media habits, behaviour and attitudes. Having a common source for these data enables you to compare, for example, the relative likelihood users and non-users of the product may have had of seeing your campaign on television or in the press, or both. Apart from helping to indicate correlations between seeing the advertising and buying a brand, or registering details about it, this kind of work is useful for forward planning. It can indicate the media patterns of those who have not yet been encouraged to try a product, so that media can be better selected in the future.

Advertising research studies

Concept tests

The purpose of this operation is basically to quantify reactions towards one or more advertising concepts. Often the concepts are very simple propositions, e.g.:

'A breakfast cereal that contains bran but is still liked by children "because it has just a little honey to flavour it"'

But – depending on the philosophy and practice of a particular advertiser – an advertising concept may take a more complex form, e.g.:

A presenter is shown in illustration. She is a housewife and a mother. She tells the reader of her concern to offer her family a worthwhile food instead of just any ordinary cereal. Now she has found this brand which contains bran and just enough honey . . . . A second illustration shows her children with empty bowls, announcing gleefully that 'It tastes great!'

Whether the latter is a concept or an 'embryonic treatment' can be debated endlessly. As regards research, it is a question of exposing the test concepts – usually in rotated order – to a representative sample, and analysing reactions. The 'answers' given are usually expressions of interest in the brand, or suspicion of it, etc. Diagnosing the reasons for superficial reactions is very important if the study is going to be helpful towards developing a good campaign.

Advertising pre-tests

When one or more rough treatments have been prepared as expressions of the agreed advertising strategy, a pre-test may be conducted. Here material that is still unifinished, but is nevertheless considerably closer to a final version of an advertisement than anything under (a) (above), is exposed to a representative sample, and their reactions are analysed. The locations may be in specialized theatres, in home, or even in mobile units.

Sometimes use is made of standardized questions, so that the answers (e.g. the degree of enthusiasm for the brand after exposure to the test ad) can be compared to norms. Great care should be exercised before deciding that normative data is relevant to the kind of product that is being tested, or the sample concerned. But intelligent use of norms enables researchers to interpret what a set of results really means for the chances of success of a future campaign.

Tests of finished advertisements

In both press and TV various services exist for assessing the effectiveness of a finished advertisement before it is used very widely, but real-life viewing conditions reduce the 'hot house' element of other testing methods. Most of this research is concerned with recall scores. This has some meaning in terms of advertising impact, but is not in itself any guarantee of advertising success.

Tracking studies

This kind of research is traditionally mounted just before an advertising campaign breaks, and then is repeated at the end. The difference between these two tracking waves in terms of:

- Spontaneous awareness of the brand
- Knowledge of what the brand is or does
- Brand usage
- Trial of the brand
- Intention to try, or to use the brand
- Advertising awareness

can be imputed to whatever has happened in between. Although it is the advertising campaign that is likely to be the main factor responsible for any changes in these measures, it is never the *only* factor. For this reason, in complex markets, control areas are sometimes used as well, to show what proportion of change is likely to be the result of the advertising.

The optimum timing for second and subsequent tracking waves is a matter of some controversy. Weight of advertising, the purpose of the campaign, and the particular market circumstances (e.g. distribution, competitive activity) will often influence the choice.

Product tests

The conventional product test is expected to give information on consumer reactions to one or more formulations of a product. In a blind test (i.e. when the informants are not shown which brand is which) the information shows the extent to which there may be a genuine preference for one's own brand, or the main competitor. Comparing these data with an identical test conducted when both products are labelled shows the extent to which brand image influences the appreciation of the one as compared with the other. Sometimes, as with beer, the difference between the findings in the two situations can be very great. When one proceeds further, to analyse the reasons for preference in both situations, a clear idea is given of the relative strength in image terms that each brand has. This relates to the kind of claim that is likely to be consistent with the current image of the brand, and with the actual benefit that a consumer perceives in it, when it is asked for by name.

Sometimes a product test is added on to a test of an advertising concept, or an advertising treatment. In this case, some reactions to the promise can be compared with reactions to the actual performance of the product tested. This could provide useful clues on the extent to which advertising may be likely to under-sell or over-sell the product overall, and in respect of each product characteristic.

Packaging tests

A change of pack may often be an integral part of a change in the advertising. Defining consumer reactions to packs tells one how far the new pack may be complementary to an advertising change. The method pursued is often a variation on a product test: identical products are placed in dissimilar packs, and first the informant is required to indicate ways in which he thinks the products are likely to be different; secondly, he is asked to take them away and try them, and then report back to an interviewer his feelings about each of the different products.

Other kinds of packaging research include finding out how clearly visible a new pack may be on a shelf, and whether it indicates to people the right kind of information about the product, clearly and quickly. Sometimes, for this purpose, shelf displays are simply shown to a sample of informants on a screen or in a supermarket; alternatively, use is made of such elaborate machinery as the tachistoscope, which allows for exposure of a pack for a brief time period.

Observed behaviour

There are many kinds of observation study. Sometimes they are set up simply to watch what consumers do as opposed to what they might say they do in a market research interview, but at others they are combined with a formal interview in order to get the benefit of consumers' comments on his or her recent behaviour while it is still fresh in the memory. An example might be the purchase of a new brand in a supermarket. When a consumer is seen buying that brand, she may be watched to see how she approaches the shelf. Does she read the label carefully, or compare it with others, etc.? Subsequently she may be stopped outside by an interviewer and asked if she had heard of the brand before entering the shop; this might show whether she had made an impulse purchase or not.

Other uses of observation methods include the study of children and parents in, for example, a supermarket or a CTN (confectioner, tobacconist or newsagent). It may be important for the advertiser of a brand to know how far a child influences the choice of cereal or how far the mother exercises influence on the sweets that are bought. In some markets observation is the most satisfactory means of determining the profile of the buyers, as opposed to the users, of the product. Mystery shopper studies can be included here. These examine what actually happens in a given situation where a 'buyer' approaches a sales assistant, a car sales-man, or a bank clerk, etc. The results show the advertiser what the reality of the point of purchase actually is.

Consumer audits

One of the problems of surveys in which questions are asked about purchasing is that very often the informants do not know exactly what they have done, partly owing to lack of interest in the items. Consumer audits, of which the best known is Television Consumer Audits (TCA), enable measurements to be made of the number of packs entering a household or consumed by that household week after week. Because a panel is used, an exact indication of relative increase or decrease of purchase of different brands is possible.

When media exposure data are used as well, links between changes in purchasing pattern and relative degrees of exposure to advertising can be observed. Because the packs are scrutinized in a special dustbin by trained interviewers, the uptake of promotional offers can be noted, and allowed for when attempting to calculate the effects of advertising over time. In many parts of the world supermarket purchases are being recorded automatically by electronic scanners that read the UPC markings on each product that is bought.

Qualitative research

Many forms of qualitative research are important in the advertising scene. Usually the qualitative exercise is on a small scale, but not always, and it should be remembered that quantification of some of the data in a study that is otherwise tackled in a qualitative way can sometimes be useful.

In quantification work there is a premium on accurate and meaningful question formulation, on sampling and the selection of coding categories in data processing, and on the adroit use of analysis by computer. In qualitative work sampling is, arguably, often more important; but a high premium is put on the individual skill of the interviewer at developing the interview in a way that seems appropriate to the task, and on the interpretative skill of whoever is analysing the data and reporting on them. The main qualitative research techniques are the following.

Individual depth interviews

Often these are unstructured, and a skilled interviewer, probably a psychologist, organizes the kind of conversation in which his own role is of an encouraging sympathetic listener, allowing the talk to range freely but following up by means of verbal probes any leads that appear important to the information requirements of the study.

Semi-structured interviews

This demands a lower level of skill, but needs specially trained interviewers. A questionnaire is used, and certain question forms are standardized both in content and in the order in which they may be given. But there is scope for development of the interview in any way that the informant feels is natural and important. This part of the questionnaire consists merely of a list of points that need to be covered at some stage.

Group discussions

Practitioners vary considerably about what they regard as the ideal number for a group. Some prefer 'mini-groups' of four or five, whereas others are confident they can control as many as twelve. More than that should probably be avoided. To become a group discussion moderator requires skills of a social kind as well as possession of some kind of psychology and marketing background. Use is made of a discussion guide, in which the order and content of the main features of the discussion are specified. However, there is much personal flair involved in developing the discussion fruitfully and naturally within this structure.

Ordinary living-rooms are often preferred for group discussions, because they approximate to normal home conditions. But special rooms are favoured by those who want the groups to be observed through one-way mirrors, for the edification of the creative team. Closed circuit television can be used for observation as well; alternatively, the group may be filmed on video-cassette.

Paired interviews

Sometimes it makes sense to put together, for a combined interview, two informants, one of whom uses a brand while the other has stopped using a brand. Their argument can be instructive, so as to devise advertising to defend the brand or to recoup lapsed users. Similarly, pairs of informants who react in opposite ways to a campaign may be brought together.

All these techniques may be used in the course of creative development – from an initial trawl for ideas for a creative platform, through a test of concepts and consideration of rough treatments, to examining the reactions to finished treatments themselves. They may also be used (even in conjunction with quantification work) to analyse more closely consumers' reactions to a campaign after it has begun.

Quantitative research

Sometimes a figure has to be put on a particular finding. It may not do, for example, to say simply that 'most people noticed advertisement A.' One may need to know exactly how many. Were they *more* than the total who noticed B? Was it a high score relative to other similar research experience? If these questions are to be answered, you need numbers, and therefore quantitative research.

Standardization of technique is important in all research, but the freedom allowed to individual ways of tackling respondents in a depth interview cannot be extended to the quantification exercise. The more informants in a sample, the less control you have over how many variations in technique might be influencing the results. Therefore, you have to limit such variations to a minimum.

Brand name registration by informants who are exposed to it (either in a pre-test or in the real media situation) is a frequent subject for quantified research. Two matched samples of 200 informants might be shown a folder that is identical for each sample except for one particular ad. A comparison is made between the proportion in each sample who, later on, can mention accurately the name of the brand featured in the test ad. There are also other kinds of information that can be collected about the effects of a brief exposure of an ad. in a folder test. But for any comparisons to be valid, you need strict standardization of sampling, of interview technique, of the length of exposure, etc., between the two samples. Some work has suggested, too, that you need the same interviewers employed to work with both the samples.

Briefing

Sometimes research is undertaken in order to comply with the general feeling that it is the professional marketing thing to do. There is some sense in this, but in order to be really effective, research has got to be specific. There must be a clear rationale of why the research is being done; otherwise it may be developed according to the whim of those who are running it, so that important areas of investigation are left untouched, and the interpretation may be tangential to primary needs.

When a brief for a research proposal is put forward, two things should be made abundantly clear: first, the kind of information that is needed, and, second, the purpose to which this is to be put. Distinguishing between these two is important, to avoid any misunderstanding. For example, 'Research is required to examine users' and non-users' attitudes towards Brand X, and the competition. This information is required to aid the planning of the next advertising campaign for Brand X.' This is perfectly clear.

It is important to know both these points, in order that the researcher should not be misled into interpreting attitudinal data about Brand X from the point of view of possible product improvement rather than the application to advertising strategy. Any confusion will affect interpretation and the report produced. Similarly, merely to say to a researcher that we want information that will help us plan our advertising better may be to invite all kinds of examination of, say, circumstances of use of products in the Brand X product field, which may be perfectly well known already.

It follows that, as well as giving a clear brief, it is vital to make sure that the researcher understands the brief. It needs to be discussed, not simply noted with the assumption that the words will mean the same to everybody. Each company tends to develop its own research jargon.

One would expect to cover the following points in a comprehensive research brief:

1 Statements of the ultimate purpose (as outlined above).
2 Statements of the immediate objective (as outlined above).
3 Indication of the type of people who are concerned.
4 The timing requirement.
5 The degree of accuracy required.
6 Indications of any other existing data that would make for better understanding of the problem before the researcher starts to tackle the job.
7 Indication of other surveys with which the information must be comparable, so that, for example, changes over time can be observed.

In the above list the fifth point requires some comment. Depending upon the purpose for which the research is done, the findings may need to be very accurate indeed, or simply to give a general indication of numbers. It is worth making clear at an early stage within what limits you expect to be using any particular statistic.

Sampling

Obtaining a representative sample is really the cornerstone of all market research. It is no use asking ingenious questions, applying the latest data-processing techniques, and making a brilliant interpretation of the findings, if the people among whom the information is gathered have been inexpertly recruited or assembled.

The best kind of sample consists of people drawn at random, in an arrangement whereby everyone who would theoretically qualify for interview has an equal chance of being selected. In practice the perfect random sample never happens. But it is possible to get a very good random sample that misses out only the least accessible potential respondents.

The procedure usually begins with a selection of sampling points after the decision has been taken as to how many sampling points would be appropriate. The terms 'universe' and 'population' are used to describe the total number of things or people that are eligible for interview, and the sample must represent this universe (or population) as well as possible. To do so, the sample must be well distributed across the population. If the population is of men in Great Britain, it may be thought unlikely that fewer than about eighty sampling points would be acceptable, as likely to give a representative sample, but this number will vary widely depending on the reliability you need in the results – and of course the numbers of interviews which you take at these points. There is a very powerful relationship between the number of interviews per point and the sampling error (cf. Moser and Galton, and the MRS conference papers 1976–9, by respectively Holmes; Harris; Goodhart and Collins; Boyd, Godfrey and Twyman).

In a 'random' survey of the population the procedure would be selection of areas by a random choice method in which the opportunity to be selected is proportional to the number of people living in each area. A weighting factor may be applied to yield a representative list of sampling points in terms of area type and distribution across the country. Electoral registers may then be used, in order to pick a sample of households, evenly spread across each sampling point. Since there is more than one person living in most households, a rotation rule has to be given to an interviewer to make sure that different kinds of people (heads of household, housewives, other adults, and children sometimes) have got an equal chance of selection. Individuals selected may not be at home at the time. An appointment has to be made. Three call-backs may be the rule used by the research company to limit negotiations with one household before it is abandoned in favour of a substitute.

All this is very time-consuming and very costly. Most market research relies on 'quota sampling' methods, in which the choice of sample points may still be randomly determined, but a quota of respondents of certain types is issued to each interviewer working on each sampling point. The quota will specify certain controls (e.g. social class groups, age groups, presence of children in the family, etc.) beyond which the interviewer may not stray. Interviewers have complete freedom to go to whichever household they like (so long as that household is not personally known to them), to find informants who will fit the quota. They determine quota eligibility before proceeding with the interview itself. If one knows the characteristics of the universe, it is perfectly possible to issue quota instructions that will ensure the population is representative, *but only in terms of the controls.*

Quota samples are sometimes described as 'Station Road research'. This comes from the natural tendency of the interviewer to go to the most convenient road in a new sampling point, in order to achieve the quota – the goal is to achieve the object satisfactorily, as quickly as possible. To get round this, some research companies favour 'random walk' in-structions. Starting points are chosen on local maps; then the interviewer proceeds to every third household down one side of one street, turns right, then turns left, and so on. This spreads the interviewing better, but can make for administrative difficulties if the area chosen for the random walk is completely wrong for the interviewer's quota.

The more precise the quota controls are in terms of market behaviour, the less reasonable it is to insist on other controls being strictly observed, and on the interviewing being spread evenly across each sampling point. The argument is that if one is organizing research in order to compare frequent against infrequent users of Brand X, meeting the criterion of usage frequency is the most important of the quota instructions; whether the informants are evenly distributed among age groups may be much less relevant. On the other hand, one can take this too far, as in the case where older users of Brand X are very different from younger users. Each sampling problem needs to be solved at leisure, in the light of all the information one has about the universe concerned. The constraints of time and money soon obtrude. A sampling expert may need to advise on the degree to which economies in money and time are consistent with maintaining the adequacy of the sample for the demands of the research brief. Unfortunately the sampling expert is not always listened to and sometimes not even consulted!

Interview methods

Most reputable research companies have their own procedure whereby they can make sure that an interviewer meets their requirements, and see if he or she has a potential for qualitative work as well as 'nosecount' operations. Although a certain level of competence and intelligence can be assumed when dealing with an interviewer of the latter kind, it makes sense, when there may be particular points of potential difficulty in the interview or in the questionnaire itself, to organize a briefing. Here the interviewers will be taken through the questionnaire, and told how to apply each part of it. They should also be asked to do dummy interviews among themselves to make sure that the lessons have been brought home.

The interviewers must be aware that a proportion of their work will be validated. This means that an independent check will be made (by telephone or personal interview) on whether an interview actually took place, and some questions will be repeated to determine whether it was done thoroughly.

Pilot work is essential to make sure that an interview works. Reasons for an interview not working are often a question of the ratio between the time required to find a suitable respondent plus the time required for the interview itself, relative to the total amount of time planned for fulfilling the quota. The pilot may indicate that less stringent quota controls are needed if the job is to be completed on time. It may indicate that certain questions are ambiguous or that some careful explanation of a question is required either to the interviewer or to the informant.

Some interviews allow for a certain amount of 'self-completion'. Where attitude scales are administered, the respondent may be asked to tick his level of agreement or disagreement with particular statements on a page offering him a battery of questions. It sometimes makes good sense to use this method, particularly where the nature of the questions may make an informant less confident about expressing his true feelings in front of the interviewer.

It is contrary to the Market Research Society Code of Practice to use any kind of interview method that does not allow informants to suspend the interview at any time they please, or includes recording or invigilation without their knowledge. Hidden tape-recorders, hidden cameras, one-way mirrors, and film equipment may be used, provided the informant is told about them. Another protection afforded to the public by the Code of Practice is that the names and addresses of individual informants cannot be disclosed by the research company unless formal permission has been given by the informants themselves. It follows that in surveys where lists of eligible people (e.g. buyers of a particular car, etc.) are supplied by the research company's client, these names must never be linked to any particular piece of information going back to the client.

In the best interview work a rapport develops between interviewer and respondent, giving the latter the confidence to express precisely what he feels about a given subject. Anything that threatens this rapport – overlong questionnaires, tedious repetitive questions, assumptions that are in any way insulting, etc. – is to be avoided. Sometimes it is important not to indicate the precise reason for the research being done. The degree to which interviewers are told about the purpose of the research must be viewed against this requirement. It is dishonest to pretend to informants that they are being interviewed for something quite other than the real reason; the area for manoeuvre is *suppressio veri* as opposed to *suggestio falsi*. For example, before making it clear that he is primarily interested in reactions to Brand X, the interviewer should elicit spontaneous comment about good and bad brands within the product field.

Data processing

When questionnaires come back from the field, they have to be put through a procedure that extracts and combines the data they contain. The sequence is traditionally the following:

- Questionnaires return from field.

- Editing (some questionnaires that contain obvious mistakes are referred back: interviewing may be repeated).

- Extractions (samples of answers to open-ended questions are drawn, and studied).

- Code sheets prepared (common categories of answers are given codes, which are applied by coders).

- Coding of questionnaires.

- Coded questionnaires are 'copied' on to punched cards; possibly on to computer tape.

- Hole count (this gives, on a printout sheet, a summary of all the figures for each code on each question, based on the total sample).

- Further simple analysis (e.g. breakdowns of the hole-count information by sex, age, etc. in tabular form).

● Multivariate analysis (e.g. factor analysis of the results of attitude scaling, to determine what patterns of answers may exist among the sample, or a sub-sample).

Obviously questionnaires with only pre-coded questions (e.g. Yes = 1; No = 2) need no coding. Nowadays questionnaires suitable for optical scanning are sometimes used, and in these the proportion of pre-coded data form the bulk of the questionnaire. CATI (computer-assisted telephone interviewing) bypasses a lot of the above work, since the answers are entered directly into a computer. But the need for sensitive assessment of the open-ended questions still exists.

Where qualitative data are concerned, there is a more meticulous study of each questionnaire, of each tape or film of an interview or a discussion, and of the comments reported back by the interviewer at a debriefing. Content analysis in some form is usually preferable to simply reading through everything and going by the 'feel of the data'. Such analysis means picking out all references to each of a range of aspects that you decide are important: e.g., all references to the taste of a product might be written out, then subdivided, then linked with other attitudes expressed by the informants.

BIBLIOGRAPHY

Henry, H. *Motivation Research*. (Crosby Lockwood, 1986)
Kish, L. *Survey Sampling*. (John Wiley & Sons, New York, 1965)
Lovell, M. and Potter, J. *Assessing the Effectiveness of Advertising*. (Business Books, 1976)
Worcester, R. and Downham, J. S. *Consumer Market Research Handbook*. (Elsevier Science Publishers, 1986)

9

Media research

Alan Copage

Introduction

The objectives of media research are:

- To match the media to advertising markets.
- To examine the value and efficiency of the individual media.
- To set campaign objectives.
- To measure the effectiveness of advertising campaigns.
- To provide the information most relevant to the efficient use of the media.

This chapter confines its discussions of media research to television, press, radio, cinema and outdoor.

The inherent different properties of the media themselves has meant different requirements of audience measurements by media planners. For example, television is, on the one hand, fleeting, and on the other, sequentially dominant of the screen. Whereas with press, the reader may be selective of his take-up of material – including advertising content. For these and other reasons, television research has been heavily biased towards the minute-by-minute measurement of audiences, in particular to commercials. As a result, the depth of detail of the viewers has tended to be shallow. With press readership research the belief is that the audiences (readers) tend to be more regular across time, with far less volatile changes. This has resulted in far more depth of press research into the demographics and/or product usage of readers than is the case with television viewers. On the other hand, there is very little press research which will help the media planner to select between issues of a publication. Other variables, too, in the case of the press, are thinly researched: time spent reading, source of copy, place of reading, amount read, etc.

Another important factor in the quality of media research is the advertising revenue of each medium. Radio, cinema and outdoor media *between* them currently take less than one-tenth of the advertising revenue of the press. The radio contractors – the AIRC – invest a far higher proportion of their revenues in audience research (JICRAR) than do the independent television companies – the ITVA – as their share of the television research contract (BARB). However, the radio medium currently enjoys an advertising revenue only some 6.5 per cent that of the television medium.

Current methods of media research do not appear to measure the effectiveness of advertising. The measurements are of exposure, or of an *opportunity* to see (or hear) a specific advertisement or campaign. In the case of television audience measurement, for example, the criterion is simply that the person was present in the room, with the advertisement being shown. No account is taken of attention, or 'eyes-open-in-front-of' the television set. Similarly, analyses of the reach (net coverage) and frequency with which a specific target group is exposed to an advertising campaign present measurements of opportunities to see or hear (often referred to as 'OTS' or 'OTH').

However, media research does enable the media planner to set 'goal-posts': to be able to demonstrate the relative values of various combinations of media.

It is true that this measurement of potential exposure is only the first hurdle in the advertising race. Ideally, the advertiser would like to know the 'sales' effect of each specific advertisement, and of his overall campaign. Between current media research and that ideal lie other 'fences', for example:

- Opportunities to see/hear which are *taken*.
- Resultant changes in attitude or perception of the brand or service.

A great deal of experimental work has been carried out in these areas, notably with the use of electronic laser scanners of bar codes on purchased goods, linked with the identity of the purchaser, and the use of electronic diaries for the collection of media exposure information. Cable TV is also suggested as a means of measuring the links between advertising and sales, by virtue of the flexibility of varied advertisements on cable, combined with the knowledge of home reception of the commercials. As yet, such measurements are still in the future – but not too far distant. Meantime, this chapter examines the *current* state of media research.

Press circulation and readership

Circulation

The most common source of information concerning the number of copies of each issue of a publication which are distributed is the Audit Bureau of Circulations (ABC). This authoritative body regularly issues statements as to the average sales of the majority of paid-for newspapers and periodicals. Where any copies are distributed free, or sold at less than normal trade terms, these are also reported by the ABC.

In the case of free publications, e.g. free local newspapers, the ABC has a separate form of measurement of the numbers of copies distributed: Verified Free Distribution (VFD).

For specialist publications, e.g. the business, professional and specialist consumer journals, the ABC provides regular volumes entitled *Media Information Files*. These contain media data forms (MDF) of the details of each publication: circulation, methods of distribution, fields or markets served by the title, etc.

In many cases, the ABC supplies information on the proportion of copies circulated abroad, which can be extensive in specific instances.

Of course, there are many press titles which either prefer not to join the ABC, or are not accepted by the ABC. In these cases, the publication may present its own audited figures, or a publisher's statement of circulation, some of which statements are sworn. Most media planners feel more reassured by an ABC circulation figure, however.

Readership

There is often little clear relationship between the circulation and the readership of publications. At the same time, groups of publications by type are perceived to have similar ratios of readers per copy as Table 9.1 demonstrates.

There are a number of regular readership studies, some of a specific nature, either in terms of the selection of respondents, or in terms of the questions asked. Some of the more widely known of these surveys include:

- JICNARS (or NRS) – the Joint Industry Committee for National Readership Surveys.
- TGI – the British Market Research Bureau's Target Group Index.
- BMRC – the Business Media Research Committee.
- FRS – NOP's syndicated Financial Readership Survey.

Table 9.1 Readers per copy

Daily Mirror	2.8	What Car	11.3
The Sun	2.7	Classic Car	13.8
Daily Star	3.3	Performance Car	11.0
Today	3.3	Golf Monthly	9.2
Daily Mail	2.4	Golf Illustrated	8.8
Daily Express	2.6	Woman	3.2
The Daily Telegraph	2.4	Woman's Own	4.1
The Times	2.5	Woman's Weekly	2.5
The Guardian	2.9	Woman's Realm	2.8
The Independent	2.9		

Source: NRS January–December 1988

Other specialist readership surveys cover farmers, doctors, etc. This chapter confines its report to the NRS, the survey still considered by publishers and media planners/buyers as the main standard trading 'currency' of the press.

The JICNARS (NRS) methodology was considerably changed in 1984, to the 'Extended Media List' (EML) method. In broad terms, the method is as follows. Named respondents are randomly selected from the electoral rolls. Secondary interviews are conducted with 15 to 17-year-olds. The interviewee is handed a pack of some fifty-five postcard-sized cards. On the face of each card appear the titles of six (or so) related titles – motoring, home interest, etc. The title names are typeset – mastheads are not used. There are four variations in the card packs and accompanying questionnaires – two by varying the position of the titles on the cards, and two by alternating the order of the cards in the pack. Three major readership questions asked. They can be summarized as:

1 A card 'filter' question.
2 A frequency of reading question.
3 A recency of reading question.

1 The interviewee is asked to sort the pack of cards into three piles – a 'yes' pile for those where *any* title on the card has been read or looked at, at any time in the past year; a 'no' pile where the respondent has not seen any title on the card, and a 'not sure' pile. Both the 'no' and 'not sure' piles are checked through by the interviewer. This 'screening', or filter, question results in an average of some six 'yes' cards per respondent. Included in the filter question are some important statements by the interviewer. They include: 'It doesn't matter *who* bought the publication, *where* you saw it, or how *old* it was.' Thus, the

main NRS does not measure source of copy, place of reading, or specific issue read. Separate studies into these factors have been undertaken by JICNARS.

2 The frequency of reading questions are on the reverse of the card. Displayed at the bottom of each card are the same frequency statements for all titles on the NRS:

- 'Almost always' (at least three issues out of four).
- 'Quite often' (at least one issue out of four).
- 'Only occasionally' (less than one issue out of four).
- 'Not in the past year'.

Respondents are asked, for each 'yes' card, which newspapers/magazines they read within each frequency band.

3 The 'recency' questions are also similar for all titles, regardless of the frequency of the publication itself. Respondents are asked which titles (on the 'yes' cards) they read yesterday, within the past seven days, and – for the remaining titles on the card – when they last read a copy.

The NRS analyses and reports produce, first, 'average issue readerships' (AIRs). These AIRs are the sum of those who have claimed to have read or looked at a copy of the title within its publication frequency. For daily publications, only those who read an issue 'yesterday' are valid. For weekly publications, those who read a copy within the past week are also included. For monthly titles, those who saw a copy within the past four weeks are also added.

It must be reiterated that the NRS *main* survey cannot measure the readership of specific single issues of publications – it measures the *average* issue readership of titles.

Two other factors also need consideration:

1 Replication
2 Parallel readership

1 Replication is the repeated, re-reading of the title in question. Such 'double counting' of readers tends to inflate true AIR.
2 Parallel readership refers to the reading of several different issues of a publication within its apparent life-cycle; e.g., the reading of several issues of a monthly title within one month. Such reading of old copies would be counted as one issue readership.

To attempt to clarify these problems, and until 1990, Question 4 on the NRS questionnaire asked respondents further details of those magazines read 'yesterday'. These questions cover the age of the issue(s) read, and whether any other issue(s) were read.

Cumulative readership

The combination of frequency and recency questions enables the calculation of the probability of a respondent to see any one issue – or any number of issues. Tables of this cumulative effect are published in the (twice yearly) NRS volumes of data (Table 9.2).

Table 9.2 Cumulative readership of *The Sun* newspaper

Issue number	Percentage reach (adults)	Incremental reach %
1	25.0	–
2	30.5	4.5
3	32.9	2.4
4	34.6	1.7
5	35.9	1.3
6	37.1	1.2

Source: NRS January–December 1988

Table 9.2 shows that, on any one day, *The Sun* is read by one in four adults in Great Britain. But, of course, these are not precisely the *same* one in four adults each day. Some readers will drop out on day two; others will take their place. The table shows that this 'out/in' phenomenon is in the order of one in twenty-two adults (4.5 per cent) – the incremental loss and gain of the second issue. The third and progressive issues have an ever-reducing 'out/in' gain and loss of readers, in the form of a geometric progression.

Within a few issues, any one title will cease to add other than a very marginal number of new readers, not reached by any previous issue. This effect is not necessarily bad – a media planner wishing to add *frequency* of OTS rather than net *coverage* would use such a phenomenon to good effect.

A word of caution is essential. The method of calculation of cumulative readership figures varies between research/computer bureaux. Research Services, the current NRS research contractor, uses a simple binomial expansion formula for such calculations. Other computer bureaux with a licence for such NRS analysis, e.g. Telmar and IMS, use more complex algebraic formulae. All three companies produce different answers to the same cumulative readership question – from the same NRS base data. None can be accused of producing 'wrong' figures – the limitations of the NRS means that we do not know a truly 'right' cumulative readership figure – all are modelled. in some fashion.

Scope

JICNARS is a *Joint* Industry Committee. On its main and other committees, the bodies represented are:

- The Institute of Practitioners in Advertising (IPA).
- The Incorporated Society of British Advertisers (ISBA).
- The Press Research Council (PRC).

Between them, these three bodies are the sponsors of JICNARS. The publishers (PRC) are the major sponsor, paying around three-quarters of the total cost of the survey.

The interviews are conducted with adults aged 15 plus daily through the year, totalling around 29,000 in any twelve-month period.

The Extended Media List method has enabled the number of titles included in the survey to be increased to around 240. Data are published in volume form every six months, based on one year's fieldwork on each occasion: January to December, and July to June. The data overlap by a period of six months' fieldwork from volume to volume.

The volumes include:

- Readership penetration.
- Readership profiles.
- Exposure to other media (TV, radio, cinema).
- Cumulative readership.
- Duplication tables.

Most tables confine themselves to the demographics of readers – age, class, sex, region, terminal age of education, etc. Some tables are concerned with product (or service) usage, although other surveys (e.g. TGI) are used more frequently when such media/product consumption analyses are required by planners/buyers.

Analyses

The NRS data are supplied to bona fide computer bureaux, who, in turn, offer their own software packages for computer analyses. These analyses are conducted: 'on-line', via modems and the telephone network; or on batch, by postal or verbal request; or locally, by the supply of the complete NRS data, in electronic form, to advertising agencies and media owners. The software packages available enable users to analyse the NRS data in various ways. In the main, these include:

- *Rankings* of titles, by their individual efficiency in reaching a specific target group. Rankings can be by cost per thousand readers, individual coverage, profiles of the target group when compared with a larger base (e.g. ABC1s as a target, all adults as a base), etc.
- *Schedule analyses*, comparing the overall reach, OTS and frequency distributions of a number of choices of media schedules.
- *Schedule building*, where, given the criteria involved, a computer model will produce an 'optimum' schedule.
- *Cross tabulations*, where stipulated columns (across) and rows (down) give resultant cells of 'anything by anything' analyses, including vertical and horizontal percentages.

Developments

Various plans are in hand for the future developments of the NRS. These include:

- The measurement of the readerships of separate newspaper sections versus their main parent newspaper titles.
- The qualification of readers, by such criteria as place of reading, source of copy, time spent reading, and date of issue read.
- The use of miniaturized mastheads on the backs of the cards (to lessen title confusion), rather than the current typesetting.
- Readership amongst people down to the age of ten, examining their leisure, consumption and income details.

Conclusion

JICNARS is Great Britain's major tool for the negotiation of the buying, selling and planning of press media. It continues to develop and adapt to meet the changing needs of the media marketplace.

Television

The major sources of industry research regarding people's viewing of television include:

- JICNARS: the National Readership Survey.
- TGI: the British Market Research Bureau's Target Group Index.
- BARB: the Broadcasters' Audience Research Board.

JICNARS

JICNARS (NRS) is explained elsewhere in this chapter, where the NRS's collection of 'other media' data is mentioned. Useful mainly as a check for media planners in examining the weight of viewing television characteristics of a title or of a press schedule, the NRS is not a tool primarily used for the planning or buying of television airtime.

TGI

The Target Group Index is a 'single source' of data. The British Market Research Bureau continuously distributes self-completion questionnaires entitled 'What do you buy?' to respondents contacted by their Omnibus survey. These questionnaires, covering some 200 or so product fields and around 2000 products by brand name, also include questions concerning the viewing, listening and reading habits of respondents.

The returned, usable questionnaires total some 25,000 in number during a TGI fieldwork year, which runs from April to March. Thirty-four volumes of product consumption information are published annually, in August. For each product field and brand, demographic data and media exposure levels are shown, including weight of viewing of television.

By computer anlaysis of the TGI database, subscribers may interrogate the data more thoroughly, including far more detailed media exposure information.

TGI has become a heavily used source of market and media data by account planners in advertising agencies, as well as – increasingly – media planncrs.

However, by the time new TGI data are released, the earliest fieldwork is already some seventeen months old. In a fast-changing media environment, and, in particular, in the case of the television medium, TGI cannot be used for other than general trends and tendencies in media consumption by product users.

BARB

BARB is the UK's major source of television viewing data, and it is on BARB that I shall concentrate in this section of the chapter, looking at:

1 Structure of BARB.
2 Establishment survey.
3 Data collection and collation.
4 Data delivery and analysis.

5 Audience appreciation indices.
6 Future developments of BARB.

Structure of BARB

The Broadcasters' Audience Research Board consists of representatives of the broadcast companies. Currently, these are the terrestrial television companies: the BBC, ITVA and Channel 4 companies. At the time of writing, two satellite TV contractors have expressed their wish to join the Board of BARB.

It should be noted that neither advertisers nor advertising agencies/media independents are represented on the Board of BARB. They are represented on some of BARB's various committees, including its Technical Sub Committee: but BARB is not a true 'JIC' (Joint Industry Committee) in the sense of, for example, JICNARS (see elsewhere in this chapter).

Establishment survey

This BARB annual survey of homes is designed to produce details of the total populations and television populations of each ITV area. The survey is conducted each March, currently, but is due to become a continuous study in 1991. Such continuous fieldwork enables trends and seasonality to be better monitored. The establishment survey has three major objectives:

- To establish details for households and individuals in each ITV area and BBC region of television ownership, reception, other TV equipment (e.g. VCRs), and detailed demographic information.
- To obtain targets of various demographic and television reception characteristics, to which the BARB panels should conform (more of which later). These criteria are known as 'panel controls', and include control criteria regarding: age of housewife; size of household; presence of children; social class; total ITV/BBC weight of viewing; age; sex; working status (adults); stations received; number of sets; set characteristics; ownership of other TV equipment.
- To provide a master sample, from which households can be selected for inclusion in the panels, representative of the whole.

The sample size of the current establishment survey is in the order of 20,000 interviewees. From these interviewees, a representative sample is recruited, to become members of the BARB metered panels as described in the next section.

Data collection and collation

The current BARB methodology entails the use of metered homes. These homes, representing the country at large as described above, number some 3000 in total, but are specifically selected by ITV area. The number of metered homes will increase to 4500 in August 1991.

The area panels currently range, in terms of numbers of metered homes, from 100 to 350 homes per area, as shown in Table 9.3.

Table 9.3   BARB panel target homes

Area	Target	Area	Target
London	350	Wales and West	300
Midlands	300	South, S. East and Channel Islands	380
North West	300	East of England	300
Yorkshire	250	South West	150
North East	200	Ulster	100
Central Scotland	200	Border	100
North Scotland	100	Total	3030

The main meter may be sited anywhere in the home. It contains a quartz digital clock, and an electronic memory. The meter frequently monitors the status of each TV receiver (at the moment, limited in number to four such units, including VCRs as well as television sets) in the home. Any change in status of the receiver – from off to on, changed channel, number of individuals present in the room is stored in the meter memory.

'People' data, i.e. presence in the room, is measured by the use of a remote control handset. Individuals in panel homes are asked to press and re-press numbered keys when entering or leaving the room. These data are collected by a remote detection unit (RDU) on the set.

AGB's main computer retrieves each panel home's meter data by telephone, in the early hours of the day. These data are then collated together with the TV companies' transmission log information. The transmission log data, also delivered on-line contains details of the programmes and the commercials transmitted. The resultant computer tape thus contains information regarding the size and demographic profiles of audiences to television programmes and specific commercials, minute by minute.

The new BARB specification for the contracts to begin in August 1991 includes the need for all channels to be monitored individually, whether broadcast off air, by satellite, or by cable. In addition, the recording and playback of programmes and commercials must also be monitored.

Audience appreciation indices

The BBC carry out some 3000 face-to-face interviews daily, asking adults to recall the television programmes they viewed the previous day. Also included in the interview is a semantic scale, ranging from 0 to 6, to score the programmes. The resultant scores are used to produce audience appreciation indices (AIs). Access to these data is restricted to the broadcasters: BBC, ITVA, etc. They are not available to advertisers or agencies.

Future developments of BARB

In the near future, BARB may be able to capture information of 'presence in the room' in an automatic manner, without the need for any action by the viewing panel members. There are various means by which such measurements might be taken. Current experiments involve the use of infrared sensors, transponders, etc.

The next most likely development in television audience research, however, may not directly involve BARB. Several of the current ITVA contractors have introduced, or are introducing, supplementary measurement systems. London Weekend Television has recently introduced a system entitled 'Support', which involves the placement of interactive viewdata sets in short-term panel homes. These sets are programmed with a questionnaire which may be altered every twenty-four hours. The questions are currently concerned with respondents' viewing of yesterday's television transmissions, quarter hour by quarter hour. Importantly, viewers' opinions of the programmes concerned may also be gathered, together with their product usage and lifestyle characteristics.

The short-term panels may be selected to match any required demographic sub-group (e.g. 16–24 year-olds, business people, etc.), in order to supplement the BARB panel.

There is little doubt that the needs of advertisers and media planners to understand more of why people view specific programmes (and the resultant effects upon the viewer of the commercials involved) will lead to the expansion of research of a qualifying nature, such as LWT's Support system. These developments are all the more likely as programmes and channels increase their 'narrowcasting', to reach minority sub-groups.

Outdoor advertising

Posters are a particularly difficult medium, in terms of audience measurement. To interview individuals asking them to recall the posters they have passed/seen/can remember having seen is a technique which has been tried in the past, and found wanting. Over the past few years, however, considerable advances have been made in poster audience measurement, in two ways:

1 Estimates of traffic (pedestrian and vehicular) past poster sites.
2 Site classification; the grading of sites in accordance with factors concerning their relative visibility.

Estimation of traffic

There are two ways in which estimates of traffic past poster sites can be made:

1 Location card or sketch map. The Copland model relies upon interviews with respondents, who are asked to trace their journeys during the past week, with the aid of a sketch map of the area.
2 Oscar (Outdoor Site Classification Audience Research) uses an actual count of observed traffic past each site by pairs of enumerators. Both pedestrian and vehicular traffic are measured. In the latter case, the counts are adjusted to take into account the numbers of passengers in, for example, cars versus buses.

Site classification

Oscar, through NOP, collect highly detailed information concerning some 125,000 poster panels in the UK. The criteria measured in addition to details of site addresses and ownership include:

- Road type.
- Location.
- Traffic flow.
- Bus routes.
- Speed limits.
- Traffic lights.
- Vehicle entry points.

Visibility is also measured. Criteria include:

- Furthest distance from which panel is clearly visible.
- Angle to the road.

- Deflections from natural eye line.
- Obstructions.
- Height from the ground.
- Illumination.

Such information allows Oscar to classify and grade sites, and enables Oscar to provide information regarding site quality.

In addition, Oscar provides two estimates of the audience to each site: vehicular, and pedestrian. In each case, the estimates given are themselves twofold: (a) *gross* site audiences, and (b) *net* panel audiences.

(a) *Gross site audiences* – these data are produced by a model which combines the NOP site characteristics information with actual audience figures collected by AGB. (The latter AGB research is for a representative sample of sites.)

(b) *Net panel audiences* – the gross figures are adjusted, to produce measures of the audience who will have 'opportunities to see' the panel, rather than simply passing by the site. This adjustment procedure is carried out using 'visibility' factors. Once again, the factors concern themselves with (i) vehicular traffic, and (ii) pedestrian traffic.

   (i) *Vehicular traffic* – the vehicular visibility index uses the following factors:

   - Length of visibility.
   - Angle of vision.
   - Competition.
   - Height.
   - Deflection.
   - Obstruction.
   - Illumination.

   The first three of these factors could have a perfect sum score of 100 maximum. The latter four factors are multiplicative. The last of these, illumination, can be scored as high a factor as 1.3. Thus a full perfect score from factors 1 to 3 of 100 maximum could then be multiplied by perfect factors (4–7) of $1.0 \times 1.0 \times 1.0 \times 1.3$: a final *net* score of 130. For this reason, it is possible (but improbable) for a perfect panel to have a higher net than gross audience.

   (ii) *Pedestrian traffic* – The pedestrian visibility index takes into account only three factors: the proportion having an opportunity to see, competition and illumination.

These visibility indices, in practice, appear harsh when applied as netting factors to the gross site audiences. On average, the effect of these applications is to reduce the gross audience by some 70 per cent. Only 30 per cent of those passing the site are considered as having a true opportunity to see a specific panel.

The future of Oscar

First, it must be emphasized that Oscar measures only those sites owned by those contractors which belong to the Outdoor Advertising Association. These amount to some 90 per cent of all panels – and all of the higher quality sites.

On a question of net coverage and frequency data other than within the specific local area of the site, work has been completed by the poster industry to adapt the Copland model. This adaptation gives reach and frequency information on a national scale, rather than – and in addition to – town by town data.

Oscar information is still often derided by media planners, who are sceptical of so much modelling of data. At the same time, Oscar continues to improve its efficiency in the measurement, calculation and delivery of audience data. Advances within reach and frequency estimates will help Oscar to become accepted as the industry currency used by planners, buyers and sellers of the medium.

Cinema

To a large extent, the cinema medium is measured by the numbers of (a) admissions and (b) visits to the cinema.

Admissions

Data are provided by the Cinema Advertising Association (CAA), from surveys conducted by Marplan. These are based upon 80 per cent actual returns from 80 per cent of cinemas, and a 15 per cent sample of the remaining 20 per cent.

Visits

Visits to the cinema details are available from surveys including the National Readership Survey (JICNARS – see Press section of this chapter) and the Target Group Index (TGI – see also Press section). Both sources give clear indications of the profiles of those most likely to visit the

Table 9.4   Regular cinemagoers

		Regular cinemagoers (000s)	(%)	Population 15+ (%)	Index (population profile = 100)
Age	15–17	628	20.2	50.4	374
	18–24	1464	47.1	14.2	332
	15–24	2092	67.2	19.5	345
	25–34	612	19.7	17.9	110
	35–44	218	7.0	17.0	41
	45–54	115	3.4	13.5	27
	55–64	59	1.9	13.0	15
	65+	15	0.5	19.2	3
Social	A	137	4.4	2.9	152
grade	B	691	22.2	15.2	146
	C1	915	29.4	22.6	130
	C2	786	25.3	28.1	90
	D	444	14.3	17.5	82
	E	137	4.4	13.7	32
All adults		3111	100	100	100

Source: NRS January–December 1988

cinema. Table 9.4 gives an example of such demographic profiles by age and social grade for 'regular' visitors to the cinema. In the case of JICNARS, 'regular' refers to those who go to the cinema once a month or more often.

Several major points arise from Table 9.4. First, it is clear that regular cinemagoers have a strong tendency to be young: over two-thirds are aged between 15 and 24. Second, only some 3.1 million adults go to the cinema once a month or more often: 7 per cent of the adult population. The NRS currently shows that almost two out of three adults (63 per cent) say that they never go to the cinema. Third, the major industry surveys, such as JICNARS and TGI concern themselves only with adults aged 15+. The profile shown in Table 9.4 suggests that there may be a high proportion of children of under 15 years in the cinema audiences.

On this latter point, it is logical to suppose that the cinema audience profile will differ by type of film: e.g. 'Bond' versus horror versus Disney. The cinema industry, under the auspices of the Cinema Advertising Association, are appreciative of these points. As a result, a number of 'sweeps' (surveys) have been carried out by CAVIAR: Cinema and Video Industry Audience Research. Each study has been sponsored by the industry itself (CAVIAR is not a Joint Industry survey) interviewing persons down to the age of seven. The survey, as its name implies, also covers the watching of video films. Some examples of the resultant profiles are shown in Table 9.5, which shows that, of ten popular films of the last two to three years, only one matches the population profile aged 35+, in terms of audience profile. At the same time, the profiles of the audiences vary greatly by type of film, within what is, basically, a very young group.

Table 9.5   Audience profiles from top ten films seen in the cinema in last 2–3 years

	7–14 (%)	15–24 (%)	25–34 (%)	35+ (%)
Population	11	17	16	56
Jungle Book	31	17	22	30
Master of the Universe	31	35	15	19
Three Men and a Baby	14	46	20	20
Innerspace	20	49	15	16
Good Morning Vietnam	*	62	25	13
Coming to America	*	76	13	11
Last Emperor	*	24	20	56
Fatal Attraction	*	40	26	34
Witches of Eastwick	*	48	33	19
Selected arts films	3	40	22	35

Source: CAVIAR 6 (November 1988)

Currently, the cinema medium is enjoying high – and rising – audiences. Screen time is at a premium, due largely to the ability of a media planner to measure audiences and their demographic profiles with a reasonable degree of accuracy.

Radio

It could be argued that commercial radio is a relative newcomer to Britain's media mix. In fact, the first independent local radio (ILR) station to begin broadcasting under the auspices of the IBA was LBC in 1973. The oldest commercial radio station (in terms of its English service) is Radio Luxembourg, which has been in operation since 1934.

The ILR network now consists of forty-six stations, many now transmitting on split frequencies; different programming is transmitted on the AM and FM wavelengths.

Shortly after the launch of ILR, a Joint Industry Committee for Radio Audience Research (JICRAR) was set up. JICRAR's function is to provide measurements of the audiences of ILR stations and programmes, in a form which can be used as a buying and selling currency. The resultant research is that upon which this section will concentrate. However, three other widely available sources of radio audience research are worthy of mention. They are Radio Luxembourg, JICNARS, and TGI. The latter two sources are discussed under the Press section of this chapter. Of course, the BBC, too, carries out its own research into radio audiences, by day-after recall interviews. The BBC data are not made available to media planners.

JICRAR

There have been several changes to the JICRAR methodology since 1986. The current method is to place self-completion diaries, by random location sampling. The areas within which the diaries are placed are defined as the Total Survey Area (TSA) of each ILR station. The TSA is provided to JICRAR by the IBA, and is based upon reception/transmission strengths and political boundaries. These areas have changed over the years and comparisons of historic JICRAR surveys for trend data are difficult, as a result.

The sample size of JICRAR across all stations totals around 2500 in any one year. The sample size, station by station, varies – as does the size of the populations of the areas. Samples normally range between 500, 800 or 1100 adults aged 15+.

Each respondent is asked to complete a listening diary for one week. The diary has each day divided into quarter-hour segments from 0600 to 2400, and into half hour segments between 2400 and 0600. At the top of each page, the various relevant radio stations are shown as column headings. These include the ILR station itself, the BBC national and local radio stations, Radio Luxembourg, and an 'any other station' heading. Respondents may write in the name of any other radio station in the latter column. The demographics of respondents are collected before the diary is placed by face-to-face interview.

The JICRAR published reports contain:

- The weekly reach of each station.
- Cumulative reach over four weeks.
- Total hours of listening.
- Half hourly audience averages.
- Audiences by rate card time segments, both average and cumulative.
- Reach and frequency data for packages and spots.

The number of demographic subgroups for which these data are published varies according to the sample sizes available.

JICRAR is not a true 'Joint Industry Committee' in terms of funding: the research is sponsored entirely by the AIRC.

Special analyses are available: only one of several such computer analysis facilities uses the original database. This is the Radio Audience Terminal System (RATS), operated by the JICRAR research contractor, RSGB. Schedule analyses for non-standard packages can be produced.

There are also several computer models available which will estimate the reach and frequency of radio schedules. These include: Rascal, a J. Walter Thompson system; RAM, an RSGB on-line model; MRC System R, for use on programmable calculators; and COMBAT, a system for use on microcomputers, by Total Marketing Services.

The future of JICRAR is important, in that the number of competitive commercial radio stations is due to increase rapidly. Community radio, Independent National Station, split frequency transmissions, etc. will conspire to produce a demand for audience measurement of a network, regional and local nature.

Conclusion

There is a great deal of useful media research available to media planners and buyers. These sources tend to be discrete by medium. Consequently, definitions of media audiences – of 'opportunities to see' (or hear) – differ from medium to medium. Intermedia comparisons by the use of media research are difficult.

The next major step in media research may well be twofold: the measurement of opportunities to see *taken*, thus producing an improved intermedia comparison; and data fusion, the combining of research sources into one database.

BIBLIOGRAPHY

Chrichley, J. *Radio Research: An Annotated Bibliography*, 2nd edn. (Dartmouth Publishing Company, 1988)

Consterdine, G. *Readership Research and the Planning of Press Schedules*. (Gower, 1988)

Davis, M. P. *The Effective Use of Advertising Media: A Practical Guide*, 3rd edn. (Business Books, 1988)

Douglas, T. *The Complete Guide to Advertising*. (Macmillan, 1984)

JICNARS National Readership Survey, six-monthly reports and bulletins. (JICNARS/Research Services)

Monk, D. *Social Grading on the NRS*. (JICNARS/Research Services, 1985)

White, R. *Advertising: What It Is and How To Do It*. (McGraw-Hill, 1980)

10

Media planning

Daz Valladares and John Standish

Two of the most important questions asked of a media planner are the ones he is no better equipped to answer now than in the late 1960s, when the functions of media planning first originated. The questions are inter-related:

- How much money should be spent on advertising?
- Which advertising media should be used?

Research provides the media planner with little or no help, and it is easy to see why. The answers presuppose that we know how advertising works and can isolate the contribution it makes relative to the other elements in the marketing mix.

Over the years, experimental studies have been conducted by media owners, advertisers and agencies to compare the effectiveness of various media groups. The published studies have revealed the extent of bias in the media owner sponsored studies. It cannot be simple coincidence that when a publisher conducted the test, the press was always superior and vice-versa for a television-sponsored test. More complex experiments conducted by advertisers, both in the USA and in the UK, have shown just how difficult it is to keep 'all other things equal' in comparative tests. A change of sales people in one area, the loss of shelf facings in the other area, competitors' attempts to muddy the water, all contribute to the difficulties of evaluating the results.

Difficult as the task is, the media planner is obliged to make recom-mendations almost every day about the choice of media groups. He or she starts with a basic aim: to maximize the effectiveness of every advertising pound available; and to do this in the realization that to varying degrees, all media are inefficient.

So how do we decide between TV and press? The first thing to establish is that the requirements of the brand must take precedence over any media theory. It follows, therefore, that media planning is a rational progression from the agreed strategies of marketing and advertising for the brand or service in question.

The four steps in the media process are:

1 *Strategy* – what the brand needs to obtain when spending money in media.
2 *Planning* – media selection and deployment.
3 *Execution* – buying the plan.
4 *Evaluation* – did we get it right?

Let us start with the strategic decisions which need to be taken.

Strategic decisions

Earlier, we stated that the needs of the brand are paramount. This means brand thinking, not media theorizing and involves understanding the role expected of advertising.

A good planner will raise questions about the brief and not try to double-guess his client's intentions. Sadly, good briefs are rare and it is dangerous and foolish to make the wrong assumptions on which the media plan is to be based. Challenging the budget provided for the task is appropriate at this stage.

The planner should consider issues such as:

- How heavily should one advertise?
- The frequency of advertising exposures.
- Accumulation and decay of brand goodwill generated by advertising.
- Ideal share of voice, bearing in mind competitive activity.

Any research available from the client's offices – syndicated sales figures, evidence from tracking and econometric studies – should be used to help guide the planner.

The start point is understanding what the objective of the campaign is.

The objective

Advertising campaigns are usually conducted for fairly obvious reasons – for example, to increase profitable sales, or to persuade people to use their telephone more often. Sometimes, however, consumer campaigns may be carried out, not only to get prospects to buy, but also to persuade retailers to stock the brand. Toy campaigns come into this category. Some consumer campaigns are conducted in order to boost the flagging morale of the sales force.

It is important that we do not confuse marketing objectives with advertising or communication goals. A marketing objective is precise and capable of measurement. For instance, the objective of increasing sales from £10 million to £12 million per year is a marketing objective. Advertising objectives may be to make people think more kindly of the company such as the British Gas campaign entitled 'banishing gripes'.

We should avoid repeating marketing and advertising objectives under the guise of describing what the media objectives are. We need only state the nature of the campaign. This could be a test marketing exercise, the advertising of a promotion or an attempt to get people to respond to a coupon.

A key decision concerns the stance to be adopted. At its simplest, this involves a conceptual translation of the marketing strategy into media terms as follows:

- Aggressive stance: relevant in crowded, competitive markets showing little or no growth. A launch of a new confectionery countline calls for an aggressive approach and will involve gaining sales at the expense of existing brands.

   or

- Defensive stance: this is a non-aggressive or protective approach, appropriate for long-established brands towards the end of their life cycle.

The decision made at this stage will affect all other considerations as we will demonstrate.

The target audience

The planner will assemble as much information about who buys, influences purchase, or uses the brand and its competitors. All brands will appeal to different groups of people in varying degrees. Social or political trends may provide more guidance. An example could be the trend to healthy eating or to 'green' issues. The purpose is to influence these key prospects by means of media advertising.

The agreed marketing stance will guide us in the correct definition of just who these key prospects are. If our stance is aggressive, the target could be users of competitive brands. If defensive, we should target users of our brand.

Prospects are usually described in demographic, psychographic, life-style or life-cycle terms. However, there is a real danger of oversophistication. It would be foolish to describe our prospects as: 'People with a terminal education age of 19+ years, at the pre-family, but independent stage, concerned about the environment but prone to conspicuous consumption!' and then recommend the use of a blunt media instrument like television. The intention should be to use descriptions which can best help identify the media behaviour of key prospects.

The coverage, frequency and impact balance

All advertising budgets are finite. Advertising campaigns require a balance between the conflicting needs of coverage, frequency and impact (as defined by the size of space or time length of the commercial message).

High coverage levels are sometimes necessary for specific campaigns such as the Water Privatization programme. However, greater emphasis on coverage means a reduction in the frequency affordable and/or a diminution of the size and colour used in the space or in the length of the TV commercial. If the creative experts demand two-minute commercials for extra impact then the number of TV regions featured may need to be restricted and the number of advertising weeks limited as well. It may be that frequency is the key priority. Established analgesic brands may need to be advertised fifty-two weeks of the year. That will mean sacrifices in coverage and in the size of the advertisements in question.

Media selection – the intermedia comparison

These strategic decisions may well throw up the 'obvious' medium for the brand. But what if it does not? Occasionally there is an impasse. Both television and press may be viable in the light of the brand's strategic requirements. In these cases, it is necessary to make a decision based on two basic considerations.

1　The relative cost efficiency of each medium in reaching the defined target audience,
2　The relative value attributed to each medium in terms of the different creative opportunities they provide.

Let us look at each stage in turn.

1 Comparison of cost-effectiveness

Cost-efficiency comparisons between media groups tend to be difficult. Great care needs to be exercised if the comparison is to be fair in the sense of:

(a) *The units of space or time lengths being evaluated* – is a thirty-second commercial equivalent to a full-page colour space? Since the over-riding consideration must be the communication needs, it seems fair to allow the creative department the units of space and time they feel are necessary. The question then becomes a flexible one – depending on the particulars of the brand in question.

(b) *The target audience* – media research in the consumer press area is capable of providing fairly detailed breakdowns of the readership of specific publications, by class age or other demographic subgroups. TV audience research, however, cannot provide this degree of precision. The danger, therefore, lies in comparing mass audience delivery, simply because TV research cannot provide precise target audience coverage figures for subgroups.

(c) *Production costs* – these costs are often ignored by media planners when evaluating the efficiency of the different media groups. Yet the cost of producing films can differ dramatically from the cost of material from which press advertisements can be produced.

(d) *Limitations of industry media research* – however fair the basic comparison is, the media planner needs to be aware of the limitations of the measurements supplied by the industry research bodies. Both TV and press audience research measure 'editorial exposure' not advertisement exposure. An individual classed as a viewer may, therefore, not even be in the room. Research carried out in 1961 and again in 1972 suggests that 20 per cent of 'viewers' are not in the room during commercial breaks. Viewers who are in the room may not be watching the set with a degree of intensity as the 'attention' studies demonstrated. The definition of a 'reader' in the National Readership Surveys basically describes an individual who claims to have read an issue of the publication during the last publishing period. Reading intensity is not implied, nor does the issue have to be the most recent one. It is therefore important to refine the basic viewership or readership information to measure 'exposure' to the advertisement in question. Great care must be exercised to ensure that the refining tools are comparable. For example, it would be incorrect to compare reading and noting scores in the press with presence in the room during the commercial break. A fairer comparison would be between 'eyes open in front of spread' with 'presence in the room'. Unfortunately, there is a danger in using 'averages', as the statistician discovered when he drowned in a pond which was six inches deep on 'average'. It seems unlikely that every publication offers the same opportunities to see an average advertisement. Programme journals with their nine-day life, must offer more opportunities for advertisement exposure than daily newspapers. In the same way, 'presence in the room' will vary according to time of transmission.

2   Communication values

Over the years, a great many myths and theories have been evolved regarding the ways in which the media work. The media planner is only, incidentally, concerned with the ways the media communicate. His aim is to discover how much a medium adds or detracts from the *communication* of the advertisement and from its *persuasiveness.*

Television, with its facility for combining sound, pictures and movement, helps to develop images, moods and atmosphere. It can be used to heighten the dramatic effect or for a soft sell. It can convince and it can demonstrate. And it sells products.

The press, without sound or movement can also lend itself to the creation of evocative, dramatic and convincing advertisements.

Never ignore the contribution made by talented writers or art directors. They have demonstrated the knack of breaking all the so-called rules such as: 'TV is best for demonstrating the product' and 'The press is useful when the need is to impact a lot of information.'

In ideal circumstances, the considered inter-media decision ought to be based on a subjective evaluation of 'finished' advertisements, prepared from the same creative brief, but in the alternative media groups. In normal circumstances, however, the interpretation of the brief is presented in a fairly rough form. Storyboards plus scripts for television, layouts and copy for press.

The team must decide on how much better or worse, the press advertisement is when compared to the TV commercial in terms of communication and persuasion. The relative difference furthermore needs to be *quantified.* For instance: 'We believe this commercial achieves our advertising objective *twice* as well, compared to the press advertisement.' Again there is a danger of using numbers to justify a preconceived choice.

The final media plan may call for the use of only one medium like television. These days, however, the larger advertisers feel the need for a multi-media approach. Multi-media campaigns work because they enhance the message delivered by the prime medium. A second medium may be used to reach people whose exposure to the main medium is slight. However, whether a single medium approach is proposed or not, the plan must be precisely costed and provide the advertisers with a real indication of audience delivery.

So far we have described a fairly simplistic process. Now consider these questions in relation to judged communication values.

- Will frequency of exposure change communication values? In other words, will a commercial work as well relative to a press advertisement, irrespective of the number of exposures each achieves?
- Will every individual in the target group respond to the advertisements in the different media groups in the same way?

Judgement, therefore, plays a vital part in the whole decision-making process. However, this judgement must be made on the basis of available research and in the context of the specific situation.

Buying the plan

Good buying involves understanding the needs of the brand and having the confidence of the advertiser.

The best buyers are aware of all the media options which exist and the ones that are coming up on the horizon. They understand the complexities of the rate cards – and most rate cards put up by TV and radio contractors are almost incomprehensible to the lay person. The very best buyers are better at deciphering the rate card than the sales executives.

It also helps to have an insight into the selling strategy of the media owner. National newspapers tend to either chase volume or are concerned with the 'yield' per page. Often they get confused and will change their strategy on a daily basis.

Good buying is *not* a function of muscle but rather of the skill of the buyer and some of the better buyers work in relatively small buying shops or agencies.

The evaluation of results

In an ideal world, the evaluation of the campaign's performance should be because you wish to learn from your mistakes and not an excuse for post-rationalization.

- Did the campaign achieve the targets set at the outset?
- Did you achieve the TV ratings planned for?
- Was the position obtained in the magazines as good as those obtained by your competitors?

Direct response advertisers are probably best at post-campaign evaluation exercises, because they have tangible results to monitor, such as cost per enquiry, cost per order and profitability of the business obtained. There is, however, a strong case for more conventional brand advertisers to conduct meaningful evaluative exercises. As the old saying goes . . . . Those who ignore the reasons of history are doomed to repeat its mistakes.

Conclusion

Media planning and buying is an art. It involves the spending of £4 billion a year in the UK and requires sound logical thinking and a deep appreciation of the disciplines of marketing and advertising.

As a specialist, the media person has earned the right to be taken seriously as the emergence of the media independent planning and buying shops illustrate.

Industrial media planning

John V. Standish

Media planning in the industrial area tends still to be much more an art than a science. Most industrial product promotion is aimed at a handful of people, relatively speaking – for instance, design engineers in the aeronautical field or manufacturing chemists concerned with the preparation of aerosols – and is largely carried out in the pages of the specialized trade, technical and professional press. Of course, in some instances, what are thought of as the mass media are appropriate for an industrial message, but this is usually where the product or its parent company has a wide appeal across many industries and/or has consumer connotations.

In addition to working on schemes concerning the support of direct product sales, the industrial planner also becomes involved in corporate projects in attempts to influence City opinion, investors, local authorities in a particular plant's area; even employee public relations exercises. The constant, overriding problem in these tasks is that while planning primarily in terms of job functions and industrial/business sectors (the latter as expressed by the 'CSO Standard Industrial Classification'); the majority of syndicated information available to the industrial planner comes in a 'consumer' context, that is in data breakdowns by socio-economic class, age, sex and geographical region. Thus the 'National

Readership Survey', even on the rare occasions where it reports on media of interest to him, is of little help. Similarly with television and radio research data.

However, as we have said, the majority of the industrial media planner's time is taken up with the specialist press, which comprises some 1,500 titles in the UK. In this field the planner has virtually no readership (as opposed to circulation) data to help. A great deal of thought has been given by various bodies and individuals to the possibility of producing an 'Industrial National Readership Survey'. However, bearing in mind the complexities and the resultant high cost a truly comprehensive survey would entail, it is doubtful if one will ever materialize. Of course, individual publishers do some work in this area; but in using such data one must be constantly on the watch, not so much flr flagrant inaccuracies in favour of the sponsoring bodies, as for significant omissions, peculiar samples and questions posed in such a way that the answers must benefit journal X.

On the brighter side, there are in planning in the architectural or farming areas, the annual 'INDAL' and 'AGRIDATA' readership surveys giving informative, unbiased data. Comparable works also exist in a handful of other fields allbeit published irregularly.

On the general business plane the 'BMRC Businessman Readership Survey' and the 'European Businessman Readership Survey', both conducted by Research Services Ltd., and multi-sponsored, are helpful too. Although a word of warning is in order if one is attempting to compare the performance of professional journals in the former – some sample sizes are small and the job functions tend to be lumped together.

On a different media front there have also been moves to enable planners to select 'industrial site' posters.

The planner's own company will sometimes conduct readership research into industrial areas, but it is hardly likely to provide enough data to meet every eventuality. Most of the time, therefore, the planner will have to work without the help of any readership research, and certainly without the kind of data his consumer counterpart often has.

Conventionally, the industrial planner will start work on a plan by selecting a candidate media list of those journals whose circulations align most closely with his required target readership. Here it is usual to consult BRAD (*British Rate and Data*) as an *aide-mémoire* for the range of media to be considered. Two criteria, at least, will usually apply – job function and industry. That is, taking design engineers in the aeronautical industry again, two groups will be considered – engineering journals with a design bias circulating to engineers as a whole, including aeronautical engineers, and also aeronautical industry journals that appeal to design engineers. Of course the brief may not be so straight-forward. While design engineers may be quoted as the main product specifiers, purchasing officers and/or production engineers etc. may also be deemed to influence brand selection, in which case the media planner may be obliged to give 'weightings' to the various job functions in analysing the suitability of one journal against another. Equally, the product may have secondary applications in other sectors of industry, which must also be taken into account in a like manner.

Having obtained a basic candidate list, the planner will normally be in possession of a number of campaign criteria, which will automatically reduce 'the field'. Among these might be the following:

1 An overriding need for maximum reader response, which will favour 'bingo card' product journals and possibly direct reply publications, and work against erudite monthlies.
2 The need for superb four-colour reproduction in line with quality presentation of the product, to the obvious exclusion of those publications that cannot provide it.
3 An urgent announcement, which requires a minimal delay – and therefore probably a weekly publication.

The next step for the planner will be to analyse closely the remaining publications against the detailed requirements of the brief in order to produce an order of journal priority. In this task all the factors set out in Figure 10.1 will be taken into account. Particular attention will be paid when comparing journals on the basis of published readership data, to the source of such information and the sample, and also the fact that information on circulation, however well authenticated by ABC certificates and Media Data Forms, cannot be taken as proof of reader-ship. This is particularly the case for free controlled circulation journals, and applies whether or not a high proportion of their circulation is 'requested' (although the latter is always a good sign).

An experienced industrial media planner will not, at least at this point, be concerned with costs per 1,000. In the field of controlled circulation publishing it is all too easy for a publisher to add on the odd 1,000 copies to get one step ahead of the opposition in the 'numbers game' in a situation where the ideal universe for any given journal is debatable.

It is as well to be wary of 'special supplements' or 'feature articles' which seem to be exactly relevant to the promotion, and would therefore appear to make a strong case for the inclusion on schedule of a particular publication – the rule of thumb here is only to schedule the issue if the journal would have qualified without the benefit of the 'special'. That is, the 'special' should be a bonus not a make-weight.

Media Data Form

Is an M.D.F. regularly completed and lodged with A.B.C.?
If not, what are publisher's reasons?
Is it fully completed,
with the information quoted backed by acceptable research?

How is it circulated?

Is it paid for,
controlled circulation,
or some of each?
Is it sent automatically to members?
Is it strictly 'requested' only?

What do readers think of it?

What is the editorial policy?
Are its articles authoritative?
Is the editorial standard high?
Is it an official organ?

Creative scope

What colours are available (specials or publisher's choice only)?
What is the printing process?
What is the quality of the paper?
Type area, format, bleed, spreads, etc?
Will odd shapes be accepted?
Type of binding?
Is the front/back cover available?

Who reads it?

Which industry or industrial Sector do readers come from?
How many are there out of the possible maximum?
Where are they geographically?
What is their management role?

Reader service facilities

Does it carry reply-paid postcards?
How much work is the publisher prepared to undertake?
Is it a product-cards-only publication?

Judging an industrial publication as an advertising medium

Economy

How do rates compare with other publications?
Are there any series discounts?
Are there special rates for special positions?
Will they do a deal?

What kind of publication is it?

Newspaper ... magazine ... journal?
Is its content horizontal — or vertical?
across a wide sector —
How frequently is it published?
What is the advertising — editorial ratio?
Does it carry new product items, recruitment advertising?
Does it have special issues?

Figure 10.1 *Factors in journal priority*

No mention has yet been made of publishers' representatives. Space salesmen can be particularly useful in the industrial area, providing one appreciates from the outset that no matter how helpful they may appear to be, their job commits them to total bias in favour of their own publication. The truest picture of the aims and potential advertising uses of their medium is obtained when they are encouraged to talk generally without the benefit of knowing which product the planner has in mind – a tactical advantage, incidentally, that the industrial agency planner possesses and that the single product advertiser is denied. The media planner will get the representatives to talk about their competitors if possible, then cross-check to see what their competitors say in return.

A cardinal fact for the planner to remember, although surprisingly easy to lose sight of, is that one is attempting to select the best publication, not the publication with the most plausible and sympathetic space salesman. The crunch comes when a decision has to be made against the journal of an extremely helpful representative and in favour of another journal, with marginally better claims, whose representative has been curt on the telephone, unwilling to travel out to explain his medium and generally acts as though he does not care whether he gets the business or not. While on the subject of the staff of publications, it should be mentioned in passing that magazine editors can prove to be a fruitful source of information on the technical aspects of industrial products and their applications.

Clearly the number of journals reaching the ranked candidate list will be dictated partly by the complexity of the campaign – perhaps requiring coverage of many separate industrial areas, each of which will have its own 'short list' – and partly by the way in which media have evolved to cover a given field. For instance, BRAD quotes eight journals under the heading of 'Fuel Industry' but 207 under 'Medical'.

The construction of a media insertion schedule from the candidate list naturally requires decisions on the size of space to be taken in each journal, positioning within the journal, the desirability of colour and the number of insertions that should be adopted over a given period. An agency planner might find that some of these decisions have been made in advance as the creative requirements of the original brief, a budget, and some idea of a possible start date and the most advantageous campaign periods.

However, regardless of any considerations that may work to the contrary, the overriding preoccupation will be to follow the golden media planning rule of restricting selection to those journals in which there is a guaranteed adequate exposure. 'Adequate' here is the key word. Adequate exposure in terms of insertion frequency is bound to bears a direct relation to the attention-getting power of the advertisement creatively, and from the point of view of size, positioning, and, indeed, competitive activity.

Judgements on the cost effectiveness in attention value terms of industrial journal pages against smaller sizes will have to be made, as will judgements on special positions against run-of-paper, and colour against black-and-white. Here again the advertising specifically under consideration will be the main determinant, together with the nature of the particular publications under review. There is little or no research evidence available in this area, although McGraw-Hill's *Laboratory of Advertising Performance*, based on US results, shows what can be done to help, but not to replace, the judgement factor.

One last point remains to be made about industrial media planning – that the planner is often working in a highly specialized industrial area with few tools, so that it is very important he or she explains the reasoning, preferably in writing, step by step to whomsoever is agreeing the expenditure. Only in this way can any flaws in the planning process – perhaps originating in an ambiguous briefing – be illuminated and corrected. It is a sign of an experienced, not an immature, planner when one reads such an admission in a report accompanying a proposed schedule as the following: 'We were in doubt finally as between journal X and journal Y, but decided in favour of the latter purely on the basis of its marginally superior coverage of production engineers – although admittedly its cost exceeded X by some £30 per insertion.'

11

Rules and advertising – legal and self-regulatory systems

Peter Thomson

Introduction

Advertising, like any other business, is hedged about by rules. Some of them, such as the legal rules that deal with conditions of employment, liability for damage, tax and similar matters are common to all businesses; they are not considered further here.*We shall be concerned instead with the rules that are peculiar to this business *because* it is advertising – the rules about where you may advertise, what you can advertise and how.

To list even these rules, and to explain and analyse each of them, would take us well beyond the confines of the present book. This chapter does not attempt the impossible. It is concerned not with rules in particular – though it ends with some recommendations about trustworthy sources of advice about them – but with advertising rules in general; who makes them, how they are enforced and what they are for. Its aim, in short, is to provide you with a framework of understanding of the nature of the rules that control advertising, their relationships to one another and the way they are enforced, into which you can fit your developing knowledge of the detail of the rules themselves.

Law and self-regulation

Writers about advertising in Britain habitually divide the rules we are concerned with into two groups – those that are backed by law, and those that are self-imposed (and contained, principally, in the British Code of Advertising Practice [the Code, or BCAP] and the British Code of Sales Promotion Practice [or BCSPP]). The two kinds of rule are different in the

---

* Though this chapter will mainly be concerned with rules about advertising, I shall, where appropriate, also mention rules about sales promotion.

way they have evolved, and often in the way they operate, so some division along these lines is inevitable, and we shall observe it in this chapter. But, before we examine them separately, let us enquire what these two kinds of rule have in common, and how they differ.

All rules, whether legal or self-regulatory, are aimed at shaping conduct, or controlling behaviour. They are instruments of social control, ways of ensuring that the individuals who make up a society conduct themselves in a way that conforms to what those who have power or influence within that society wish to see. The society concerned may be the nation, or it may be the advertising business; the function of rules is the same in either case.

What, then, are the differences between the legal and the self-imposed rules that affect advertising?

To some extent they are a matter of scope. The rules in the British Code of Advertising Practice are concerned, almost entirely, with the content of advertisements. Many legal rules go further and seek to control the conduct of advertisers, as well as what their advertisements say. But this greater scope is not in itself sufficient to distinguish legal from self-regulatory controls. The British Code of Sales Promotion Practice, for example, deals with the conduct of promotions as well as their form. And both the law and the Code seek to confront the fundamental issues of honesty and fairness in advertisement content.

This can be seen from the considerable similarities which there are between the rules that apply to advertising in the 'electronic media' – radio, television and cable – and those that apply elsewhere, to posters, press advertisements, cinema commercials, direct mail and so on and which are set out in the British Code of Advertising Practice.

Television and radio advertising are subject to legal control, under the terms of the Broadcasting Act 1981. The Independent Broadcasting Authority (IBA) regulates both the amount and content of commercials on television (ITV and Channel Four) and independent radio. The IBA issues and maintains a Code of Advertising Standards and Practice to which all commercials are required to adhere. This code is implemented on a day to day basis by the Copy Clearance Department of the ITCA (Independent Television Companies Association), which clears scripts, tapes and film commercials for use in independent broadcasting.

Despite the formal differences in the origin of the IBA's rules, and those in the self-regulatory Codes, they are very similar in detail, and identical in approach, or motivation. This makes possible the very close cooperation which exists between the IBA and the two bodies responsible for the self-regulatory system, the Advertising Standards Authority and the Committee of Advertising Practice. These similarities and this cooperation underline the fact that, whether legal or self-regulatory, the rules that govern advertising have a single purpose and thus normally work harmoniously together. Of course, it is true that the overlap in scope between the law and the British Code of Advertising Practice can, from time to time, cause problems; and these problems can, in turn, lead to arguments about which set of rules has priority. As to that, there can be no argument. In a society, such as ours, based on the rule of law, legal rules must take precedence over self-imposed rules in the event of any conflict between them. What is sometimes forgotten is that an acceptance of the primacy of law does not necessarily involve agreement with the view that legal rules are, for that reason, somehow 'better' – more sensible, more effective – than self-regulatory ones, or that they are necessarily well adapted for use in all control situations.

The two sorts of rule differ noticeably in the ways in which they seek to ensure compliance with what each requires,. Legal rules (and not only those in the criminal law) are backed by the power of the State; ultimately, by threats of imprisonment and fines. The system of self-regulation that adminsters the Codes disposes of apparently less impressive sanctions – non-publication and adverse publicity. Is the main difference, then, between the legal and self-regulatory rules one of effectiveness? There are those that claim that it is. But, even in a traditionally law-abiding society, such as Britain, and even within a limited area, such as advertising, there are now so many laws that not all are either as well-known or as well-understood as they might be. And, sufficient resources of manpower and court time to ensure the enforceability of legal rules are sometimes both lacking. The result can be that a rule's status as a law fails to guarantee its observance.

The one certain difference between legal rules and self-imposed rules is the status of the bodies that originate them. The laws that concern us are rules made by Parliament, or under parliamentary authority, while the Code's rules are made by the advertising business itself. This tells us where ultimate responsibility lies for ensuring compliance with the rule concerned; in the case of laws, with the public authorities; and, in the case of the Codes, with the Advertising Standards Authority. It also tells us to whom we should address ourselves if we want a given rule changed or removed; the Government in the case of a law, and CAP in the case of a rule in either of the Codes.

In the next section, we look further at legal rules, who makes them, what they do, and how they are applied. (*Note*: The IBA will be replaced on 1 January 1991 by the Independent Television Commission (ITC) and the Radio Authority (RA).)

Legal rules

Lawyers distinguish between statute and common law. Common law is that body of legal rules which has grown up over generations and is embodied not in Acts of Parliament, but in the recorded decisions of judges and the writings of lawyers since the Middle Ages. Its importance is immense and its complexity considerable. Fortunately for us, it has little direct relevance to our immediate theme – advertising law, though it is Common Law for instance which has established that in most circumstances advertisements are not in legal terms 'offers', but what lawyers call 'invitations to treat'. This means that an advertiser cannot be obliged to sell what he has advertised to anybody who tenders the right money. So he is protected in circumstances where he has run out of stock or has mistakenly priced his goods too low – though in the latter case he may have problems under the Trade Descriptions Act 1968.

Advertising law is essentially a creation of statute, which is to say that the legal rules with which we need to concern ourselves are either contained in Acts of Parliament or are in the form of rules made by Ministers under authority given them by Acts of Parliament.

These Acts and Regulations, or Orders, and impressively numerous, and mostly of fairly recent date.

Their diversity is a characteristic feature of British advertising law. If we look at this country from the perspective of our partners in Europe, we are struck by the absence of any attempt to express an advertiser's legal obligations in general terms – whether to consumers and the general public on the one hand, or to his fellow businessmen on the other.

The German Law on Unfair Competition (UWG) of 1909, by contrast, encapsulates the businessman's (and hence the advertiser's) obligations succinctly in its very first clause: 'Whoever in the conduct of business for purposes of competition commits acts which are contrary to customary morality can be sued for an injunction or damages, or both.'

Nowhere in British law on advertising is there any comparable expression of a general obligation. Our law, instead of leaving it, as it is left in Germany, to the Courts to deduce an advertiser's precise legal duty in particular circumstances from considerations of general principle, typically attempts in the statute itself to lay down exactly what an advertiser should and should not do in this or that set of circumstances. The gain in certainty which the British approach offers can be offset in practice by the need for an advertiser who wishes to know the full extent of his obligations to piece them together from a wide variety of sources, not all of which, to the uninitiated, have any immediately apparent relation to the advertising business.

The situation is not made any easier by the fact that very few of the cases involving advertising that come before the Courts are the subject of easily available reports. Most criminal prosecutions are disposed of before magistrates and most civil actions are heard in the County Court, but it is only the decisions of higher courts that are published as a matter of routine. This has the consequence not only of making it difficult to discover precisely how some obscure provision has been interpreted, but of making it more likely that conflicting interpretations of the same provision are arrived at by courts in different parts of the country, thus occasionally posing a problem for national advertisers.

Again we can contrast this state of affairs with that in Germany, where the standard textbook contains thousands of pages of decisions providing guidance on most aspects of advertising.

We can break down the great assemblage of British statutory rules into three broad groups. In the first place, we have the most numerous class of rules, those that take the form of direct instructions from the state to the advertiser to do or not to do this or that. For example, the Race Relations Act 1976 prohibits advertisements that indicate an intention to discriminate on racial grounds, and the Business Advertisements (Disclosure) Order 1977 obliges traders to come clean about their status (and thus their motives), when advertising in the 'For Sale' columns of newspapers. These rules are backed by criminal sanctions. Breaches of them lead to prosecution.

The second main group of statutory rules is made up of those in which Parliament confers rights on some citizens, a process which entails corresponding duties being imposed on others. These duties are not obligations owed directly to the State, but by an advertiser to an individual consumer or competitor. It is the responsibility of the competitor or the consumer (and not of some public official) to invoke these laws against the advertiser when necessary. For example, under statutory rule of this kind, an advertiser may find that he cannot enforce a contract for the sale of goods because he has misdescribed them (Misrepresentation Act 1967); or he may be obliged to withdraw a comparative advertisement because it makes use of a competitor's trademark (Trade Mark Act 1938).

The last main group of statutory rules with relevance to advertising are those that establish public bodies and/or give them powers (and sometimes duties) to enforce or oversee the law. We have already discussed the role of the IBA. Now we should note that it was under the Fair Trading Act 1973 that the Office of Fair Trading came into being, and it was the Trade Descriptions Act 1968 that, for the first time, imposed a duty on local authorities to enforce the law on misleading claims.

This brings us back to the question of how legal rules are put to work. Once again, the contrast with Germany is very noticeable. Their Law on Unfair Competition began as a charter of fair dealing among traders, and later came to be the vehicle whereby consumer protection was provided. Thus it is that, in Germany, responsibility for ensuring that an advertiser conforms to the law lies, in the first place, with his competitors, and in the second,with consumer associations, both asserting their rights under what English lawyers would call civil law. Only in a narrow range of circumstances is there any question of state intervention or of criminal penalties.

We have seen that in Britain, statutory rules in our second group confer rights which can be asserted by individuals – whether businessmen or consumer. But, overwhelmingly, in this country the weight of consumer protection is based upon the application of criminal law and is dependent upon enforcement by local authority officials usually known as Trading Standards Officers. There are both advantages and disadvantages in this solution. On the one hand, the involvement of public officials, duty bound to enforce the law, minimizes the risk of legal action being used as a means of hampering legitimate competition, and increases the chance of the public interest being served. On the other, by institutionalizing enforcement, the possibility arises of matters being pursued which are of no genuine concern either to consumers or to competitors; and by the use of the criminal law, a situation is created in which it is sometimes more difficult to deal with rogues, because of the quite proper insistence in criminal proceedings that the burden should be on the prosecution to prove their case and not on the accused to prove his innocence.

It is partly for that reason that the role of self-regulation in the United Kingdom is more substantial than in some of our European Community partners – or indeed our fellow common law jurisdictions such as the United States.

Britain's membership of the European Community means that Parliament is no longer the only source of legislation affecting those in advertising. A Directive (that is, an instruction which must be obeyed, to a member government) on misleading and unfair advertising was issued in 1984. This led in 1988 to the introduction in Britain of the Control of Misleading Advertisements Regulations which provide through the Office of Fair Trading valuable back-up for self regulation. Other directives and regulations are on the way and will come to play an important part in the life of anyone in advertising.

Self-regulation – the codes

We must now turn to a consideration of the self-regulatory system which exists alongside the law. This system's rules are embodied in two Codes, the British Code of Advertising Practice and the British Code of Sales Promotion Practice. In 1959 the advertising business took the decision to draw up a single, unified advertising code to replace the many, sometimes conflicting, codes that existed at that time in different parts of the advertising business. In 1974, the guidance which the ASA had given over the years on such matters as premiums and competitions was incorporated into the Sales Promotion Code. /

One of the main advantages that a code has over statutory provisions is that it is more flexible, and can be more readily adapted to changing circumstances. In 1988 the eighth edition of BCAP was published. As much as possible of the guidance given since 1962 is now incorporated into the body of the Code itself. The eighth edition of BCSPP was published in 1988. But those who are responsible for them do not see either Code as a completed achievement; if they are to remain able to deal with changing problems in a rapidly developing society, they must be flexible and capable of further growth and change.

This is not the place to spell out the detailed provisions of the Codes; everybody in the advertising business should have his own copies and should refer to them regularly, but two key points are worth stressing because they go to the heart of the matter. The essence of both Codes is expressed by saying that 'A Code is applied in the spirit as well as in the letter'. It is this adherence to the spirit that marks one of the two most crucial differences between Codes and the law. The other great difference is the requirement (and the system's ability to demand) that substantiation for claims, descriptions and comparisons in advertisements should be provided to ASA and CAP without delay. Advertisers and agencies are required to hold such substantiation ready for production. In other words, ASA and CAP do not have the burden of disproving claims that are challenged; it is for an advertiser to make out his case to the Authority's or the Committee's satisfaction. This would not be acceptable under a legal system of control but it is freely accepted as one of the essential elements of cooperation within a voluntary system.

The mechanics of self-regulation

A Code, no matter how comprehensive, is worthless unless it can be and is vigorously enforced. An administrative system is required. Since 1962 the self-regulatory system has been in essence what it is today; a two-tier tripartite system. Two-tier because it consists of an industry-wide executive body under the general supervision of an independent controlling body and tripartite because the three elements – advertisers, agencies and media – which go to make up the advertising business, are all represented on the industry-wide executive body.

The first edition of BCAP was launched at the Advertising Association's Conference in 1961; the standing committee established to supervise its operation and to ensure that it was kept up-to-date was christened 'The Code of Advertising Practice Committee'. It swiftly became better known as the CAP Committee, or simply 'CAP'. In 1988 it changed its name to The Committee of Advertising Practice. In 1962, taking note of doubts that had been voiced about the extent to which a purely industry body was capable of being firm enough, or of bearing the consumer interest sufficiently in mind, Conference endorsed the establishment of the independent Advertising Standards Authority (ASA), whose objects were defined as 'The promotion and enforcement through the United Kingdom of the highest standards of advertising in all media, so as to ensure, in co-operation with all concerned, that no advertising contravenes or offends against these standards'.

The Advertising Standards Authority

Formally, the ASA is a company limited by guarantee. Its directors are the Members, including the Chairman of the Authority. The Members of the Authority form a Council, so that membership of the Authority and its Council is identical.

The Chairman, who is paid a salary, is appointed by the Advertising Standards Board of Finance in consultation with Council members and the Department of Trade and Industry. The Chairman, who must be wholly independent of all advertising interests, serves for three years (a term which is renewable) and appoints the other members of the Authority, at least half and not more than two-thirds of whom must also be completely independent of all advertising interests, while the remaining members must be persons with knowledge and experience of advertising. All members serve in an individual capacity and none represents or reports back to any other organization. Members serve for three years, also renewable.

The Authority meets once a month and issues an annual report and regular reports of cases upon which it has adjudicated.

The Authority's function is supervisory. It ensures that the system of self-regulation set up by the advertising business works effectively in the public interest. This it does by ensuring that the Code is properly and fairly applied and kept up-to-date; that CAP functions smoothly and that all complaints are properly investigated. Complaints from the public are investigated by ASA staff who also monitor advertising continuously to check on advertisements that have not been the subject of complaint. Increasingly, research is becoming a major preoccupation of the Authority. ASA also represents the control system to the outside world. It maintains close liaison with the Department of Trade and Industry and other Government departments, the Office of Fair Trading, consumer bodies, Trading Standards Authorities, trade associations, organizations such as the Equal Opportunities Commission, and many others which, although not directly concerned with advertising, have an interest in its work. Trading Standards Authorities, Citizens' Advice Bureaux and Consumer Advice Centres, as well as Chambers of Commerce and Trades Councils, are supplied by ASA with copies of the Codes. So is every major public library. Perhaps the most visible of the ASA's functions is its own substantial advertising campaign, which informs the public of what is being done on their behalf.

Committee of Advertising Practice

The Committee consists of representatives of nineteen advertising organizations representing advertisers, agencies and media. The independent radio and television companies are represented by their associations (Independent Television Association and Association of Independent Radio Contractors), even though advertising on television and radio are controlled by a public body (Independent Broadcasting Authority). Each association may be represented by one permanent official and one member; the latter may have a named alternate for meetings, and other officials attend, at the Committee's discretion, as observers. In practice, one Association (Periodical Publishers Association) has two members, one representing general magazines and another trade and technical magazines. None of the members of the Committee is paid a fee. The Chairman of CAP is elected for a period of two years. The Committee enjoys the support of three non-member associations in the indoor and direct marketing fields.

The major functions of CAP are the regular review of the Code, the investigation of complaints from within the business, and the giving of advice and guidance, on a confidential basis, to advertisers, agencies and media. By making this guidance available, the Committee seeks to ensure that advertisers and agencies, especially those operating in sensitive areas, are encouraged to submit advertisements for advice before publication, in the knowledge that confidentiality is complete. In the case of cigarette advertising, pre-publication clearance of all advertising is mandatory.

The Copy Panel

The Copy Panel exists to give guidance on claims and general issues, particularly where interests are finely balanced. The Panel is divided into five sections, one of which is available to meet each week. The membership of each of the sections consists of one person nominated by each of the following organizations: Newspaper Publishers Association, the Newspaper Society, the Periodical Publishers Association, the Institute of Practitioners in Advertising, the Incorporated Society of British Advertisers and, importantly, the Advertising Standards Authority. Each member serves in his or her individual capacity. Each ASA nominee is chosen from the independent membership of the Council.

CAP sub-committees

In 1973, CAP took the decision to move from monthly meetings to six meetings a year (though the officials of CAP member organizations continue to meet at intervals to deal with points of detail). At the same time four standing sub-committees of a more manageable size, generally seven or eight members, were set up to deal with matters arising in some of the more specialized areas in which the Codes are involved. Three of these sub-committees deal with matters covered by BCAP: these are the Health and Nutrition Sub-Committee, which deals with the whole area of medical claims, whether made about medicines, about appliances or about foods; the Mail Order Sub-Committee and the Financial Advertising Sub-Committee which is principally concerned with financial advertisements addressed not to other specialists but to the general public. The fourth sub-committee, the Sales Promotion Sub-Committee, administers BCSPP.

Administration

The day to day business of ASA and CAP is conducted by a joint secretariat, which has its own premises where the Council of the Authority meets regularly. The CAP Committee meets at each of the major sponsoring bodies' headquarters in rotation. It has been found to be of practical advantage to have the same secretary for both ASA and CAP. The Director-General of the Authority is therefore also the Secretary of the Committee. Great care nonetheless is taken by all concerned to maintain the separate identities of ASA and CAP.

Methods of dealing with complaints

Complaints from the public are dealt with by ASA, those from within the business by CAP.

Evidence of the advertisement itself or sufficient detail to identify it must be supplied by the complainant. If on the face of it, there appears to be a case requiring an answer, the Secretariat will write to the advertiser, and the agency responsible for the advertisement, seeking their views. No action will be taken until a reasonable time has been allowed for comment (except in cases of flagrant breaches either of the Code or of an undertaking already given by advertiser or agency). On receipt of their comments the Secretariat evaluates the complaint, taking specialist advice from the system's retained expert advisors as appropriate, and drafts a recommendation for the consideration of the Authority or the Committee.

The Secretariat's recommendations may be overturned, or reserved for future discussion or investigation; but once accepted, an adjudication by the Authority or the Committee becomes binding on all concerned, though there is provision, in rare circumstances, for appeal from a CAP decision to the ASA Council.

The number of complaints before the Advertising Standards Authority's advertising campaign had begun in 1975 was about 600 per year to the ASA (of which somewhat over half concerned mail order transactions) and 150 to the CAP Committee. Both have increased substantially as a result of the initiatives in the field of publicity described below, and complaints at present are running at a rate of 9,500 per year, of which just under 8,000 go to the Authority.

Further detailed information about ASA/CAP procedures is available from the joint secretariat on request (Brook House, 2–16 Torrington Place, London WC1E 7HN).

Compliance

The primary sanction for breaches of the Code is non-publication by media. Each of the three press media bodies circulates confidential memoranda to its members, and if a particular advertisement is found to be unacceptable, no member should accept the advertisement. The procedure is thus one of recommendation of non-acceptance. The same sanction is applied, *mutatis mutandis*, by other media. The regular publication of details of the cases considered by ASA and CAP also acts as a deterrent to those who are shown to have broken the Code; the Authority reserves the right to make a public condemnation of those who flagrantly or repeatedly breach the Code.

Education

The staff of ASA and CAP lecture and instruct at many different colleges and schools each year, and take part in seminars, courses and discussions of various kinds. The ASA also acts as host to the advertising business and others interested in its work in four or more provincial towns and cities each year. The Editorial, with which each issue of the ASA cases reports is prefaced, is also a source of detailed guidance to practitioners.

Publicity

For the first 13 years of their existence, the policy of ASA and CAP was not to seek direct publicity for their activities; rather, every effort was made to ensure that those agencies to which the public was likely to turn for advice (in circumstances where advertising seemed to them to be to blame) should be fully informed as to the existence of the self-regulatory control system and of the rules of the Code. In 1975 the greatly increased funds that became available as a result of the establishment of ASBOF (see below) permitted for the first time an advertising campaign, based on extensive use of national and regional media, addressed to the general public, telling them what the Advertising Standards Authority was and did, in particular how it could help them when they had a complaint about an advertisement. The campaign has been developed and continued with great success, resulting in a greater number of people seeking the Authority's advice and assessment and a substantial increase in public knowledge of the Authority's role as well as a significant increase in the level of complaint.

The funding of the system

Since January 1975, the system has been funded out of the proceeds of a 0.1 per cent surcharge on the cost of display advertisements. The collection of this surcharge is in the hands of the Advertising Standards Board of Finance (ASBOF) from whom details of its operation may be obtained. In 1988, the surcharge produced an income of over £2 million.

Conclusion

Thus it can be seen that, since 1962, a sophisticated and extensive system has been developed to implement the advertising industry's self-regulatory Codes. It may reasonably be asked whether the advantages claimed for codes have succeeded in delivering a worthwhile benefit to the consumer, and how successfully this system, different in its construction and way of operating, meshes with the legal provisions which were described earlier. The Director General of Fair Trading is on record as saying that 'The greatest contribution of my country to the control of the content of advertising has been the combination of legal controls, enforced in the courts, and voluntary self-regulation, devised, financed and provided by the advertising industry itself.' After a somewhat lukewarm reaction in its early days, self-regulation is now seen on all fronts as an indispensable element in any practical scheme for the control of advertising content. The Office of Fair Trading undertook a thorough review of the system in 1978. This demonstrated for all to see the high level of success which the system had attained. The few suggestions for improvements which were made have all since been implemented. Discussions subsequently concentrated on improving the fit between the legal and self-regulatory systems, and particularly the creation of a swift-acting power in the hands of the OFT to prevent publication of advertisements in circumstances where neither our system, nor the normal legal control could act, or could act swiftly enough. This goal was finally achieved, as noted above, with the introduction of the Control of Misleading Advertisements Regulations 1988.

The fact is that neither law nor self-regulation acting alone can deliver as much in society's interest as can the two working together. They require to be deliberately designed and developed so that they do not merely work in parallel – and certainly do not cut across each other – but rather divide the field between them with each doing what it is best at.

This is now the conventional wisdom, and the concept of a partnership between legal rules and code rules is embodied in statute, with the Fair Trading Act placing a responsibility on the OFT to sponsor industry codes. This they have energetically done since 1974 and now there are Codes in many distinct areas of trade. Some of these Codes, such as that of the Association of Mail Order Publishers, provide more detailed guidance on advertising matters than would be appropriate in BCAP. But BCAP is in all of them accorded primacy so far as advertisements are concerned.

Sources of further information

As we have seen, the British law as it affects advertising is a complicated subject. The advertising practitioner is best advised to consult a lawyer specializing in this area if he seeks advice on a specific problem. But there are some trustworthy sources of general information which may help you to understand the advice you get.

Croner's Consumer Law and Product Liability
ed. R. G. Lawson (Croner Publications Ltd., New Malden) This is a loose-leaf book which is kept up-to-date by the regular despatch of new material. It covers in brief but authoritative style a variety of topics, including advertising law.

Consumers and the Law – Ross Cranston
(Weidenfeld & Nicolson 1979)
This volume in the 'Law in Context' series is aimed at a professional readership, but is clearly written and particularly interesting on the social context. Its treatment of self-regulation is, however, inadequate.

Three interesting subscription-only journals are:

Consumer Affairs
(Consumer Relations Bureau, J. Walter Thompson)
Consumer Law Today
(Monitor Press)
Bee Line – a digest for consumer protectors and advisors
(Office of Fair Trading)

BIBLIOGRAPHY

Circus, Philip and Painter, Tony. *Sales Promotion and the Law: A Practical Guide*. (Butterworths, 1989)
Food Manufacturers' Federation. *Food Labelling – A Guide to the Statutory Requirements*, 2nd edn. (Food Manufacturers' Federation, 1973).
Woolley, Diana. *Advertising Law Handbook*, 2nd edn. (Business Books Ltd, 1976).

12

International advertising

David Hanger

There was a time when 'international advertising' was relegated to the backroom – but not any more. The last five years have seen international advertising elevated very much to the front office in agency financial, planning, creative and media departments. Industrial companies around the world that once boasted '20 per cent of our production is exported' now realize that to survive, let alone succeed, they need at least to treble that percentage. To match all of this, new media opportunities abound on every horizon (or in every sky), while the accepted international publications, with a head start, flex their muscles and demonstrate their true international product advantage of not just worldwide reach but also a relevant editorial environment.

Why the change? Is it just 1992 in Europe? There is little doubt that this is a major factor, though pan-European advertising is not new and pan-Asian advertising is by now a well-recognized reality. Indeed, long before Marshall McLuhan or Professor Levitt and friends proposed theories of globalism, companies and products were being advertised internationally.

What is international advertising?

So what has changed? Well, let us start with some definitions.

Traditionally, international advertising has simply meant advertising beyond a company's home market, with a common message to a definable international audience. It was accepted that invariably within the 'home' market, a company's depth of market penetration was greater than abroad, its market was broader, its sales message more detailed, and its advertising created to match actual or perceived local nuances. 'International' has not meant the Colgate toothpaste campaign appearing in

Spain, Sweden or Hong Kong, even though they might all have relied upon a translated version of the same or similar copy line. These campaigns were seen as attacking a 'local' market. With all but a few exceptions, international advertising was initially limited to products and services which were common across borders, and often aimed at the frequent traveller – cigarettes, upmarket drinks, expensive luxury goods, hotels and inevitably, airlines. The other important categories which have developed progressively have been corporate image advertising from the large multinationals, and the industry which has overtaken even airlines in its internationalism, – banking and its related round-the-clock global services. All of these relied historically, and still do, upon the existence of international media, which was, and still is, predominantly the published word, and in English/American.

The traditional international advertisers are still there, but even more companies from many diverse sectors of business now think and act internationally. The pan-frontier media opportunities continue to grow, still mainly press but also broadcasting in Europe. The globe has become smaller thanks to improved communications, both physical and telecommunications, round-the-clock computer links and facsimile transmission. The world can now read and watch news, sports, current affairs, opinions from afar and even the occasional common soap opera such as *Dallas* within roughly the same time frame. It is no wonder that people in general, but businesspeople in particular, are finding that their interests, tastes and needs are converging.

Being an international person is no longer the prerogative of the few elite, frequent-travelling, businesspeople – now a much wider audience thinks and behaves in a like-minded way. Advanced marketers recognize that national boundaries are not the only, nor necessarily the best, descriptives of a market. Indeed, there may be more differences between Manhattan and the Bronx than between mid-town Manhattan, Knightsbridge in London and the seventh arrondissement in Paris. It is now accepted that 'consumer convergence' is here. Remember, the travelling elite were not always there in such great numbers nor were they readily definable, yet now we take them for granted. It is therefore surprising that some minority of marketers still insist that 'consumer convergence' is a myth that can only be applied to the now accepted elite and never to a broader audience – why not the housewife? Why not indeed, in media terms, simply ask why has *Prima* been so successful? As Gruner and Jahr, the publishers, claim – the behaviour patterns of women across Europe are now broadly the same – same tastes, same interests. Sony, Canon, Jaguar, Mercedes, IKEA, Braun and many more enjoy an image which is so common across borders that it surprises even the internationalists. Do the businessperson's requirements of a telephone, a photocopier, a computer, change because of a national border? Rarely, they are more likely to change because of the commercial discipline in which he/she operates.

But is it all simply the technological advancement of improved communication and growing international media? No, it is commerce which has been and still is the real driving force. Commerce has become global, no longer can a company concentrate solely on a single market and feel safe behind a national frontier. The multinational business will eventually enter every market. The economies of large-scale international production have moved the advantage irreversibly in favour of the global producer. The global producer needs the size of a global market, and the more common the basic product requirements the better. So believe not yesterday's fashionable adage 'think global, act local', the successful companies of today both think and act globally – even in advertising and marketing terms.

Is international advertising synonymous with 'global'? By definition:

- Global implies a universal way of thinking, of acting, a common message.
- Multinational suggests an approach to many markets, but probably a different approach, and certainly in different languages.
- As we have seen, international means attacking markets beyond your home market and has traditionally meant a common message, often a single language.

So where are the lines to be drawn and does the reason for growth in international advertising lie partly in a movement between and within these definitions? In tomorrow's world, will a company even be able to retain a different image in its home market versus its international markets? It seems unlikely. International advertising will continue to develop, and as it does, so we must expect it to embrace global marketing and aspects of multinational marketing.

To understand this change, we need to examine the basics of how a company sells, starting as far down the line as the direct customer contact, by salesperson or retailer. This customer contact is only partly influenced by the producing company, indeed, there is often a surprising lack of awareness on the part of a company as to exactly what an individual salesperson says to secure the sale, even the written word has to conform more to price than any specific description of the goods or services. Each salesperson sells in a different way, emphasizing different product advantages. So, other than sales training, what does the company do to control the reaction of its customers? They advertise, but at differing levels of detail. Regional advertisements will differ, even within a country – the advertisement for the local showroom sale in Bournemouth will differ in approach from that in Newcastle. It is therefore not surprising that on an international scale differences occur across borders in the detailed sell. So do the marketing chiefs of the world's internationals do anything towards influencing our perceptions? Do they even need to? *Image* – it is not just Carl Schwarz or Clarence Smith the salesperson who walks through the door, no, it is the image he takes with him of Sony, Nissan, Unisys, IBM, Bosch, British Aerospace, Federal Express, Wrangler, BMW, Tefal. Yes, they do aim at achieving a universal image and they need to – otherwise why even make goods to the same standard – why even believe that your goods will command a premium price? Companies must control that image – they cannot leave it to Clarence Smith, who will sell himself as much as the company. The company can and must influence the branding and the image.

So what we see is local sales action, but branding (company or product) nationwide initially, but then internationally, often regionally, Europe/Asia at first, and then for a growing number of companies, globally to the eventual point where even the internal (home) and external markets converge. Does Sony have a higher-priced image than Aiwa everywhere? – that is their aim. Can BMW command a higher price and even better technical image than the most advanced Ford, at home and abroad? A resounding yes.

This trend towards global imagery will continue, it does not preclude local or national advertising, but it will mean more international advertising, more commonality within advertisements as they cross borders.

Why not *always* totally global in action at first? Companies cannot always cope with such pressure for organizational reasons, and it does take longer to build an internationally uniform image. As, however, prescribed regions become more definable, so we shall see more pan-frontier activity within definable regions – South East Asia and Europe being the two recognized powerhouses and the best developed beyond the USA, a region within itself.

Marketers will look more and more towards how to define their market in demographics/common interest groups/product usage/need to influence. They will be guided less and less by national boundaries. For some of these groups, the media and creative expertise are there, for others, they still have to develop, but develop they will and language will not be a barrier, translation technology and the ability and desire to communicate in another's or a common language will continue to grow apace. Albeit that it may continue to favour the English writer, particularly in areas of business.

So we have established that there is and will be more international advertising, and why.

The practical side of international advertising – creative, media, budgets, research

Many of the guidelines which apply to creative apply equally to media planning. The questions vary little – What is the company trying to achieve?, Who is the audience? and then What should the budget be?, or What is the budget?

What is the company trying to achieve? This is important, for it will influence creative, media and timing both the span and start-point. Is the company trying to enter a market, create a brand image which will affect market share or price, or both? What position versus the competition are they aiming at in the market, and by when do they hope to reach various levels on the way to their ultimate goal?

The new entrant invariably needs heavy up-front expenditure to create an immediate impact, but the message must then be sustained. The mature product will already have a marketplace position and an image – where it wants to be and what image it wants will affect the frequency, spend and media to be used. All of this will affect the creative.

So the steps:

- Where does the company want to be?
- Where is it now?
- The audience?
- How great and immediate is the resultant task?
- What kind of creative approach?
- Start point?
- Time span?

Remember that the failing of many agencies is that they think only in one-year terms. If a company is thinking internationally, then invariably the task will be greater, the goals spread across a larger time span, with very specific plans. Do not just think longer, but plan further ahead.

Audience

Think demographics/interest groups/business *before* you think geographics. Remember it will not just make the media plan more efficient, but if the creative department is thinking the same way, it will help to increase the relevance and the impact of the message. Try to encourage all involved to think this way first, beyond those normal boundaries.

The organizational problem referred to earlier will present problems. Many companies are organized into regions of the world, and you may have to come back to fit these organizations, but push them into global thinking first. Remember no one aims campaigns at 'Europeans' or 'Asians' or 'Germans'. The demographics of the group are far more important.

Creative

As we have seen, audience is the start-point for the successful international advertisement.

Establish the target audience *demographically* or by *interest* group, or *product* usage, then, and only then, worry about the geographic limitations – Europe, Asia, Africa, Middle East, America, the world. Second, as in all cases, define what conscious image you want them to have of your company, or product, or range, in order that they buy *the product or service you wish to sell more frequently* and *at the price you dictate*. Third, remember it is more difficult to create a successful international advertisement, but not impossible. Do not accept the bland, the too safe, the advertisement agreed by a committee of ten local offices, or the translated version of someone else's 'good national' idea. Above all, do not accept the 'not invented here' rejection. When it comes to image, the global approach is winning.

The fact is that when advertising moves beyond the nationalistic norms and the comfortable acceptance of a local language and out into the big wide world, it does have to abandon some of its accepted creative ambitions and seek new ones. Think as a foreigner, avoid clever word play with its double meaning and references to yesterday's local event. Remember, clever can often mean incomprehensible, and do not forget that visuals often travel better than words. So many cautions, and we have not even mentioned the boring textbook pitfalls such as the meanings of different colours, legal problems, the humour that is not universal, etc.

So can international advertising work? The answer lies in simple disciplines as stated – define the audience, establish the message/branding, make sure it is relevant and understandable, be certain that your *language* is understood by them. If you combine these simple guidelines with the marketing rules covered earlier, then your international campaign can and will work. For example, your audiences, the specialists are likely to have the same interests and business requirements wherever they may be. So discover what motivates the buyers of telecommunications systems, international trade financiers, company relocation experts or whatever the product may be, wherever they may be. Remember also that the really new products in this world are new to everyone, a *walkman*, with its incredibly wide audience, was a *walkman* to everyone – Sony was the brand to which the customer aspired. A facsimile transmission machine was just that, and it was perceived in the same way by most businesspeople – so never mind the product, your office-to-office salesperson will demonstrate that, never mind the discount, your local newspaper advertisement will do that, never mind the list of distributors, your 'national' campaign will do that, but *do* concentrate on the international brand image – for if you do not, your competitor will.

Many of the thoughts covered here are not new, indeed they were covered as long ago as 1986 by P. Townsend of The Creative Business in a paper to the IAA congress in Chicago.

Budget

Inevitably, the budget will affect all stages of the final thinking process.

In the perfect world, the budget should relate simply to the task in hand, in reality the task is often governed, in the short term, by the budget. That is why if you cannot achieve the goal all in one week or one year, the company should plan out further and test its theories in as much detail as possible. Three, five and ten year planning is vital in international marketing.

When the budget is established in terms of what can be achieved at different expenditure levels and within different time spans, then and only then can a company be taken seriously. The budget will dictate your media approach – it will affect the type of media, achievable penetration levels and the type of media mix to be used.

International advertising is also affected by *control of the budget*. Is HQ setting and providing the budget along with the aims, or is it a collection of countries or regions who all want their say? This organizational point has a tremendous effect on the long-term planning. It all too often results in the overinvolvement of too many self-interested parties. The result is committee/bland advertisements, delayed campaigns, and detrimental stop-start planning. Strong central direction and purpose is vital to the successful international campaign, but the various interested/involved parties must be carried along and convinced at every stage. Yet avoid detailed involvement by endless committees at all cost. Remember, in 'far away' places, advertising is often your main/only sales thrust, so you should spend a disproportionately larger amount of your budget in relation to sales.

The media opportunities

Theoretically, every medium in the world falls within the remit of the international media planner to be dictated only by the audience definition. C, DE socioeconomic groups across the countries of the European common market would mean mass market press or television in each country. However, mass markets can at present only be reached by national media and as such are more often the prerogative of the local planner. This may well change as companies and agencies treat regional markets as one and look more and more at budget, objectives and markets as a single problem. Bringing all advertising thinking together, the many national campaigns and the international, have so far happened more at the detailed buying stage rather than the planning stage. This may change as more satellite television channels begin to cut across borders, reaching not just a specified elite but lower down into the television-viewing public. To date, however, these penetrations are limited and vary enormously from country to country. As such, pan-frontier satellite television in most instances still falls within the bounds of the international planner's responsibilities.

Within the broadest descriptions laid out in this chapter – common message, brand, image, relevance to audience, definable audience – international planning is at present limited to:

- The top end of the consumer market, with ABs across a region being the loosest definition, though just as that is often too loose even within most national markets, so it is loose when thinking globally or of international regions.
- Businesspeople – but even here most companies would and should have a tighter target audience definition within that, just as they would nationally, i.e. what type of businesspeople, which interest group, which business?
- International interest groups, the traveller being the most traditional within this sector.

So what of the media? Well it is impossible to list them all here, but they include, in pan-frontier terms:

- Satellite television, with its current limitations.
- Lifestyle magazines – *National Geographic, Asiaweek, Asia Magazine, Time, Newsweek*, etc.
- Newspapers such as the various editions of the *Wall Street Journal*, the *IHT* and, to a lesser extent, the *Financial Times*.
- Current affairs and business publications, such as *The Economist, Far*

Eastern Economic Review, L'Express International, and *Businessweek* and *Fortune* out of the USA.

• The endless list of specialist category media.

Does the planner stop there? Not necessarily, and again, it will depend on message, objective and budget, but most would also consider specific 'national' additions to a schedule. Not simply because most pan-frontier media are in English, for certainly in the business arena, that has become the *lingua franca*, but a company may need to penetrate deeper into specific sectors in specific countries.

So, what should we look for in international media? First does it cover the audience? Is it cost-efficient, is the environment right, what is its editorial stance, is it respected within its field, is it truly an international, or is it simply an overspill publication with most of its circulation in its country of origin and an insignificant amount outside? How does the reader perceive the medium? Is it, as we have demanded of the advertising message, relevant? Are any additional national media needed to achieve the media planning objective – or vice versa?

We can only answer all of these questions if the media research is available. Well, even in the most sophisticated countries, the constant cry is for more information, and in some countries and about some media, there still remains only limited and rather suspect information. The international scene has moved a long way from the early 1970s, when there was none. There are now over fifteen pieces of independent international research, all of which help the experienced planner.

The future – it seems certain that as the world becomes more like-minded, so international pan-frontier media, with common editorial across borders, will continue to flourish.

Research

Where should international advertising start? Obviously with research, and specifically market research. Do not always believe a company's own explanation of how well known they are in foreign markets. There are too many examples of companies which are household names or well-recognized in business circles within their home country but are unknown abroad. Indeed, it is often said that it is the Japanese belief and understanding that no one could possibly have heard of their brands which led them to market them so successfully outside Japan.

The rule then is research the market, and remember if you wish to post-test, then you need to pre-test. Common sense, but is there any difference when doing it internationally?

International research means employing a company or a group of associates who are used to working in different countries. The simple rules are:

- Allow more time.
- Be sure the questions 'work', translated or not – if translated, be sure the translation works; job titles and definitions change – varying tax regimes mean that people talk about salary in a different way, etc.
- In some countries, people open doors/answer mail-shots more readily than in others.
- Personal questions are sometimes seen as intrusive and therefore upset response.
- Research companies have different ideas as to what represents an acceptable standard.
- Be certain that having responded to the need for minor variations across borders you can still create a common statistic if needed.

Tomorrow

The exciting factor about international advertising is that whatever is written will soon be out of date. The world will continue to become 'smaller', we will continue to communicate better, we will become more common in our tastes and interests, and language will decline as a barrier. This does not mean that we will become a planet occupied by clones. It simply means that the discriminators in defining groups of people will not be those sacred national borders that have dominated history, but people as people, their interests, their ambitions, their tasks.

BIBLIOGRAPHY

Bernstein, David. *Corporate Image and Reality.* (Cassell Educational, 1989)
Doyle, P. and Hart, N. A. *Case Studies in International Marketing.* (Heinemann, 1982)
Paliwoda, Stanley J. *International Marketing.* (Heinemann, 1986)
Porter, Michael (ed.). *Competition in Global Industries.* (Harvard Business School Press, 1982)
Porter, Michael. *Competitive Advantage.* (Free Press, New York, 1985)
Walsh, L. S. *International Marketing.* (Pitman, 1982)

13

Training for a career in advertising

Vivienne Kriefman

There have always been many misconceptions about working in advertising. Advertising had a questionable image – high pay for little expertise, big expense accounts, lavish lunches and a high degree of superficiality. The preceding chapters should have allayed these suspicions.

Today any career in advertising – whether with an agency, an advertiser, a media owner, a market research company, a media or creative independent, is tough, challenging and competitive. It demands trained, informed specialists who can work within strictly defined disciplines. Increasingly, organizations are looking for people prepared to earn a qualification.

There used to be a variety of alternative training courses and examinations for students of advertising and marketing. The Advertising Association, the Chartered Institute of Marketing and the Institute of Public Relations all sponsored their own diploma schemes. Currently, CAM (Communication, Advertising and Marketing Education Foundation) provides a comprehensive set of qualifications leading from Certificate to Diploma level as does the Chartered Institute of Marketing. Both CAM and CIM courses are available at recognized colleges. The actual content of these qualifications is described later in this chapter.

First, it will be useful to describe some of the jobs available within the advertising industry.

Working for an advertiser

The needs of different types of advertiser vary enormously, so that it is difficult to generalize about company organization. Chapter 2 outlines the differences between companies that operate a brand management system and those that have an advertising department. The variety of organizational structures may appear confusing, but it is necessary to tailor advertising and marketing requirements very precisely to individual products, services or communication needs. Opportunities are not limited to manufacturers of fast-moving consumer goods. Other advertisers include: the Government (Central Office of Information), retailers, publishers, companies involved in travel/tourism, companies manufacturing industrial products, companies offering financial services (a recent rapid growth area), and charities.

Brand managers, marketing managers, and marketing services or communication managers, tend to be recruited to manufacturing companies and are often recruited to a general management or marketing training scheme. They are likely to be graduates, although the precise discipline they have read is relatively unimportant. Each brand manager is responsible for the total marketing policy for a given brand or group of products and for its implementation. Brand managers have some knowledge of every stage of the marketing process, from research and production to distribution and promotion and their success depends on a sound marketing training and good communications with the specialists inside and outside the company who must be briefed and whose recommendations have to be evaluated.

Working in an advertising agency

Those contemplating a career in an agency rarely realize how small a business world agencies represent. The 300 or so advertising agencies in membership of the Institute of Practitioners in Advertising range from the handful of London giants employing up to 500 people to small-town two-person businesses. They are the focal points of the advertising world, though in fact they employ only about 15,000 people. Of these, about 10,000 work in London. It is estimated that there is also a similar number of small, non-IPA agencies which are primarily active in one sector of the business but do not provide a full service.

For anyone with the persistence and determination to find an opening, working in an agency has a good deal to commend it. An agency applies its skills across a range of product fields and advertising problems, and so offers much more variety than an individual advertiser. It tends to attract lively people with original minds and rewards them with early responsibility, in an informal and stimulating atmosphere. Inevitably there are disadvantages, too. Agency life is not secure. Advertising is subject to the vagaries of the economy and agencies rarely have long-term contracts with their clients. If a budget is cut drastically, or a large advertiser moves an account, a number of jobs may suffer. Chapter 3 describes the main roles and how they interact.

Briefly, the agency's job is to interpret the message that the advertiser – in agency language, the client – wants to get across and to suggest how and where to say it, within the budget that the client has available. Having agreed the form of the campaign, the agency then prepares the advertisements, gets them approved by the client, and ensures that they appear in the right place at the right time according to the plan. This work breaks down into a number of stages.

It should be borne in mind that not all agencies perform all the functions described below 'in-house'. Some buy them as required from service houses, and employment opportunities among these suppliers of services should not be ignored.

The account team is the prime point of contact between the client and the agency. Account executives work with the client to decide the aims, budget and broad outlines of a campaign.

The creative department, made up of artists and copywriters, translates the broad outlines into ideas for advertisements, producing visual concepts, slogans, copy and story-lines for all the media and for support materials (such as what is known as 'point-of-sale' in shops).

Account planning has become a separate function in the account teams of many, but by no means all, agencies. Essentially the planner's job is to represent the consumer's point of view at each crucial stage of the advertising cycle from developing an advertising strategy, through the development of creative work to the assessment of effectiveness in the marketplace. Research evidence can be crucial at each of these stages and one of a planner's key tasks is to interpret that evidence into advertising judgements which provide useful guidance to account management and creative staff.

Production departments arrange for commercials to be made and for the production of the artwork from which press advertisements are printed. This involves the work of a large range of specialists such as photographers, illustrators, typographers, typesetters and film and radio production teams.

Traffic (sometimes called 'control') involves what industry calls 'progress chasing', making sure that proofs of printed matter flow smoothly in and out, artwork is delivered to the media on time, the necessary clearance is obtained from the authorities for TV commercials, and that the thousand and one other items moving through the agency arrive at their destination on time. Traffic has been called 'the heartbeat of an agency', and demands meticulous attention to detail, acute awareness of time and careful record-keeping.

Media

The space in which advertisements appear is selected by media planners, who allocate the advertising appropriation to reach the appropriate audience in the most economical way. They need to consider creative requirements as well as marketing objectives, and must evaluate competing demands and alternative schemes. Once the media planner has prepared an approved schedule, the media buyer negotiates with the suppliers for press space or airtime. Smaller agencies may combine the two functions of planning and buying, but larger ones may not only separate them but have, for example, specialist buyers for press, television and outdoor. Buyers not only need special knowledge of media costs but also technical knowledge, as a poorly printed advertisement may entitle the advertiser to a free insertion or a rebate.

Graduates of any discipline may be recruited as trainee buyers or planners, but school leavers may also join media departments as juniors. Numeracy is essential for media buyers. Keyboard/computer skills are useful too, since much of the research information on which media decisions are based is available on computer.

There has recently been a growth in media 'independents' who provide media expertise to clients not wishing to use a full-service advertising agency. Several are in the Advertising Agency Top Ten.

The quality national papers often contain job vacancies in selling magazine, newspaper and radio space/time. These jobs provide a challenging entry point into the world of media.

Research

Independent market research companies may handle a wide range of research studies – social studies and public opinion polls as well as shop audits and consumer research. A range of research services has already been outlined earlier in the book. Research executives must be objective and analytical. They need sympathy with figures, an orderly and methodical approach, accuracy and the ability to express themselves clearly and unambiguously.

Other suppliers and services

A number of organizations provide services for advertisers or their agencies ranging from creative independents (providing copywriting and art expertise), designers, finished art studios, film production companies, packaging specialists and sales promotion specialists. Many of these are not exclusively concerned with advertising, but can provide a starting point. For example, an apprentice with a printing company could later move to a specialist print or packaging department, and knowledge gained with a typesetter could be valuable experience for the production department of an agency. Anyone fortunate enough to be trained by a design studio might be able to move into an art department.

Whatever the starting point, an approved course of study leading to a recognized qualification is clearly an advantage.

Education and training

Full details of the CAM system of qualifications are available from: The CAM Education Foundation, Abford House, 15 Wilton Road, London SW1V 1NJ but are described in some detail here.

The Chartered Institute of Marketing scheme may also be of interest. This is described further in the chapter.

CAM Educational Scheme

The qualification is at two levels – the Certificate in Communications Studies (Part I) is broad-based and can be regarded as an ·industry introduction. The CAM Diploma (Part II) is management orientated but 'industry specific', and is for those wishing to make a career in middle or senior management in their chosen sector.

Entry qualifications for CAM

Candidates must be at least eighteen, and must meet one of the following criteria:

1 Hold any UK degree, or two GCE passes at 'A' level or GSCE – one of these must be in English Language.

or

2 Have been in full-time employment in a relevant part of the com- munication business for at least one year, *and* have five GCE 'O' level passes, or GCSE passes, including English Language.

or

3 Hold a BTEC or SCOTVEC National Certificate or Diploma in Business Studies (see BTEC address in final paragraph).

or

4 Have passed the London Chamber of Commerce and Industry Third

Level Group Diploma in Advertising, Marketing and Public Relations *or* the International Advertising Association Basic Certificate in Advertising *or* a CAM recognized foundation course.

All candidates will be required to provide proof of their eligibility. Certain higher education qualifications may qualify a student for exemption from part of the certificate course. Contact CAM for details.

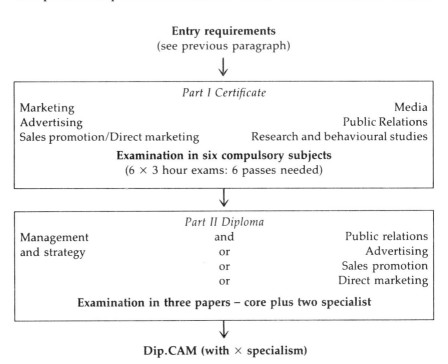

Entry requirements
(see previous paragraph)
↓

Part I Certificate	
Marketing	Media
Advertising	Public Relations
Sales promotion/Direct marketing	Research and behavioural studies

Examination in six compulsory subjects
(6 × 3 hour exams: 6 passes needed)

↓

Part II Diploma		
Management	and	Public relations
and strategy	or	Advertising
	or	Sales promotion
	or	Direct marketing

Examination in three papers – core plus two specialist

↓

Dip.CAM (with × specialism)

The CAM Certificate

The CAM Certificate in Communication Studies is awarded to a candidate passing six subjects over any period of time. The subjects for the Certificate Stage are as follows:

Marketing

An introduction to what marketing is and how it operates – the marketing concept. The marketing mix and factors which influence it. How marketing is organized, planned and controlled. Applications including business-to-business, international and social marketing.

Advertising

A general review of the advertising business as a whole – its origins and history, its place in business and in society; the way it is organized and controlled. The roles of advertisers, advertising agencies, media owners, professional bodies and associations. The way advertising works in practice. How advertisements are created and delivered to target audiences. Legal aspects and voluntary controls.

Public relations

The role of public relations in relation to the many different publics with which an organization is concerned, and the means of communication by which those publics can be reached. The organizational and professional context in which people working full time in public relations operate.

Media

A basic knowledge of the principles of media selection and media planning, ways of defining and reaching selected groups by the use of press, television, radio, posters, cinema, direct mail, exhibitions. Media research and audience measurement.

Sales promotion and direct marketing

The nature and scope of sales promotion and direct marketing, and their roles within the marketing function. Codes of practice, and basic elements of a sales promotion and direct marketing campaign.

Research and behavioural studies

The fundamentals of psychology and market research. The development of a market research programme. Types of research – their applications and limitations. Basic research techniques and their application to typical marketing and communication situations. Legal and self-regulatory controls.

The CAM Diploma

The aim of the Diploma level is to develop deeper content knowledge and, more specifically, the ability to apply that knowledge. It provides an industry-specific qualification, with the possibility of subsequent endorsements, built on the common foundation provided by the Certificate level. A core subject (management and strategy) is included, plus a number of specialisms which consist of two subjects. The exception is advertising, where the specialism consists of three subjects, two of which must be selected for study. Thus candidates study three subjects: the core and the two subjects constituting a particular specialism. Both specialism examinations are based on case studies. The content of the Diploma course is as follows:

Management and strategy

(Compulsory core paper)
The organization, structure and financing of enterprises. Elements of corporate and strategic planning, management techniques, procedures and practice. Development of strategy in pursuit of organization objectives, and specific applications to the communication industry.

Public relations management

The application of PR management principles to programme development and organizational activity. The integration of PR into overall management planning and decision making.

Public relations practice

The practical application of PR principles, techniques and management to problems and opportunities faced by different types of organizations and situations.

Consumer advertising

Application of advertising and other forms of marketing communication to the overall marketing framework. The elements of marketing communication planning, including media, research and evaluation. Organizing for advertising.

Business-to-business advertising

The practice of business-to-business marketing and advertising with emphasis on planning integrated campaigns. The way the business-to-business marketing operation is organized in companies, and the methods of obtaining facts about the marketplace. The different types of communication channels and the data available to assess them.

International advertising*

Variations in marketing and advertising practice when applied in more than one country. Primary emphasis is placed on advertising and marketing in the countries of your own region so that the lessons learned can be developed in some depth, but the underlying objective is to extend principles to global marketing considerations.

Sales promotion management and structure

The management and structure of sales promotion. Devising a sales promotion campaign. The role of sales promotion agencies, promotion, distribution companies, the trade and fulfilment houses. Administration and controls. How to apply sales promotion campaigns and techniques.

Sales promotion practice

The terminology of, and the role of sales promotion techniques. The different type of sales promotions, their uses, advantages and disadvantages; the application of sales promotion techniques.

Direct marketing

This is the BDMA Diploma, and intending candidates should contact: The Direct Marketing Centre, 1 Park Road, Teddington TW11 0AR.

Tuition

Certificate

CAM is not responsible for tuition leading to the examinations.

Candidates for the Certificate may sit for as many or as few subjects as they wish at any one time. Most study three subjects a year and cover the complete Certificate in two years. Candidates can choose from the following methods of study:

- Guided Studies (see below)
- Evening or part-time day classes at a local college
- Full-time studies
- Private studies
- Residential weekend courses
- Distance learning

A list of colleges offering courses leading to the CAM examination is available from CAM.

Guided Studies

Guided Studies are a series of learning aids which are designed to help candidates improve their knowledge and prepare themselves for the examinations. All of the material within the scheme has been specially compiled by experienced CAM tutors and examiners; it is directly related to the syllabus and is regularly updated. The scheme provides a home study course (with textbooks, learning notes and self-test questions), and a whole day of intensive instruction. Full details of the Guided Studies programmes and application forms are available from Guided Studies, PO Box 332, London WC1H 9TL.

Diploma

Candidates for the Diploma must attempt three subjects (or two if an exemption is granted) at their first examination sitting. Both specialisms are attempted together. The core paper can be sat either at the same time or at an alternative session. Candidates can choose from the following methods of study:

- Residential weekend courses
- Evening or part-time day classes at a local college
- Full-time studies
- Private studies

Registration

All candidates studying for CAM examinations must be registered with the CAM Foundation. You are strongly advised to register with CAM before beginning a course of study. Enrolling at a college is not the same as registering with CAM.

Candidates resident overseas

There are no permanent overseas centres, but in most cases the British Council provides accommodation and invigilation for the CAM examinations.

A CAM qualification is no guarantee of a job in advertising or public relations. It is, however, evidence of achievement of a worthwhile and recognized standard, and a relevant and practical training course.

Additional routes into advertising

As you will have realized, advertising does not have a *single* recognized entry qualification. A good Degree is obviously helpful, as well as an ability to work well with people on a team basis. The degree can be in any subject. For younger entrants, many sixth form colleges offer BTEC qualifications (four 'O' levels is a normal entry qualification). The BTEC Diploma in Business and Finance often includes a 'marketing' option. BTEC Higher is available at Colleges of Further Education and often includes marketing/advertising options too. It is useful to read the trade press (*Campaign, Marketing Week* and *Marketing*). CAM students are offered a substantial discount for subscriptions to *Campaign* and *Marketing Week*. (Apply to the publisher for details, quoting your CAM Registration Number).

The Chartered Institute of Marketing

Sometimes people take a job in marketing with an advertiser and from there take a sideways step into the advertising business itself. The Chartered Institute of Marketing offers a course of study which leads to relevant and practical qualifications in the broadly based marketing field. The CIM professional diploma qualification is accepted as a higher education diploma under the European Council directive 89/48/EEC and will be recognized in all member states from January 1991.

CIM Certificate course

Students are examined in eight subjects including an optional choice subject depending on the qualification required.

Fundamentals of Marketing
Principals and Practice of Selling
Economics
Statistics (Quantitative Studies)

Business Law
Behavioural Aspects
Financial Aspects of Marketing

Practice of Sales Management	— or —	Practice of Marketing
↓		↓
Certificate of Sales Management		Certificate in Marketing

CIM Diploma course

Students are examined in four subjects including the main Marketing Case Study – Marketing Management (Analysis and Decision):

- International Marketing
- Marketing Planning and Control
- Marketing Communications
- Marketing Management (Analysis and Decision)

BIBLIOGRAPHY

Association of Graduate Careers Advisory Service (AGAS). *Advertising.* Careers Information Booklet, 1986*

Careers and Occupational Information Centre (COIC). *Working in Advertising* (Working In Series No. 01), 1987†

Hart, Norman and Waite, Norman. *How to Get on in Marketing.* (Kogan Page, 1987)

Pollard, Michael. *Getting into Advertising.* (The Advertising Association, 1986)

Taylor, F. *Careers in Marketing, Public Relations and Advertising,* 3rd edn. (Kogan Page, 1987)

* For further details contact Central Services Unit, Crawford House, Precinct Centre, Manchester M13 9EP

† For further details of the Working In Series contact Sales Department, COIC, Freepost, Sheffield S1 4BR

USEFUL ADDRESSES

British Direct Marketing Association
Grosvenor Gardens House, 35 Grosvenor Gardens, London SW1W 0BS

Business and Technician Education Council
Central House, Upper Woburn Place, London WC1H 0HH

The Chartered Institute of Marketing
Moor Hall, Cookham, Maidenhead, Berks SL6 9QH

Communication, Advertising and Marketing Education Foundation
Abford House, 15 Wilton Road, London SW1V 1NJ

Incorporated Society of British Advertisers
44 Hertford Street, London W1Y 8AE

Institute of Practitioners in Advertising
44 Belgrave Square, London SW1X 8QS

Institute of Public Relations
Gate House, St John's Square, London EC1M 4DH

Institute of Sales Promotion
Arena House, 66–68 Pentonville Road, London N1 9HS

Market Research Society
175 Oxford Street, London W1R 1TA

PTT (the organization of training in periodical publishing)
Imperial House, 15–19 Kingsway, London WC2B 6UN

Appendix:
Trade and professional bodies

THE ADVERTISING ASSOCIATION

The Advertising Association, founded in 1926, is a Company limited by guarantee without a share capital and is a non-profit-making concern. Of more recent times its nature has been akin to that of a Federation, as its main member organizations are Trade Associations in the advertising, marketing and related fields. The main aims of the Association are as follows: To promote public confidence in advertising; to establish that responsible advertising is an essential factor in the marketing of goods and services, and in the economic life of the country; to demonstrate the efficiency of the service that advertising can give to Government, industry and the public; to safeguard the common interests of those engaged in or using advertising by the promotion of common action and the support of protective measures; to persuade officials and legislators in this country, Europe and elsewhere so as to remove or modify regulatory provisions adverse to the interests of the advertising industry, and industry generally; to encourage in all milieus a continuing improvement in standards and efficiency in communication, of which advertising is a part.

ADVERTISING CREATIVE CIRCLE

The Circle is a peripatetic society (founded in 1945) for people engaged in creative work connected with advertising. Its main objectives are the following: to encourage the highest standard of creative skill in advertising; to extend the influence and opportunity of advertising writers and artists; to further the training of creative personnel; and to provide regular occasions for the interchange of ideas among its members and between its members and others.

ADVERTISING STANDARDS AUTHORITY

The ASA is an independent body set up and paid for by the British advertising business. It exists to protect the public from advertisers whose advertisements mislead, misrepresent, or offend. It has a responsiblity of overseeing the implementation of the British Code of Advertising Practice and also the British Code of Sales Promotion Practice. The majority of the members of the Authority's Council must be entirely unconnected with advertising, as must the Chairman. Those members of the Council with experience of advertising sit as individuals and not as representatives of any sectional interest (*see also* Code of Advertising Practice Committee.)

ASSOCIATION OF MAIL ORDER PUBLISHERS
The Association was formed to acquaint the public at large and the media in particular with the nature of its activities, the protection it offers to the consumer and the advantages inherent in shopping by post. Mail order promotion techniques and the problems arising out of the customer/company relation have frequently been misunderstood, and have given rise to criticism in the past. The purpose of the Association is to correct misconceptions and to explain to the consumer his rights and privileges in the trading relation. It comprises leading publishers of books and audio products who trade directly with the consumer primarily by use of the mails.

THE ASSOCIATION OF MEDIA INDEPENDENTS
The Association represents media specialist companies. Members must hold ITCA, NPA and PPA recognitions, be independent of advertisers or advertising agencies, and satisfy Council of their professional and financial standing. More than two-thirds of the turnover of the independent sector is handled by AMI members.

AUDIT BUREAU OF CIRCULATIONS
The ABC provides advertisers and advertising agencies, by ABC certification, independently and professionally audited circulation figures for most publications booking advertising space. The audits are conducted to identical rules agreed by the ABC Council, and are for universal periods, so ensuring full comparability between each publication's results.

CHARTERED INSTITUTE OF MARKETING
The Chartered Institute of Marketing is the professional body for all executives engaged in marketing management. Membership is open to all those responsible for management within the marketing area. For over 60 years the Chartered Institute of Marketing has taken a lead in promoting a professional approach to marketing.

CODE OF ADVERTISING PRACTICE COMMITTEE
The CAP Committee is the central executive and policy-making organ of the advertising industry's system of self-regulation. Subject only to the general superintendence of the Advertising Standards Authority, whose function is to ensure the operation of the whole system in the public interest, the CAP Committee accepts responsibility for seeing that the *Code* itself is kept up-to-date and that its member organizations work harmoniously together, with each playing its due part in making sure that the *Code* is complied with. Anyone in the advertising business, whether a member of the sponsoring organization or not, may seek the Committee's advice, ask it to investigate a complaint or make suggestions to it as to how the *Code* or its own procedures might be improved.

COMMUNICATION, ADVERTISING AND MARKETING EDUCATION FOUNDATION LTD
CAM is the nationally recognized examining body for the communications industry. It was formed in 1969 by combining the educational bodies of

the Advertising Association, the Institute of Practitioners in Advertising and the Institute of Public Relations. CAM is an educational charity set up to integrate a system of education and training in the related fields of communication, public relations, advertising and marketing, leading to the professional qualifications in the industry.

CREATIVE SERVICES ASSOCIATION
The Association was formed in 1953 in order to achieve better reproduction standards in all mechanical printing process. This objective necessarily entails the advancement of production knowledge and techniques through education, and, consequently, better liaison between advertising agencies, suppliers, printers and publishers.

DEBATING GROUP
The Group meets six times a year to debate motions on all aspects of advertising and marketing. Its aim is to focus attention on specific, relevant and topical issues, and to broaden the industry's outlook by bringing 'outsiders' into debates. At the same time, it hopes to provide entertaining discussion in a lively way. Debates take place in a committee room in the House of Commons, and are open to members of the IPA Society, The CAM Graduates Association and the Publicity Club of London and their guests.

DIRECT MAIL PRODUCERS' ASSOCIATION
The principal aims of the Association are to promote the wider use of direct mail advertising; to maintain the highest standards in its creation, production and despatch; to represent the producers of direct mail advertising; and to express the views of all those engaged in its creation and promotion to Governments, postal authorities and other official and unofficial bodies in the United Kingdom and all parts of the world. The Association consists of companies, firms and individuals who are principals engaged in or allied to the business of direct mail advertising as defined in its schedule of Qualifications for Membership.

INCORPORATED ADVERTISING MANAGEMENT ASSOCIATION
The Association is open to persons responsible for advertising, publicity, sales promotion, marketing and public relations in commercial, public and other undertakings.

INCORPORATED SOCIETY OF BRITISH ADVERTISERS LIMITED
The ISBA was formed in 1900, and is the only organization that exists in Great Britain solely to look after the needs of the advertiser. It represents the interests of the advertiser on all matters relating to advertising and sales promotion codes of practice. The Society aims to enable advertisers to speak with one voice, and to represent the views of members on advertising matters to Government, opinion leaders, media owners, advertising agencies and the public. Membership comprises large, medium and small advertisers from all sections of industry and commerce. Any company except media or advertising agencies can belong to the ISBA.

INDEPENDENT BROADCASTING AUTHORITY
Responsible for both Independent Television and Independent Local Radio in the United Kingdom, the Authority was created by Parliament in 1954 (as the

ITA) to provide public television services of information, education and entertainment additional to those of the BBC; and in 1972 its responsibilities were extended to include local radio. The IBA's four main functions are to select the programme companies, to supervise programme planning, to control advertising and to transmit the programmes.

ITV ASSOCIATION
Incorporated as a company limited by guarantee, ITV Association is the trade association of the programme companies appointed by the Independent Broadcasting Authority (see above). It is a voluntary non-profit-making organization, which provides a channel for joint action on matters of concern to the programme companies.

INDUSTRIAL MARKETING RESEARCH ASSOCIATION
The objectives are to establish the Association, both in the United Kingdom and elsewhere, as the organization representing the profession of industrial marketing research in all forms; to improve technical standards and quality in industrial marketing research, and to maintain a high standard of efficiency and service in the profession; and to promote the understanding and the proper use of organizations, professional institutions, trade associations, research associations, educational institutions, marketing research and marketing organizations.

INSTITUTE OF PRACTITIONERS IN ADVERTISING
The Institute is the representative professional body of service advertising agencies in this country, and acts to safeguard and promote agency interests *vis-à-vis* media, advertisers and suppliers. As the voice of the UK agency business, it represents the interests of its member agencies both in Government, commerce and industry, and in negotiations with media and advertising organizations. Through its specialist departments, guided by experts in their own fields, the Institute gives its members immediate and practical help on problems from complex legal queries to questions about media, marketing and research; it can also advise on the international front through its close working relations with agency organizations throughout Europe and in many other parts of the world.

INSTITUTE OF PUBLIC RELATIONS
The Institute of Public Relations is the only organization in the United Kingdom devoted exclusively to the study and development of all aspects of public relations. It was founded in 1948 by a group of public relations officers from commerce, industry, and central and local government, all of whom felt the need for an organization to represent the rapidly expanding profession in which they were engaged. The main objectives of the Institute are the following: to promote the development, recognition and understanding of public relations; to establish and prescribe standards of professional and ethical conduct, and ensure the observance of such standards; to encourage the attainment of professional qualifications; to provide via meetings, conferences, seminars and printed material, information, discussion and comment on all aspects of the practice of public relations; and to maintain two-way contact between the public relations profession in the U.K. and public relations practitioners in other parts of the world.

INTERNATIONAL ADVERTISING ASSOCIATION

The primary goal of the IAA is to encourage and maintain a high standard in advertising and marketing proficiency throughout the world, emphasizing strict adherence to codes of ethics, such as the International Code of Advertising Practice of the International Chamber of Commerce. In doing this the IAA helps to advance the cause of advertising and provides a strong element of consumer protection against bad or misleading advertising. Since it was founded in 1938, the IAA has advised its members throughout the world of current trends and developments affecting their business interests, stimulating its members to exchange ideas, experience and skills. Any executive who is associated with the business of advertising and marketing, be it on a domestic or international level, is entitled to apply for membership. There is also a category of Sustaining Membership covering companies that have an interest in the communications field, believe in the principles of the IAA and wish to support this work. They may each appoint an executive, who will have all the rights and privileges of an individual member. Similarly, organizations such as associations, academic institutions, and Government departments that share the IAA's interests can also join in membership and designate an official to represent them.

INTERNATIONAL MEDIA BUYERS' ASSOCIATION

The Association was founded in November 1965 to provide social and business activities for advertising media executives engaged wholly or partly in international buying, and to give them a united voice in the advertising world.

MARKET RESEARCH SOCIETY

The incorporated professional body for those using survey techniques for market, social and economic research, the Society is the largest organization of its kind in the world. It runs monthly luncheon and discussion meetings, annual conferences and a full educational programme.

MARKETING SOCIETY

The Society caters for the needs of practising marketing specialists and managements, using theory as a bridge between junior and senior marketing personnel, specialists and generalists, tactics and strategy; it is also concerned with developing and fostering profitable, practical business methods.

MEDIA CIRCLE

Founded in the late 1950s, the Circle's membership is open to people working in the media departments of advertising agencies. Its activities normally cover four ranges of activity, although its policy is to cater for any operation in the interests of its members. It holds functions at which selected speakers promote discussion on matters of topical interest. One of its committees looks after media relations, and can act speedily and constructively when disputes occur. The research committee is available to assess research projects, while education plays a major part in the Circle's curriculum. An extensive lecture course, which is run each year in the autumn, is open to non-members. Weekend seminars have also been run from time to time.

MEDIA RESEARCH GROUP

The Group provides a forum for discussion of media research and its part in media planning, and coordinates as far as possible requirements for future media research. Membership is open to those concerned with the collection, study, evaluation and use of data relevant to the understanding of the way in which people use media.

MEDIA SOCIETY LIMITED

The principal objects of the Media Society are to promote and encourage independent research into the standards, performance, organization and economics of the media; to provide a forum for the exchange of knowledge and opinion between people working in the media and those in public and political life, the professions, industry, education; and to ensure that members of the public take part in a continuing debate on the role of mass communication in a democratic society. The Council is anxious that no occupational, political or other sectional interest should predominate, and for this reason has decided that admission should be subject to approval by the Council. This limitation apart, the only qualification necessary for membership is a desire to support the objects and take part in the activities of the Society, and an undertaking to observe the provisions of the Society's Memorandum and Article of Association.

NATIONAL ADVERTISING BENEVOLENT SOCIETY

The National Advertising Benevolent Society was established in 1913 'for the charitable purpose of relieving distress among persons who are, or have been, engaged in advertising'; dependants of such people are also eligible. NABS reckons to have dealt with most kinds of trouble in its time, but those that occur most often are redundancy, sickness and bereavement. Assistance given is usually but not always financial; advice is given on entitlement to various forms of state benefit and on other matters.

NEWSPAPER PUBLISHERS ASSOCIATION

The Newspaper Publishers Association was formed in 1906 as a trade association. Membership is open to publishers of newspapers with national circulation, and the association is financed by members' subscriptions. The objectives of the NPA are to promote and regulate relations between members and their employees; to facilitate the exchange of views between members; to arrange consultation with legislative, public, trade and industry bodies; to take such joint action as agreed to protect, preserve and promote the interests of members; and to provide services on behalf of members.

NEWSPAPER SOCIETY

Founded in 1836, the Society is the oldest-established publishers' association in the UK, and probably in the world. It was for many years the only such body in the country. More recently it has become the organization which, in particular, represents and promotes the interests of the regional and local newspapers. The signal attribute of the local newspaper is that it maintains and develops close and constant contact between its readers and every aspect of local community life. It is this vital function the Newspaper Society protects and supports.

THE OUTDOOR ADVERTISING ASSOCIATION OF GREAT BRITAIN LTD

The OAA is a new organization, formed as a result of the merger of two previous Poster Associations. It represents the trade interests of 37 contractor companies who own over 95 per cent of the poster facilities in the UK. Its purpose is to protect the interests of its members companies with Government, local authorities and the public by any lawful means; to promote the concept of poster advertising by advertisers and their agents, and to improve the standards of presentation of poster sites in general.

OVERSEAS PRESS AND MEDIA ASSOCIATION

The Association exists to provide UK advertisers, their agencies and international media consultancies in the UK with reliable international marketing and advertising information; to help improve relations between UK advertising agencies and overseas media owners; to raise the professional standards of media representatives and thus help create a greater confidence and understanding between all those engaged in international advertising and marketing; to increase the volume of business overseas media owners receive from the UK; to affirm its belief in free competition both within and outside OPMA; and at the same time to stress that close cooperation between members is in their best interests and those of the media owners they represent.

PERIODICAL PUBLISHERS ASSOCIATION

The PPA was incorporated in 1913 as a trade association, and today it is the only association wholly devoted to the interests of magazine and periodical publishers in Britain. The major part of the magazine publishing business is represented within the PPA, and all members are drawn together by the overriding aim of the association to coordinate, initiate and participate in work that will assist members' profitable development, protect their interests, and safeguard the freedom and well-being of the periodical press. They all recognize that coordinated and united activity can often be more effective in achieving these aims than the individual actions of even the most powerful single members.

PRESS ADVERTISEMENT MANAGERS' ASSOCIATION

The Association was established in 1907 to give opportunity for mutual aid in matters concerning advertising. It is not an academic body, but exists to assist in the exchange of ideas and information regarding day-to-day problems, situations, and techniques and to discuss confidential matters relating to the everyday running of the advertising business. Membership is confined to the suburban, regional, local trade and specialist press.

PUBLICITY CLUB OF LONDON

Founded in 1913, the Club is the oldest organization in the UK representing all sides of publicity and advertising. It is a meeting ground for informed opinion on all aspects of advertising, marketing and promotions as they affect the business of communication today. The Club played a leading role in the establishment of the Advertising Association in 1926, and was also active in the setting up of a large number of clubs and associations in major towns throughout the country. As a founder member, it has played its part in fostering contact with clubs overseas, individually and through the International Federation of Publicity Clubs.

PUBLIC RELATIONS CONSULTANTS' ASSOCIATION

This is a trade association of public relations consultancies, bound by a code of consultancy practice. It provides guidance for members and potential clients, and organizes research and many activities for members.

ROYAL TELEVISION SOCIETY

Founded in 1927, the Society serves the interests of all those working in television by providing an organization and facilities for them to meet and talk, exchange information and ideas, and generally advance their experience and under-standing. Membership covers the whole field of television activity – engineering, programme-making, production services, education, the manufacturing industry and many others, including retailers and individuals who have been attracted by the opportunity to meet and discuss television. There are also many overseas members.

Glossary

Derek Lovell

General advertising terms

A4
Standard paper size: 297 mm × 210 mm (11¾ in × 8¼ in). *Note:* A5 is the size of a folded A4 sheet 210 mm × 148 mm (8¼ in × 5⅞ in).

ABC
Audit Bureau of Circulations. Audits total number of copies of a given publication actually sold.

ADAPTATION ('ADAPT')
An advertisement modified to fit a different size/shape.

ADSHEL
A poster contractor, often used as a shorthand way of denoting a 4-sheet poster in a shopping precinct or a High Street.

ADVERTISING STANDARDS AUTHORITY (ASA)
The organization responsible for handling public complaints about advertising (other than TV and radio) and administrating the application of the British Code of Advertising Practice

AGENCY COMMISSION
Commission, usually 15 per cent of the gross, paid by the media to the agency on the cost of space/time in return for booking space/time with the relevant medium. Not to be confused with volume or series discounts.
Also, the agency's remuneration from its clients. Usually 17.65 per cent of the net cost of space/time and all other materials purchased on behalf of the client by the agency.

AGENCY FEE
Remuneration based on a negotiated fee as opposed to remuneration based on the commission system referred to above.

AIR DATE
The broadcast date of a TV or radio commercial.

AIRC
Association of Independent Radio Contractors.

ANIMATIC
A moving, animated element within a TV commercial or a single rough commercial made from a storyboard.

ANSWER PRINT
First complete (picture and sound) print of a film.

ANTIQUE (PAPER)
Rough surfaced paper.

ART (PAPER)
Coated paper with a smooth glossy surface.

BANK (PAPER)
Thin typing (copy) paper.

BARB
Broadcasters Audience Research Board who produce the television rating research reports for BBC and ITV.

BATTERS
Damaged or broken letters in printwork.

BELOW-THE-LINE
Also known as SALES PROMOTION. Publicity activities other than by direct advertising, e.g. displays in stores, consumer competitions, and free give aways. (See separate glossary on page 247.)

BLEED
1 Printing matter in the press, posters or the print media where the printing runs to the edge of the paper. A 'bleed space', relating to one, two, three or four sides of an advertisement usually commands an additional surcharge to the cost of space with margins.
2 The allowance on a drawing or printing plate which is trimmed off when the printed matter goes right to the edge of the page instead of having the usual margin.

BLIND EMBOSSING
Raised designs or lettering on paper without colour.

BLOCK
The piece of metal on which illustration(s) and words have been engraved or set for printing.

BOARD
Stiff paper (cardboard).

BODY MATTER
The text of an advertisement etc. as distinct from the headlines.

BOND
Heavier (than bank) typing or writing paper.

BOX
Type in an enclosed frame of rules.

BRAD
British Rate and Data – a monthly publication showing advertising costs and technical information for all UK media.

BROADSHEET
A newspaper with page size approx. 559 cm × 381 cm (22 in × 15 in) (e.g. *Daily Telepgraph*); the smaller newspapers e.g. *Sun*, *Daily Mirror* are known as 'TABLOID'.

BROMIDE
See Screen bromide.

B/W
Black and white.

CAMPAIGN
1 The total advertising programme for a specific period of time.
2 The advertising business trade journal.

CANCELLATION DATE (PERIOD)
The date before which an advertisement booking can be cancelled without payment.

CAP (COMMITTEE)
Code of Advertising Practice which lays down guidelines for the control of advertising content. The Committee

adjudicate on industry complaints when required.

CAPTION
A description relating to an illustration.

CAPTION BOARD
Artwork for film titles, e.g. artwork for studio use when making videotape titles.

CARTRIDGE
Taped copy of a radio commercial sent to radio stations (two of each commercial are required). Also a type of rough surfaced paper.

CAST-OFF
Calculate how much space 'copy' will take when typeset.

CATCHLINE
Words put on the top of a page or over a piece of type to indicate its place in the whole.

CENTRE SPREAD
Two whole pages in the centre of a publication. One complete block, mechanical or film is supplied.

CERTIFICATE OF INSERTION
Issued by publishers or their printers to confirm that loose inserts have been inserted. Sometimes also supplied in lieu of a voucher copy.

CI
Copy instruction issued to a publisher for the insertion of an advertisement.

CIBACHROME PRINT
High quality direct positive colour print from a transparency.

CIRCULATION
The number of copies per issue of a publication which are sold.

CHROMA COPY
Colour print made without a negative.

CLIP
A shot or sequence of shots from a complete film.

COLOUR BARS
A strip of process colours at the top of proofs as a guide to colour strengths.

COMBINE
A printing plate containing both half-tone and line.

CONTACTS
Photographic prints taken direct from camera film (used to select shots for enlargement).

CONTONES
Four colour continuous tone separations produced conventionally by camera with the use of colour filters.

CONTROLLED CIRCULATION
Publications with a pre-selected circulation sent direct to customers. Usually trade and business/technical/professional/media.

COPY
Has a number of different meanings

1   A facsimile in the usual sense, e.g. carbon copy.
2   The words of an advertisement etc. as distinct from the pictures.
3   A manuscript supplied to a printer.
4   A complete advertisement supplied to a newspaper or magazine (in any form).

(So if you get an enquiry 'who deals with copy on?. . .') find out whether they want to speak to the copywriter or the traffic department).

COPY DATE
The date by which the publication requires copy.

COST PER THOUSAND
(*See* CPT)

COVER DATE
The date of publication as shown on the cover (*Note:* a magazine with a 'cover date' of April may be available early in March).

COVERAGE AND FREQUENCY
A measure of the overall achievement of an advertising campaign in terms of percentage of target reached at least

once and the average number of opportunities the audience will have to see the advertisement/campaign.

COW
Gum used by artists etc. (rubber in a petroleum solution – highly flammable). Now available as an aerosol spray.

CPT
Cost per thousand opportunities to see/hear/read an advertisement within a given target audience of a campaign or of the total campaign.

CROMALIN
A substitute proof for a conventional 4-colour proof.

CROSS-HEADS
Sub-titles set centrally in a column of type.

CROWN
A paper and poster size = 15 in × 10 in (381 mm × 254 mm) hence double-crown = 30 in × 20 in (762 mm × 508 mm).

C-TYPE
A high quality colour print taken from a transparency via colour inter-neg.

CUT-OUT
An illustration with the background cut away.

CUTTING COPY
First assembly of a TV commercial made from rushes.

DATE-PLAN
Shows when and where the advertisements in a campaign will appear.

D/C OR DC
Double-column, e.g. an 8 cm. dc is a space 8 cm deep × 2 columns wide.

DEEP ETCHED
A block where the highlight dot is etched away.

DOT-FOR-DOT
A type of duplicate printing plate.

DOUBLE
Used as shorthand for 'double column' hence a 25 cm double. Also expressed as 25 × 2, but make sure whether second figure refers to centimetres or columns.

DOUBLE HEAD
Film with separate picture and sound track (next stage is to combine them on an answer print).

DOUBLE PAGE SPREAD
A misleading expression which should not be used (see Two facing pages bleed into the gutter).

DROP
Door-to-door distribution of publicity matter.

DROP LETTER (INITIAL)
Large letter at the beginning of a paragraph.

DUB (or MIX)
Sound track of a film in which voices, sound effects and music have been balanced. Also when an artiste has had his/her voice replaced on film by another (see also G-spool).

DUMMY
The rough layout of a booklet, brochure etc. showing the exact size and general arrangement of the complete job.

DUOTONE
A two-colour halftone produced from a single colour original.

'DUPE' – DUPLICATE
1 A copy of a transparency
2 A copy of a printing block
3 A copy of a film etc.

DYE TRANSFER
A high quality colour print taken from a transparency and suitable for re-touching for reproduction.

EAR-PIECE
The small advertisement space(s)

alongside the title (masthead) of a newspaper.

ELECTRO
A duplicate printing plate made electrolytically from the original.

EM
The square of the point size of type matter, i.e. the 12 point em which is 12 points high and 12 points wide.

EN
One half of an em (i.e. the letter N is half the width of the letter M).

EXTRA ORIGINATION CHARGES
Charges received from publishers for 4-colour work which required work over and above one transparency.

FACE
A particular design of type, described in general terms as 'condensed', 'expanded', sans-serif, and specifically by the name of the type, e.g. Plantin, Univers etc.

FILM MAKE-UP
Putting together elements of a photostat advertisement.

FILM MASTER
A complete advertisement on film in positive held by blockmaker from which to duplicate reproduction material.

FILM SETTING
See Photoset.

FIX
To spray a drawing etc. (with a fixative) so it will not smudge.

FLIP-CHARTS
A presentation prepared in a form (e.g. with a ring binder) so that the 'pages' can be turned.

F/M
Facing matter. Denoting that the advertisement will face editorial matter.

FORMAT
Size, make-up and general appearance of a publication.

FORME
Type and illustration blocks assembled ready for printing or block making.

FORTY-EIGHT SHEET
48 sheet, a poster size 20 ft wide × 10 ft deep.

FOUNT OR FONT
A complete set of type for a given type face.

FOUR COLOUR SCANS
Set of colour separated screened positives made by direct scanning of a transparency.

FOUR SHEET
4 sheet, a poster size (40 in wide × 60 in deep).

FULL-OUT
Starting paragraphs without any indentation.

FREEPOST
A system of enabling coupons/applications for literature etc. to be sent to the advertiser without a stamp being put on the envelope by the respondents. The Post Office usually supply a special post code, different from the company's usual address, to simplify identification.

FREQUENCY DISTRIBUTION
Describes how many people saw how many ads, in the campaign.

FVO
See Voice over.

G-SPOOL
A copy of a videotape TV commercial sent to TV stations (also referred to as a 'Dub').

GALLEY
Type matter of text as it comes from the typesetter before being arranged with headlines etc. for printing. Hence *galley-proof*. (From the long shallow tray in which type is kept.)

GATEFOLD
An extra leaf which is an extension of a

page and folded. Often part of the front cover.

GHI
Guaranteed Homes Impressions. A package of TV airtime where, for a fixed cost, the contractor guarantees to deliver a number of home impressions.

GHR
Guaranteed Homes Rating. A package of TV airtime where, for a fixed cost, the contractor guarantees to deliver a number of homes ratings.

GRADING
A laboratory process to bring about matched colour quality throughout a film – or videotape.

GRAVURE (PHOTOGRAVURE)
A printing process for which artwork and not blocks have to be supplied.

GUARD BOOK
Contains copies of all advertisements published for a client. Also used to describe a book which contains the essential information of a client's advertising activities.

GUTTER
The margin between the sides of the type or pictures on a pair of pages.

HALF-TONE
A print giving the optical illusion of continuous tone by small dots of varying size.

IFC
Inside front cover.

ILR
Independent Local Radio.

IMPRINT
Name of printer, publisher etc. on any publication.

INCORPORATED SOCIETY OF BRITISH ADVERTISERS (ISBA)
The representative organization which voices the opinion of advertisers.

INDENT
To begin a line (or lines) with a space.

INDEPENDENT BROADCASTING AUTHORITY (IBA)
The controlling body for commercial television and commercial radio.

INSERTS
See below.

INSETS
Often also called 'inserts', either loose or bound-in insets are advertising material added to a publication after it has been printed.

IPA
Institute of Practitioners in Advertising (44 Belgrave Square, London SW1. Tel: 071-235-7020). The representative organization of the advertising agency business.

ISLAND SITE
A press space which is surrounded on at least three sides by editorial matter.

ISSUE DATE/COVER DATE
The official publication date of a magazine (or newspaper) which may well differ from the 'on-sale-date' when actually appearing on book stalls.

ITALICS
Typeface with *slanting letters.*

JICNARS
Joint Industry Committee for National Readership Surveys (newspaper/ magazine).

JICRAR
Joint Industry Committee for Radio Audience Research.

JICTAR
Joint Industry Committee for Television Audience Research, *see* BARB.

JUSTIFY
Even up left and right hand sides of a column of type.

KEY
Letter, number or code in advertisement (coupon) to indicate publication from which replies have been sent.

KEY LINES
Lines on artwork to indicate position of elements on areas for tint laying or painting up solids etc.

KEY-NUMBER
A code set in a corner of a reply coupon to check response.

KEY-SIZE
Unit of photosetting type size measurement.

KODATRACE
A clean film overlay on artwork that carries additional information for printers/blockers.

LAMINATED PROOF
Clear film heat sealed onto a proof for protection.

LANDSCAPE
Shape of booklet or picture where the horizontal dimensions are greater than the vertical.

LAYOUT (CREATIVE)
The design for an advertisement.

LAYOUT (TYPOGRAPHY)
The detailed 'working drawing' for an advertisement.

LEADERS
Dots or dashes set in line to link words, phrases, figures.

LEADS
Thin strips of metal used to increase space between lines of type. Hence 'leaded' and 'lead out'.

LEAF
Two pages.

LEGEND
Another name for caption.

LETRASET
Instead of hand lettering headlines etc. 'transfers' are used.

LETTERPRESS
The process of printing from a raised image (as on the type head of a typewriter).

LINEFEED
The photosetting equivalent of 'leading'.

LITERAL
A spelling mistake in printed matter.

LITHO
See offset litho.

LITHO NEGATIVES or POSITIVES
Screened film supplied to publications.

LINE BLOCK
A printing plate (usually from a drawing) with no graduations of tone.

LIP-SYNC
Synchronization of sound in film to match movement of speaker's lips.

LOGO (LOGOTYPE)
The distinctive emblem of a company or organization.

LOWER CASE
Small letters as distinct from CAPITALS.

LUCY or GRANT
Apparatus used by artists and typographers when they want to enlarge or reduce drawings etc.

MACHINE-PROOF
The final proof, taken when the publication is on the press ready for printing.

MAKE READY
The work done by the printer on the press to achieve the best possible reproduction.

MAKE-UP
The general arrangement of a paper or book. To make-up is to put together ready for printing.

MARKED PRINT (COMBINED PRINT)
Film with picture and sound correctly synchronized.

MASK
Opaque paper or card cut so that it masks the unwanted portion of a photograph.

MASTHEAD
The individual style of the name/title of a newspaper or magazine.

MATRIX (p. MATRICES)
Mould from which type is cast.

MATTER
A general term to describe text also used by media to refer to editorial e.g. advertisements are placed 'facing' and 'next matter'.

MEAL (FIGURES)
Media Expenditure Analysis Ltd, a company that monitors advertising expenditure in national daily and Sunday newspapers; weekend colour supplements; provincial morning, evening and Sunday newspapers; general weekly and monthly magazines; women's weekly and monthly magazines, special internal magazines and television, by advertiser (and by source for a fee).

MECHANICALS
The material supplied to a publication, for the reproduction of an advertisement, i.e. headlines, pictures, text etc. assembled in precise position (*see* Paste-up).

MEDIA PLAN
The agency's media *recommendation* showing publications, dates, space sizes, TV regions, start and finish dates, money, etc. Subject to approval, bookings can be made from which the media schedule is produced.

MEDIA SCHEDULE
A record – usually computer output – of the actual *bookings* made for a campaign.

METRIC SPOT LENGTH
TV commercials in lengths of 10, 20, 30 seconds etc. instead of the 7, 15, 45 seconds etc. (indicated autumn 1980).

MEZZOTINT
A form of modification of a photograph to give a distinctive reproduction when printed.

MINI PAGE
A press space, usually about three-quarters of the width of a page and three-quarters of the depth, and surrounded by editorial matter.

MIX
see DUB.

MONO (MONOCHROME)
Black and white printing as distinct from colour.

MVO
See Voice over.

NEG/NEGATIVE
Photographic original – if something is 'on neg' further copies can be obtained.

NEWS PROOF
A proof on newsprint type paper to simulate newspaper.

N/M
Next matter. A press space which appears next to editorial.

NRS
National Readership Survey.

OFFSET
1 In letterpress printing an unwanted transfer of ink from the printed page onto another sheet.
2 Offset printing is a planographic process (lithographic). The printing image is offset onto a rubber blanket and then onto paper.

OFFSET LITHO
A type of printing for which the agency supplies artwork to the publication and not a block.

ON SALE DATE
The date on which a publication is available for sale on bookstalls. Can

differ from issue/cover date, especially monthly magazines.

OPTICAL
A trick effect made mechanically in the film laboratory or video studios to combine two or more film pictures into one by superimposition. Also see below.

OPTICAL TITLES
Sometimes called opticals. Titles superimposed on film.

ORIGINAL
A term applied to a photograph or drawing used for reproduction, also used to describe a printing plate.

OTH
Opportunities to hear, the number of times a member of the target audience is exposed to the radio station containing the advertisement. The weight of a radio campaign is often described by average OTH for all members of the target audience.

OTS
Opportunities to see, the number of times a member of the audience is exposed to the television station containing the TV commercial. The weight of a TV campaign is often described by average OTS for all members of the target audience. Also used in press advertising.

OUTSIDE BACK COVER (OBC)
The outside back cover of a publication

OUT-TAKES
Pieces of film shot but not used in edited version.

OVERLAP AREA
A geographical area in which two or more ITV stations can be received, excluding the fourth channel.

OVERLAY
A sheet of paper showing alternative or revised wording/design positioned over the original.

OVER MATTER
Type for which there is no room in the allotted space. Or additional type matter set out as an alternative to that in the main setting.

OZALID
Proof of advertisement produced in an exposure unit with a chamber for developing by ammonia vapour.

PAGINATION
The arrangement of pages. Printing the page numbers.

PANTONE
Standard range of colour guides in colour paper on colour self adhesive form.

PAPER-SET
When an advertisement is set up in type by the publication instead of being supplied with a complete block or 'mechanicals'.

PASTE-UP
Type, picture etc. Elements of an advertisement, booklet etc. are assembled and pasted on card to show correct positions.

PATCH
To change one (small) element of a layout or printing plate.

PE PLATE
The method of etching letterpress plates (powderless etch) in one operation.

PHOTO-POLYMER
A printing process that requires bromides and not blocks.

PHOTOPRINT
A copy made by photographing the original and then making a print from the negative (therefore of better quality than a photostat).

PHOTO-SET
Headlines and text composed photographically instead of using metal letters. (Also known as film-set).

PHOTOSTAT
A copy made direct from the original (e.g. Xerox).

PICA
A measurement of type equal to 12 points.

PIERCE
Cut or opening in a block to insert type or another block.

PLATE
A printing block – metal (or plastic) from which newspapers and magazines are printed.

PMT
A photo mechanical transfer – the equivalent of a proof in photographic composition.

POINT
Unit of type size measurement. There are 72 points to the inch.

POP (POST OFFICE PREFERRED)
Envelope sizes.

PORTRAIT
A picture, page etc. with the vertical dimensions greater than the horizontal.

PORTRAIT PAGES
Another name for mini pages.

PRE-EMPT
On TV, some contractors now use pre-empt rate cards. The TV buyer will elect which rate he thinks is reasonable for a particular spot however, another advertiser can pre-empt him by offering to pay the next higher rate – in which case the original booking is lost. F3, F2, F1, B1, B2, B3, B4 are pre-empt rates in descending order of cost. B1 is the basic rate, other 'B' rates are discount rates and 'F' rates are surcharged rates depending on the degree of fixing.

PRESS DATE
The date on which a publication is actually printed.

PROGRESSIVE (PROOFS)
A set of proofs taken from the individual plates of a set of 4 colour plates, printed in the correct sequence in a programme build up as a guide to the final printing.

PROOF-READING MARKS
The correct way of marking corrections on printers' proofs.

PULL
A proof or any print from a block or type.

QUARTERTONE
Screened photoprint retouched for dot for dot reproduction.

R-TYPE PRINT
Direct positive colour print from a transparency suitable for presentation layout.

RATING
Expresses what percentage of the target TV or radio audience were exposed to the commercial (e.g. a 25 housewife rating, means 25 per cent of housewives were exposed).

RC PAPER
Resin coated photographic printing paper with excellent dimensional stability.

READERSHIP
The number of people reading or looking at a copy of a publication, as distinct from circulation – the number of copies sold/distributed.

REGISTER
Accurate placing of elements to other elements in printing, e.g. different colours making up colour picture.

RELEASE (FORM)
To be signed by models or anyone being photographed or filmed, giving permission for the use of the picture for advertisement purposes.

REPRO PROOF (REPRODUCTION PROOF)
Typeset matter used to prepare finished material for printing processes.

RESPONSE (or TOTAL RESPONSE)
The value of a campaign, described by

multiplying the response function by the frequency distribution.

RESPONSE FUNCTION
A series of mathematical expressions, to describe for a specific campaign the value to the advertiser and the members of the target audience receiving additional advertising impressions.

RETOUCHING
For correction or improvement of photographs by an artist for reproduction purposes.

REVERSE
Print in opposite way to normal, e.g. when a picture left becomes right or when black becomes white.

REVERSED OUT
Type matter which has the appearance of being cut out of solid black or colour.

ROM
Run-of-month. Usually used in the context of press, TV or radio airtime. A booking which has no guarantee as to which day it will appear within a particular week/month/year.

ROMAN FACE
Upright typsetting (as opposed to 'italics').

ROP
Run of paper. Advertisements not booked into special positions – usually available at a cheaper rate.

ROUGH
A crude layout.

ROUGH CUT
A first cut of a film.

ROW
Run-of-week *see* ROM above.

ROY
Run-of-year *see* ROM above.

RUN
Actual printing, hence short run, few copies; long run, a large number of copies.

RUN BACK
Taking words from one line and placing them on the previous line.

RUN-ON
In typography to continue without a paragraph break. In printing to produce additional copies at the same time as the original requirement.

RUN-OVER
Taking over words from one line to the next.

RUSHES
The first prints of the film seen as shot (i.e. before editing).

SADDLE-STITCH
To fasten the sheets of a booklet by stitching mechanically through the middle fold of the sheets.

SANS
Type without serifs.

SCAMP
A rough sketch of an advertisement design.

SCC
Single Column Centimetre. One column wide and one centimetre high – used as a basic unit of measurement in newspaper advertising.

SCHEDULE
A record, usually computer output, of the actual *bookings* made for a campaign *see* Media Schedule.

SCRAPART
Material that is already available from photographers or magazines for use as artwork.

SCREAMER
Exclamation mark.

SCREEN
The definition of the type of halftone – e.g. coarse screen, fine screen or a specific number indicating number of dots to the centimetre, e.g. 26 screen. It is necessary to know the appropriate screen number before blocks can be

prepared for a publication. Printed letterpress.

SCREEN PRINTING
A method of printing used when comparatively small numbers of a poster, cover etc. are needed.

SCREENED BROMIDE
Screened photograph.

SCRIPT
Typed version of visual and sound content of a TV commercial, or the sound content of a radio commercial.

SECOND COLOUR
The ability to print selected elements of an advertisement or leaflet etc. in a colour other than black.

SELF-LIQUIDATOR
An offer which although apparently very attractively priced covers the cost to the advertiser.

SHEET
Unit of measurement in poster sizes, e.g. 16 sheet 120 in × 80 in.

SERIF
Short cross lines at the ends of letter in certain type faces.

SFX
Abbreviation of sound effects, used in radio/TV/film scripts.

SIDE-HEADS
Sub-titles set at the side in a column of text.

SIDESTITCH
To fasten the sheets of a booklet by stitching (or stapling) front to back on the back margin.

SIXTEEN SHEET
(16 sheet). A poster size 6 ft 8 in wide × 10 in deep.

SMALLS
Classified advertisements.

SOLIDS
Black or colour which is completely unbroken (i.e. not built up of dots like a halftone).

SOLUS (POSITION)
The only advertisement on the page – thus: 'front page solus'.

SPECIAL COLOUR
The use of a colour not normally being used in the printing of a magazine, etc. a special blue instead of Tri-blue *see* Tri-colour.

SPLIT-RUN
When (usually for test purposes) different advertisements are used in different copies of one issue of a magazine or newspaper. Split-runs are two types – by area e.g. North/South, or by copy, e.g. different advertisements are printed in alternate copies of the same issue, so giving even distribution of the alternate advertisements.

SPOT-COLOUR
The ability to add an area of one colour to an otherwise black and white advertisement.

SPRAY MOUNT
Aerosol gum used for mounting paper on to board etc.

S/S
The same size.

STOCK
Printing paper.

STRIP-IN
Method of adding an element to an illustration or existing advertisement.

STORYBOARD
Illustrations of the main events in a TV/film commercial together with a written description of the sound effects and the spoken words.

SUBSTANCE
Classification of paper in terms of weight per 500 sheets.

SUPERSITE
A very large poster site, often with cut-outs and usually hand-painted (about 30 ft wide × 10 ft deep).

SUPP
Supplementary spot on TV. A spot booked at a discount.

SWASH (letters)
Elaborate type designs of roman or italic letters.

SYNC
Synchronization of pictures and sound tracks in film.

TABLOIDS
A newspaper with small size pages (e.g. *Daily Mirror, Evening Standard*).

TAKES
The different versions of each shot of a photograph, film or sound recordings.

TAP
Total Audience Package. A package of radio airtime.

TARGET AUDIENCE
Primary market for product or service.

TC
'Til Cancelled'. A 'TC' poster site is leased by an advertiser literally until cancelled.

TCA
Television Consumer Audit. A consumer panel research into product usage, conducted by AGB.

TEARSHEET
A page containing an advertisement form from a newspaper or magazine in lieu of a proof or a complete copy of the publication.

TELECOPIER
A means by which facsimiles of typed matter, layouts etc. can be transmitted and received over telephone lines.

TEST MARKET (area)
A defined part of the country which has specified characteristics of the whole country when a product or campaign can be tested prior to launching on a wider or national scale.

TGI
Target Group Index – a survey that consists of buying behaviour and media exposure reports on a wide range of consumer purchases.

TIP-IN
Addition to a book not bound in with the whole, but gumming in.

TMU (Type mark up)
Copy on which a typographer has indicated type face, size, arrangement etc. to be followed by the compositor.

TRANSMISSION CERTIFICATE
Issued by ITV companies to confirm that a particular TV commercial has been transmitted.

TRANSPARENCY/TRANNY
Full-colour photographic positive for viewing by transmitted light. (Colloquially 'Tranny'.)

TRI-COLOUR
A standard prime colour used by a publication – hence Tri-red, Tri-blue, Tri-yellow.

TSA
Total Survey Area. Used particularly with reference to radio research where stations research a larger area than their VHF area.

TVR
Television rating. The percentage of the total potential audience viewing a particular spot, e.g. if a spot achieves a 30 per cent TVR (or rating), then 30 per cent of the total audience is viewing. TVRs are usually expressed in terms of a particular target audience, e.g. men TVRs, adult TVRs, housewife TVRs etc. TVRs can be summed to give the overall achievement of a campaign, e.g. 5 spots each achieving a 30 rating would give a total of 150 TVRs.

TWO PAGES FACING BLEED INTO GUTTER
This is the correct designation of double page spread and indicates that the advertisement must be split in the centre.

UPPER CASE
Capital letters.

USP
Unique Selling Proposition. The characteristic of a brand which singles it out from its competition.

VDU
Visual display unit connected to computer.

VHF AREA
Refers to the coverage area a local independent radio station is allowed by the IBA to claim as its primary catchment. The area is defined by the limits of VHF reception at a given signal strength.

VIDEO CASSETTE
Usually either Philips VCR or Sony Umatic are used for reference or research purposes. It is important to check which type of video transmitter is to be used when ordering the video cassette as the two brands are not compatible.

VIDEOTAPE
Recording television picture with sound electronically onto magnetic tape (alternative method of making TV commercials to filming).

VIGNETTE
1 A story or lifestyle encapsulated in a few lines.
2 An illustration in which the background gradually fades into nothing.

VISUAL
The artist's indication of how an advertisement will look.

VO (Voice over)
Initials used in radio/TV/a film script to indicate the opening of spoken words in relation to the picture. (MVO = male voice over, FVO = female voice over).

VOUCHER (COPY)
Given by publishers as proof of publication of an advertisement.

VTR
Video Tape Recording (*see* Video).

WIDOW
A single word on a line by itself ending a paragraph. Not desired in good typography.

Direct marketing terms

ACG
See Address coding guide.

ACTION DEVICES
Items and techniques used in a mailing to initiate the desired responses.

ACTIVE BUYER
A buyer (*see* Buyer) whose latest purchase was made within the last 12 months.

ACTIVE MEMBER
Any member (*see* Member) who is fulfilling the original commitment or who has fulfilled that commitment and has made one or more purchases in the last 12 months.

ACTIVES
Customers on a list who have made purchases within a prescribed time period, usually not more than one year. Also subscribers whose subscriptions have not expired.

ACTIVE SUBSCRIBER
One who has committed himself for regular delivery of magazines, books, or other goods or services for a period of time still in effect.

ADD ON SERVICE
Service of the BDMA which gives consumers an opportunity to request that their names be added to mailing lists.

ADDRESS CODING GUIDE
Contains the actual or potential beginning and ending house numbers, block group or enumeration district numbers, postal codes, and other geographic codes for all delivery service streets served by Post Office.

AIDA
The most popular formula for the preparation of direct mail copy. The letters stand for: 'Get Attention, Arouse Interest, Stimulate Desire, Ask for Action'.

ALLOWABLE COST PER ORDER OR ENQUIRY
The amount of money the advertiser can afford to pay for each order or enquiry based on the real costs of selling his product or service.

ASSIGNED MAILING DATES
The dates on which the list user has the obligation to mail a specific list. No other date is acceptable without specific approval of the list owner.

AUDIT
A printed report of the counts in a particular list or file.

BACK END
The activities necessary to complete a mail order transaction once an order has been received, or the measurement of a buyer's performance after he has ordered the first item in a series offering.

BANGTAIL
A promotional envelope with a second flap which is perforated and designed for use as an order blank.

BILL ENCLOSURE
A promotional piece or notice enclosed with a bill, an invoice, or a statement which is not directed toward the collection of all or part of the bill, invoice, or statement.

BINGO CARD
A reply card inserted in a publication and used by readers to request literature and samples from companies whose products and services are either advertised or mentioned in editorial columns.

BOUNCE BACK
An offer enclosed with mailings sent to a customer in fulfilment of an order.

BROADSHEET
A single sheet of paper, printed on one or both sides, folded for mailing or

direct distribution, and opening into a single, large advertisement.

BROCHURE
Strictly, a high-quality pamphlet with specially planned layout, typography, and illustrations. The term is also used loosely for any promotional pamphlet or booklet.

BULK MAIL
A category of class mail covering a large quantity of identical pieces but addressed to different names which are specially processed for mailing before delivery to the post office.

BUSINESS LIST
A combination or list of persons or companies based on a business-associated interest, inquiry, membership, subscription, or purchase.

BUYER
A person who orders merchandise, books, records, information or services. Unless another modifying word or two is used, it is assumed that a buyer has paid for all merchandise to date.

C/A
Change of address.

CASH BUYER
A buyer who encloses payment with order.

CASH RIDER
Also called 'cash up' or 'cash option' in which an order form offers instalment terms, but a postscript offers the option of sending full cash payment with order, usually at a saving over the credit price as an incentive.

CATALOGUE
A book or booklet showing merchandise with descriptive details and prices.

CATALOGUE BUYER
A person who has bought products or services from a catalogue.

CATALOGUE REQUEST (paid or unpaid)
A request for a catalogue by a prospective buyer. The catalogue may be free, or there may be a nominal charge for postage and handling, or there may be a more substantial charge which is often refunded or credited on the first order.

CHESHIRE LABELS
Specially prepared paper (rolls, fanfold, or accordion fold) used to reproduce names and addresses to be mechanically affixed, one at a time, to a mailing piece.

CIRCULARS
A general term for printed advertising in any form, including printed matter sent out by direct mail.

CLEANING
The process of correcting or removing a name and address from a mailing list because it is no longer correct or because the listing is to be shifted from one category to another.

CLUSTER SELECTION
A selection procedure based on taking a group of names in series, skipping a group, taking another group, and so on. For example, a cluster selection on the Nth name basis might be the first 10 out of every 100 or the first 125 out of 175. A cluster selection using limited post codes might be the first 200 names in each of the specified post codes.

CODING
1 Identifying devices used on reply devices to identify the mailing list or other source from which the address was obtained.
2 A structure of letters and numbers used to classify characteristics of an address on a list.

COLLATE
1 To assemble individual elements of a mailing in sequence for inserting into a mailing envelope.

2 A programme that combines two or more ordered files to produce a single ordered file. Also the act of combining such files. Synonymous with merge as in merge-purge.

COMPILED LISTS
Names and addresses derived from such sources as directories, newspapers, public records, retail sales slips, and trade-show registrations to identify groups of people who have something in common.

COMPILER
An organization that develops lists of names and addresses from directories, newspapers, public records, registrations and other sources, identifying groups of people, companies, or institutions with something in common.

COMPLETE CANCEL
Refers to a person who has completed a specific commitment to buy products or services before cancelling.

COMPUTER COMPATIBILITY
The ability to use data or programmes of one computer system on one or more other computer systems.

COMPUTER LETTER
A computer printed letter providing personalized fill-in information from a source file in predesignated positions in the letter. It may also be a full printed letter with personalized insertions.

COMPUTER PERSONALIZATION
Printing of letters or other promotional pieces by a computer using names, addresses, special phrases, or other information based on data appearing in one or more computer records. The objective is to make use of the information in the computer record to tailor the promotional message to a specific individual.

COMPUTER SERVICE BUREAU
An internal or external facility providing general or specific data processing services.

CONSUMER LIST
A list of names (usually with home address) compiled or resulting from a common inquiry or buying activity indicating a general or specific buying interest.

CONTINUITY PROGRAMME
Products or services bought as a series of small purchases rather than all at one time. Generally based on a common theme and shipped at regular or specific time intervals.

CONTRIBUTOR LIST
Names and addresses of persons who have donated to a specific fund-raising effort.

CONTROLLED CIRCULATION
Distribution at no charge of a publication to individuals or companies on the basis of their title or occupation. Typically, recipients are asked from time to time to verify the information that qualifies them to receive the publication.

CONTROLLED DUPLICATION
A method by which names and addresses from two or more lists are matched (usually by computer) to eliminate or limit extra mailings to the same name and address.

CONVERSION
1 The process of changing from one method of data processing to another or from one data processing system to another. Synonymous with reformatting.
2 Securing specific action such as a purchase or contribution from a name on a mailing list or as a result of an inquiry.

CO-OP MAILING
A mailing in which two or more offers are included in the same envelope or other carrier with each participating

mailer sharing mailing costs according to a predetermined formula.

COST PER INQUIRY (CPI)
A simple arithmetical formula – total cost of mailing or advertisement divided by the number of inquiries received.

COST PER ORDER (CPO)
Similar to cost per inquiry except based on actual orders rather than inquiries.

COST PER THOUSAND (CPM)
Refers to total cost per thousand pieces of direct mail 'in the mail'.

CPI
See Cost per inquiry.

CPM
See Cost per thousand.

CPO
See Cost per order.

COUPON
A portion of a promotion piece of advertisement intended to be filled in by an inquirer or customer and returned to the advertiser to complete the action intended.

COUPON CLIPPER
A person who has given evidence of responding to free or nominal-cost offers out of curiosity with little or no serious interest or buying intent.

DEADBEAT
A person who has ordered a product or service and, without just cause, has failed to pay for it.

DECOY
A unique name especially inserted in a mailing list for verification of list usage. Also called a 'sleeper'.

DELINQUENT
A person who has fallen behind in his payment or has stopped scheduled payment for a product or service.

DELIVERY DATE
The date on which a specific list order

is to be received from the list owner by the list user or a designated representative of the list user.

DEMOGRAPHICS
Socioeconomic characteristics pertaining to a geographical unit, such as county, city, post code, group of households, education, ethnicity, and income level.

DIRECT MAIL ADVERTISING
Any promotional effort using the Post Office or other direct delivery service distribution of the advertising message.

DIRECT RESPONSE ADVERTISING
Advertising through any medium designed to generate a response by any means (such as mail, telephone, or telegraph) that is measurable.

DONOR LIST
See Contributor list.

DUMMY
A preliminary mockup of a printed piece showing placement and nature of the material to be printed. Also a fictitious name with a mailable address inserted into a mailing list to check on usage of that list.

DUPE (DUPLICATION)
Appearance of identical or near-identical entities more than one time.

DUPLICATION ELIMINATION
A controlled mailing system which provides that no matter how many times a name and address is on a list, and no matter how many lists contain that name and address, it will be accepted for mailing only one time by that mailer. Also referred to as 'de-duping'.

ENVELOPE STUFFER
Any advertising or promotional material enclosed in an envelope with business letters, statements or invoices.

EXCHANGE
An arrangement whereby two mailers

exchange equal quantities of mailing list names.

EXPIRATION
A subscription which is not renewed.

EXPIRATION DATE
The date on which a subscription expires.

EXPIRE
Refers to former customer who is no longer an active buyer.

FILL-IN
A name, address, or other words added to a preprinted letter.

FIRST-TIME BUYER
A person who buys a product or service from a specific company for the first time.

FORMER BUYER
A person who has bought one or more times from a company but has made no purchase in the last 12 months.

FREE-FALL INSERT
A promotional piece loosely inserted or nested in a newspaper or magazine.

FREEPHONE
Free telephone facility offered to readers or direct mail recipients to allow them to enquire or order by phone at no cost to themselves.

FREEPOST
Postage paid address which incurs no cost to the sender when written on reply/response envelope.

FREQUENCY
The number of times a person has ordered within a specific period of time, or in toto. *See also* Recency and Monetary.

FRIEND-OF-A-FRIEND (friend recommendation)
The result of one person sending in the name of someone considered to be interested in a specific advertiser's product or service. A third-party inquiry.

FRONT END
The activities necessary for the measurement of direct marketing activities leading to an order or a contribution.

FUND-RAISING LIST
Any compilation or list of persons or companies based on a known contribution to one or more fund raising appeals.

GEOGRAPHICS
Any method of subdividing a list based on geographical or political subdivisions.

GIFT BUYER
A person who buys a product or service for another.

GIMMICK
An attention-getting device, sometimes three dimensional, attached to a direct mail printed piece.

GUARANTEE
A pledge of satisfaction made by the seller to the buyer and specifying the terms under which the seller will make good his pledge.

HOT-LINE LIST
The most recent names available on a specific list, but no older than three months. In any event, use of the term 'hot-line' should be further modified by such terms as 'weekly' or 'monthly'.

HOUSE-LIST
Any list of names owned by a company as a result of compilation, inquiry or buyer action, or acquisition that is used to promote that company's products or services.

HOUSE-LIST DUPLICATE
Duplication of name and address records between the list user's own lists and any list being mailed by him on a one-time use arrangement.

INQUIRY
A request for literature or other information about a product or service.

Unless otherwise stated, it is assumed no payment has been made for the literature or other information. A catalogue request is generally considered a specific type of inquiry.

INSTALMENT BUYER
A person who orders goods or services and pays for them in two or more periodic payments after delivery of the products or services.

INTER-LIST DUPLICATE
Duplication of name and address records between two or more lists, other than house lists, being mailed by a list user.

INTRA-LIST DUPLICATE
Duplication of name and address records within a given list.

K
Used in reference to computer storage capacity, generally accepted as 1,000. Analogues to M in the direct marketing industry.

KBN (Kill bad name)
What is done with undeliverable addresses, i.e. nixies You KBN a nixie.

KEY CODE (key)
A group of letters or numbers, colours, or other markings used to measure the specific effectiveness of media lists, advertisements, and offers (or any parts thereof).

KEYLINE
Can be any one of many partial or complete descriptions of past buying history coded to include name and address information and current status.

LABEL
A piece of paper containing the name and address of the recipient applied to a mailing for address purposes.

LAYOUT
An artist's sketch showing the relative positioning of illustrations, headlines, and copy. Positioning subject matter on a press sheet for most efficient production.

LETTERHEAD
The printing on a letter which identifies the sender.

LETTERSHOP
A business organization that handles the mechanical details of mailings such as addressing, imprinting, and collating. Most lettershops offer printing facilities, and many offer some degree of creative direct mail services.

LIST (mailing list)
Names and addresses of individuals or companies having in common a specific interest, characteristic, or activity.

LIST BROKER
A specialist who makes all necessary arrangements for one company to make use of the lists of another company. A broker's services may include most or all of the following: research, selection, recommendation, and subsequent evaluation.

LIST BUYER
Technically, this term should apply only to one who actually buys mailing lists. In practice, however, it is usually used to identify one who orders mailing lists for one-time use. A list user or mailer.

LIST CLEANING
The process of correcting or removing a name or address from a mailing list because it is no longer correct. Term is also used in the identification and elimination of house list duplication.

LIST COMPILER
A person who develops lists of names and addresses from directories, newspapers, public records, sales slips, trade-show registrations, and other sources for identifying groups of people or companies with something in common.

LIST EXCHANGE
A barter arrangement between two companies for the use of mailing lists. The arrangement may be list for list,

list for space, or list for comparable value – other than money.

LIST MAINTENANCE
Any manual, mechanical, or electronic system for keeping name and address records (with or without other data) so that 'they are up-to-date at any (or specific) points in time.

LIST MANAGER
A person who, as an employee of a list owner or as an outside agent, is responsible for the use, by others, of a specific mailing list. The list manager generally serves the list owner in several (or all) of the following: list maintenance (or advice thereon); list promotion and marketing; list clearance and record keeping; and collecting for use of the list by others.

LIST OWNER
A person who, by promotional activity or compilation, has developed a list of names having something in common. Or one who has purchased (as opposed to rented, reproduced, or used on a one-time basis) such a list from the developer.

LIST RENTAL
An arrangement in which a list owner furnishes names on his list to a mailer, together with the privilege of using the list on a one-time basis only (unless otherwise specified in advance). For this privilege, the list owner is paid a royalty by the mailer. 'List rental' is the term most often used, although 'list reproduction' and 'list usage' more accurately describe the transaction, since 'rental' is not used in the sense of its ordinary meaning of leasing property.

LIST ROYALTY
Payment to list owners for the privilege of using their lists on a one-time basis.

LIST SAMPLE
A group of names selected from a list for the purpose of evaluating the responsiveness of that list.

LIST SEGMENTATION
See List selection

LIST SELECTION
Characteristics used to define smaller groups within a list (essentially, lists within a list). Although very small select groups may be very desirable and may substantially improve response, increased costs often render them impractical.

LIST SEQUENCE
The order in which names and addresses appear in a list. While most lists today are in postal rebate code sequence, some are alphabetical by name within the code; others are in carrier sequence (postal delivery); and still others may use some other (or no) order within post code. Some lists are still arranged alphabetically by name, or chronologically, or with many variations or combinations.

LIST SORT
The process of putting a list in a specific sequence from another sequence or from no sequence.

LIST TEST
A part of a list selected for the purpose of trying to determine the effectiveness of the entire list. A list sample.

LIST USER
A person who uses names and addresses on someone else's list as prospects for the user's product or service. Similar to mailer.

LOAD UP
The process of offering a buyer the opportunity of buying an entire series at one time after the customer has purchased the first item in that series.

MAIL DATES
Dates on which a user has the obligation, by prior agreement with the list owner, to mail a specific list. No other

data is acceptable without express approval of the list owner.

MAILER
1 A direct mail advertiser.
2 A printed direct mail advertising piece.
3 A folding carton, wrapper, or tube used to protect materials in the mails.

MAILGRAM
A combination telegram-letter with the telegraph transmitted to a postal facility close to the addressee and then delivered as first class mail.

MAILING MACHINE
A machine that attaches labels to mailing pieces and otherwise prepares such pieces for deposit in the postal system.

MAIL ORDER BUYER
A person who orders and pays for a product or service through the mail. Those who use the telephone or telegraph to order from direct response advertising may be included in this category although, technically, they are not mail order buyers.

MAIL PREFERENCE SERVICE (MPS)
A service of the BDMA wherein consumers can request to have their names removed from or added to mailing lists.

MATCH
A direct mail term used to refer to the typing of addresses, salutations, or inserts into letters with other copy imprinted by a printing process.

MATCH CODE
A code determined either by the creator or the user of a file to be used for matching records contained in another file.

MONETARY VALUE
Total expenditures by a customer during a specific period of time, generally 12 months.

MPS
See Mail preference service.

MULTIPLE BUYER
A person who has bought two or more times. Not one who has bought two or more items. Also multi-buyer or repeat buyer.

MULTIPLE REGRESSION
Statistical technique used to measure the relationship between responses to a mailing with census demographics and list characteristics of one or more selected mailing lists. Used to determine the best types of people and areas to mail. This technique can also be used to analyse customers, subscribers, and so forth.

NAME
Single entry on a mailing list.

NAME ACQUISITION
The technique of soliciting response to obtain names and addresses for a mailing list.

NAME-REMOVAL SERVICE
That portion of the mail preference service wherein a customer is sent a form which, when filled in and returned, constitutes a request to have the person's name removed from all mailing lists. Used by participating members of the association and other direct mail users.

NEGATIVE OPTION
A buying plan in which a customer or club member agrees to accept and pay for products or services announced in advance at regular intervals unless the person notifies the company within a reasonable time after each announcement not to ship.

NESTING
Placing one enclosure within another before inserting into a mailing envelope.

NET NAME ARRANGEMENT
An agreement between a list owner and a list user at the time of order or before in which the list owner agrees to accept adjusted payment for less than

the total names shipped. Such arrangements can be for a percentage of names shipped or names actually mailed, whichever is greater, or for only those names actually mailed, without percentage limitation. They can provide for a running charge or not.

NIXIE

A mailing piece returned to a mailer (under proper authorization) by the Post Office because of an incorrect or undeliverable name and address.

NO-PAY

A person who has not paid (wholly or in part) for goods or services ordered. 'Uncollectable', 'Deadbeat', and 'Deinquent', are often used to describe the same person.

NOVELTY FORMAT

An attention-getting direct mail format.

Nth NAME SELECTION

A fractional unit that is repeated in sampling a mailing list. For example, in an 'every tenth' sample, you would select the 1st, 11th, 21st, 31st etc., records; or the 2nd, 12th, 22nd, 32nd, etc., records and so forth.

OFFER

The terms under which a specific product or service is promoted.

ONE-TIME BUYER

A buyer who has not ordered a second time from a given company.

ONE-TIME USE OF A LIST

An intrinsic part of the normal list usage, list reproduction, or list exchange agreement in which it is understood that the mailer will not use the names on the list more than one time without specific prior approval of the list owner.

OPEN ACCOUNT

A customer record that, at a specific point in time, reflects an unpaid balance for goods and services ordered, without delinquency.

ORDER BLANK ENVELOPES

An order form printed on one side of a sheet with a mailing address on the reverse. The recipient simply fills in the order, folds the form and seals it like an envelope.

ORDER CARD

A reply card used to initiate an order by mail.

ORDER FORM

A printed form on which a customer can provide information to initiate an order by mail. Designed to be mailed in an envelope.

PACKAGE

A term used to describe, in toto, all of the assembled enclosures (parts or elements) of a mailing effort.

PACKAGE INSERT

Any promotional piece included in a product shipment. It may be for different products (or refills and replacements) from the same company or for products and services of other companies.

PACKAGE TEST

A test of elements, in part or in their entirety, of one mailing piece against another.

PAID CANCEL

Refers to a person who completes a basic buying commitment or more before cancelling a commitment. *See* Completed cancel.

PAID CIRCULATION

Distribution of a publication to person or organizations which have paid for a subscription.

PAID DURING SERVICE

Term used to describe a method of paying for magazine subscriptions in instalments, usually weekly or monthly, and usually collected in person by the original salesperson or a representative of that company.

PEEL-OFF LABELS
A self-adhesive label attached to a backing sheet which is attached to a mailing piece. The label is intended for removal from the mailing piece and for attachment to an order blank or card.

PENETRATION
The relationship of the number of individuals or families on a particular list, e.g. in toto by county, post code, or SIC, compared to the total number possible.

PERSONALIZING
Individualizing of direct mail pieces by adding the name and other personal information about the recipient.

PHONE LIST
A mailing list, compiled from names listed in telephone directories.

PIGGY-BACK
An offer that hitches a free ride with another offer.

POLY BAG
Transparent polyethylene bag used instead of envelope for mailing.

POP-UP
A printed piece containing a paper construction pasted inside a fold and which, when the fold is opened 'pops-up' to form a three-dimensional illustration.

POSITIVE OPTION
A method of distribution of products and services incorporating the same advance notice technique as 'negative option' but requiring a specific order on the part of the member or subscriber each time. Generally, it is more costly and less predictable than 'Negative option'.

POSTCARD
A single sheet self mailer on card stock.

POSTCARD MAILER
A booklet containing business reply cards which are individually perforated for selective return to order products or obtain information.

PREMIUM
An item offered to a buyer, usually free or at a nominal price, as an inducement to purchase or obtain for trial a product or service offered via mail order.

PREMIUM BUYER
A person who buys a product or service to get another product or service, usually free or at a special price or who responds to an offer of a special product (premium) on the package or label, or sometimes in the advertising, of another product.

PREPRINT
An advertising insert printed in advance and supplied to a newspaper or magazine for insertion.

PRIVATE MAIL
Mail handled by special arrangement outside the Post Office.

PROSPECT
A name on a mailing list regarded as a potential buyer for a given product or service but who has not previously made such a purchase.

PROSPECTING
Mailing to get leads for further sales contact rather than to make direct sales.

PROTECTION
The amount of time before and after the assigned mailing date during which the list owner will not allow the same names to be mailed by anyone other than the mailer cleared for that specific date.

PSYCHOGRAPHICS
Characteristics or qualities used to denote the life style or attitude of customers and prospective customers

PUBLISHER'S LETTER
A second letter enclosed in a mailing package to stress a specific selling point.

PURGE
The process of eliminating duplicates or unwanted names and addresses from one or more lists.

PYRAMIDING
A method of testing mailing lists in which one starts with a small quantity and, based on positive indications, follows with larger and larger quantities of the balance of the list until finally one mails the entire list.

QUESTIONNAIRE
A printed form to a specified audience to solicit answers to specific questions.

RECENCY
The latest purchase or other activity recorded for an individual or company on a specific customer list. *See also* Frequency and Monetary.

RECENCY-FREQUENCY-
MONETARY-VALUE RATIO
A formula used to evaluate the sales potential of names on a mailing list.

RENEWAL
A subscription that has been renewed prior to or at expiration or within six months thereafter.

RENTAL
See List rental

REPEAT BUYER
Multi-buyer.

REPLY CARD
A sender addressed card included in a mailing on which the recipient may indicate his response to the offer.

REPLY-O-LETTER
One of a number of patented direct mailing formats for facilitating replies from prospects. It features a die-cut opening on the face of letter and a pocket on the reverse. An addressed reply card is inserted in the pocket, and the name and address which appears thereon show through the die-cut opening of the letter.

REPRODUCTION RIGHT
Authorization by a list owner for a specific mailer to use that list on a one-time basis.

RESPONSE RATE
Percentage of returns from a mailing.

RETURN ENVELOPE
Addressed reply envelope – either stamped or unstamped, as distinguished from business reply envelopes which carry a postage payment guarantee – included with a mailing.

RETURN POSTAGE GUARANTEED
A legend that should be imprinted on the address face of envelopes or other mailing pieces if the mailer wishes the Post Office to return undeliverable mail.

RETURNS
Responses to a direct mail programme.

RFMR
See Recency-frequency-monetary-value ratio.

ROLL OUT
To mail the remaining portion of a mailing list after successfully testing a portion of that list.

ROP
See Run of paper or run of press.

ROUGH
A dummy or layout in sketchy form with a minimum of detail. Sometimes called a 'scamp'.

ROYALTIES
Sum paid per unit mailed or sold for the use of a device such as a list, imprimatur, or patent.

RUNNING CHARGE
The price charged by a list owner for names run or passed but not used by a specific mailer. When such a charge is made, it is usually made to cover extra processing costs. However, some list owners set the price without regard to actual cost.

RUN OF PAPER OR RUN OF PRESS
A term applied to printing anywhere on regular paper and presses as distinct from separately printed sections. Also sometimes used to describe an advertisement positioned by publisher's choice in-other-than-a-preferred position for which a special charge is made.

SALTING
Deliberate placing of decoy, sleeper, or dummy names in a list to trace list usage and delivery. *See also* Decoy, Dummy, Sleeper name.

SAMPLE BUYER
A person who sends for a sample product, usually at a special price or for a small handling charge, but sometimes free.

SAMPLE PACKAGE (mailing piece)
An example of the package to be mailed by the list user to a particular list. Such a mailing piece is submitted to the list owner for approval prior to commitment for one-time use of that list. Although a sample package may because of time pressure differ slightly from the actual package used, the list user agreement usually requires the user to disclose any material differences when submitting the sample package.

SCAMP
Minimum detail layout of mailing, advertisement design.

SCENTED INKS
Printing inks in which a fragrance has been added.

SELECTION CRITERIA
Definition of characteristics that identify segments or subgroups within a list.

SELF-COVER
A cover of the same paper as the inside text pages.

SELF-MAILER
A direct mail piece mailed without an envelope.

SEQUENCE
An arrangement of items according to a specified set of rules or instructions. Refers generally to postal rebate code or customer number sequence.

SIC
See Standard Industrial Classification.

SLEEPER (*See* Decoy)
A unique name inserted into a mailing list to monitor usage.

SOFTWARE
Set programs, procedures, and associated documentation concerned with the operation of a data processing system.

SOLO MAILING
A mailing that promotes a single product or a limited group of related products. It usually consists of a letter, brochure, and reply device enclosed in an envelope.

SOURCE CODE
A unique alphabetical or numeric identification for distinguishing one list or media source from another. *See also* Key code.

SOURCE COUNT
The number of names and addresses in any given list for the media or list sources from which the names and addresses were derived.

SPLIT TEST
A technique in which two or more samples from the same list – each considered to be representative of the entire list – are used for package tests or to test the homogeneity of the list.

STANDARD INDUSTRIAL
CLASSIFICATION (SIC)
Classification of businesses, as defined by the Department of Industry.

STATE COUNT
The number of names and addresses in a given list for each state.

STATEMENT STUFFER
A small printed piece designed to be inserted in an envelope carrying a customer's statement of account.

STEP UP
The use of special premiums to get a mail order buyer to increase his quantity of purchase.

STOCK ART
Art sold for use by a number of advertisers.

STOCK CUT
Printed engravings kept in stock by the printer or publisher for occasional use, in contrast to exclusive use.

STOCK FORMATS
Direct mail formats with illustrations or headings preprinted and to which an advertiser adds his own copy.

STOPPER
Advertising jargon for a striking headline or illustration intended to attract immediate attention.

STUFFER
Advertising enclosure placed in other media, e.g. newspapers, merchandise packages, and mailings for other products.

SUBSCRIBER
A person who has paid to receive a periodical.

SWATCHING
Attaching samples of material to a printed piece.

TABLOID
A preprinted advertising insert of four or more pages, usually about half the size of a regular newspaper page, designed for inserting into a newspaper.

TEASER
An advertisement or promotion planned to excite curiosity about a later advertisement or promotion.

TEST PANEL
A term used to identify each of the parts or samples in a split test.

TEST TAPE
A selection of representative records within a mailing list designed to enable a list user or service bureau to prepare for reformatting or converting the list to a form more efficient for the user.

THROWAWAY
An advertisement or promotional piece intended for widespread free distribution. It is generally printed on inexpensive paper and most often distributed by hand, either to passers-by or house-to-house.

TIE-IN
A co-operative mailing effort involving two or more advertisers.

TIL FORBID
An order for continuing service which is to continue until specifically cancelled by the buyer.

TIP-ON
An item glued to a printed piece.

TITLE
A designation before (prefix) or after (suffix) a name to more accurately identify an individual. Prefixes: Mr, Mrs, Dr, Sister. Suffixes: MD, Jr, President, Sales Manager.

TOKEN
An involvement device usually consisting of a perforated portion of an order card which is designed for removal from its original position and then placed in another designated area on the other card to signify desire to purchase the product or service offered.

TRAFFIC BUILDER
A direct mail piece intended primarily to attract recipients to the mailer's place of business.

TRIAL BUYER
A person who buys a short-term sup-

ply of a product or who buys the product with the understanding that it may be examined, used, or tested for a specified time before he must decide whether to pay for it or return it.

Planning and research terms

AB/C1/C2/DE
The four most commonly used definitions of socioeconomic class (upper and professional middleclass/white collar class/skilled working class/unskilled working class, and below, plus pensioners).

AD HOC SURVEY
Survey of particular topic at one specified time; one-off research; non-continuous.

ADVERTISEMENT RESEARCH
Research into the likely effect of an advertisement or a part of an advertisement on the audience at which it is directed.

AIDED RECALL
An interviewing technique in which subjects are asked to select the appropriate response to a question from a given list of suggestions.

ATTITUDE
The opinions and interests of individuals or groups towards other people, things or institutions which predispose them to certain types of behaviour.

CONCEPT BOARD
An illustration, with words used for research purposes to describe creative concepts.

CONSUMER RESEARCH
Research into the numbers, characteristics, preferences, behaviour etc. of buyers, potential buyers and non-buyers of a product, brand or service.

CONTINUOUS RESEARCH
Research in which data is collected on a continuing basis to reflect performance trends and changing conditions.

DATA PROCESSING
The processing of answers to questions on to the computer so that the results can be summarized and printed out on computer tables.

DEMOGRAPHICS
The division of the public into various groups, e.g. sex, age, socioeconomic class.

DESK RESEARCH
Research using internal records, published data and other existing material, without recourse to data collection in the field.

GROUP DISCUSSION
Interview of a number of people (group) at the same time, in which the response of individuals, resulting from their group association, is sought.

HALL TEST
A central location test, research conducted from a central point, for example a hall in a busy shopping precinct. Respondents are selected from the street and invited into the hall for an interview.

IN HOME PLACEMENT
Product testing by placing the product in the home of the tester.

MARKET SEGMENTATION
The process of identifying different groups or segments of buyers in a particular market according to their special characteristics, e.g. age, sex, social class.

MOTIVATION RESEARCH
A form of MR through which relationships between people's behaviour and their underlying motives, desires, emotions, etc. are sought. A technique to find the real answers to the question, 'why?'.

POPULATION
Also universe. Group of persons which is being investigated and from which some are selected in a systematic fashion to form a sample.

PRE-TESTING
Research to test advertising, either in

rough form or as a concept, before it is used as part of a campaign.

QUOTA SAMPLE
A sample in which the interviewers are instructed to collect information from a predetermined number of people, according to certain specified, observable characteristics, but the selection of particular respondents is not prescribed.

RANDOM SAMPLE
A sample selected by random method, i.e. in which each item or member has an equal probability of being selected.

RESPONDENT
The consumer who is being interviewed. .

RETAIL AUDIT
Also shop audit. Continuous research with a panel of retail distributors to study inventory levels and the performance of specific products at the retail level.

SAMPLE
A selected and representative part of a group of units (the population or universe).

SAMPLE SIZE
The number of members of a sample.

STRATIFICATION
The division of a population into parts (strata); particularly for the purpose of drawing a sample in which a predetermined proportion of the same is drawn for each stratum.

SUB-SAMPLE
A small sample drawn from a larger sample; a part of the larger sample.

U&A
User and awareness study – likely to form part of a quantitative research study.

UNIVERSE
See Population.

WEIGHTING
The adjustment of data by assigning definite proportional values, according to the desired degree of importance of various parts of the results.

Sales promotion terms

ADVERTISING ALLOWANCE
An allowance given to the retailer by a manufacturer in cash, as a discount or as extra product in exchange for the inclusion of the manufacturer's product being featured in the retailer's advertising sometimes called key money.

BANDED PACK
On-pack premium attached by tape or similar means to product package. Also used to describe several units banded together.

BONUS OFFER
Trade offer where cash discount is given.

BOUNCE-BACK
Consumer receives details of a further premium offer on product when he gets give-away or self-liquidator; bounce-back goods are sometimes related to those initially offered.

BUBBLE-PACK
Bubble of rigid transparent plastic attached to product package to hold and protect on-pack premium.

CHARACTER MERCHANDISING
The use of well-known characters, usually from the cinema, TV or comics as basis for premium offer on other forms of promotion.

CHILDREN'S CLUB
Children join club connected with product or character and get membership badge and card and possibly a 'secret' code; they are then entitled to special privileges.

COLLARETTE
Card with die-cut hole which fits over the neck of a bottle; give-away premium can be attached to card.

COMPETITION
Prizes are offered for correct answers to a test of skill. Tie-breakers to ensure the required number of major prize-winners are normally used, and proof-of-purchase is usually required for entry.

CONSUMER CLUB
Similar idea to children's club for adult consumers; often run by magazines as circulation booster.

CONTAINER PREMIUM
The premium is a special reusable container in which the product is packed. Usually give-away, but occasionally self-liquidating with the product at a special unit price.

COUPON OFFER
Coupons or vouchers are given to consumers allowing them money off promoted product.

COUPON PLAN
Premium merchandise is offered in exchange for coupons, labels or vouchers from products on a continuous basis (e.g. cigarette coupons).

DEALER INCENTIVE
General term used to describe any incentive or premium aimed specifically at the retailer or wholesaler, sometimes known as a dealer loader.

DEALER LOADER
See above.

DOOR-OPENER
Premium (usually inexpensive) given away by salesman to persuade housewife, retailer or any buyer to listen.

DOZENS OFFER
Trade offer where extra quantities of product are given free.

EVALUATION
Self-explanatory; but worthwhile ensuring that the techniques used are satisfactory to really check on effectiveness.

FACTORY PACK
Any give-away premium attached to, used as or inside the product package.

FGA
Free give-away *see* Free offer.

FMI
Free mention *see* Free offer.

FREE OFFER
Premium given away at no extra cost (apart, possibly from postage) to purchaser of promoted product. Scrupulous care must be taken about the exact use of the word 'free'. Sometimes abbreviated as FMI – Free Mention or FGA – Free Give-Away.

GIVE-AWAY
Low-cost premium, either a factory-pack, off-peak or mail-in, given away free.

HANDLING HOUSE
An organization providing specialized service in dealing with checking, packaging and mailing of premiums, etc.

INCENTIVE
Any premium offered in return for performing a specified task and normally used in the context of salesmen and dealer incentives. Also used as alternative word for premium.

IN-PACK
Give-away premium actually inside promoted product package.

ISP
Institute of Sales Promotion. The professional body of the promotion business.

KEY MONEY
See Advertising allowance.

MAIL-IN
A premium for which the consumer has to write in; either self-liquidator or give-away.

MERCHANDISING
Particular facet of marketing, aimed at securing maximum product movement at retail level.

MULTI-PRODUCT GIFT PLAN
Free (consumer) gift redemption scheme jointly sponsored by several non-competitive products.

MYSTERY SHOPPER
A manufacturer's representative who poses as an ordinary shopper and calls on retailer; if retailer shows and/or demonstrates manufacturer's product he is rewarded. Also used to motivate consumers in the store.

OFF-PACK
Give-away premium not attached to product package but dispensed at point-of-sale.

ONE-CHAIN
See Tailor-made.

PART-CASH REDEMPTION
Used in coupon plan to enable consumer to obtain premium more quickly by sending cash in lieu of some coupons.

PARTY PLAN
Products are sold through demonstration parties at the home of a consumer-hostess, who receives a premium gift as her reward.

PERSONALITY PROMOTION
Manufacturer's representatives – suitably garbed – call on homes awarding cash or goods in return for housewife showing product and answering product question. Also used as form of dealer incentive.

POINT-OF-SALE DISPLAY
Display material used in retail outlet to draw attention to product; alternatively called point-of-purchase display. Premiums often form part of these displays.

PREMIUM
Generally, any item of merchandise offered by a company to its consumers, retailers, wholesalers or salesmen. Specifically, any product offered with another product, usually conditionally on purchase of that product.

PRE-PROMOTION TESTING
Used to test the appeal of a promotion before a large-scale launch.

PROOF-OF-PURCHASE
Token from product package enabling consumer to qualify for a premium; usually label, box-top, brand symbol or special offer token.

REDEMPTION CENTRE
Trading stamp company's store where stamps can be exchanged over the counter for goods.

REDUCED PRICE OFFER
Price reduction printed on-pack.

RESPONSE
The actual number of consumers who respond to a promotional activity.

RISER CARD
Card attached to product package to give extra space for attaching on-pack premium or for illustrating premium offer.

SALES INCENTIVE
Any incentive aimed at company or wholesaler salesmen, usually in return for meeting set targets, getting display, etc.

SELF-LIQUIDATING PREMIUMS
See below.

SELF-LIQUIDATOR
Any premium where the cash required from the applicant covers cost of premium, handling charges and postage. Generally cheapest to run (often known as SLP – Self-liquidating Premium).

SHELF TALKER
A small point-of-sale display piece which is fitted onto self-service unit shelves.

SHRINK-WRAP
Flexible plastic sheet drawn tightly across premium on product package by heat shrinking process.

SPONSORSHIP
For the most part devoted to sports, but also in the fields of art and other cultural activities.

TAILOR-MADE PROMOTION
A promotion specifically designed for one retailer (multiple, chain or group) sometimes known as one chain.

TIE-BREAKER
Device used in competitions to ensure required number of major prize-winners; usually takes form of writing a slogan or completing a sentence.

TRADING STAMPS
Given to consumer at participating retail outlets, based on value of purchase. Consumers fill stamp saver books and exchange these for gifts or cash at stamp firm's redemption centres.

TRAFFIC BUILDER
Store promotion – generally in self-service or supermarket – designed to stimulate traffic through the store.

USE-THE-USER
Scheme in which a premium is offered to a consumer who helps company to sell product to a friend or relative.

VAT
A familiar enough abbreviation, but an item to be borne in mind when offering goods. Check carefully on current limitations.

Computer terms

ALPHANUMERIC
Consisting of both 'alpha' and 'numeric' characters, e.g. A1045/BL43.67M. Punctuation marks, i.e. non-numeric characters are regarded as alpha.

BATCH PROCESSING
See Real-time.

BINARY
The mathematical system in which all characters, i.e. numbers, letters, punctuation marks, etc. are represented by 'ones' and 'zeros' which are represented in the computer as electrical 'on' or 'off' states.

BYTE
Literally 'by eight'. A group of eight binary digits (each with a value of either 0 or 1) representing a single character or number, or part of a number or a set of indicators e.g. 1 = YES, 0 = NO). Bytes are normally considered as units, and are the basis on which capacities of storage devices such as disks, or the computer's memory are measured. A kilobyte (kb) is approximately one thousand bytes, and a megabyte (Mb) one million bytes.

CENTRAL PROCESSOR
The heart of the computer, where calculations are carried out and program instructions obeyed.

COMPUTER
An electronic device for the high-speed processing of information according to given instructions.

CONTINUOUS STATIONERY
The 'fan-folded' continuous strip of paper on which computer results are printed. May consist of plain listing paper or preprinted types such as invoices, orders, etc. It is divided into individual sheets at each fold. Generally known as printout.

CURSOR
The (blinking) indicator on a VDU screen which shows where the next character to be typed will appear.

DISK
Also disk pack or disk cartridge. A magnetic storage system which consists of a series of flat disks, about 14 in diameter, attached to a central spindle and coated with metal oxide, similar to the coating on a magnetic tape. Mounted on a 'disk drive', the assembly spins at high speed, and is 'read' or 'written' by heads which move over the surface of the disk, under the control of the computer. All programs and files in frequent use are held on disk, and are thus instantly available to the computer. Each surface can hold about 16 million characters, and data can be transferred at an enormously high speed, several thousand characters per second.

FILE
A sequence of related information, i.e. a list of media bookings, or clients and products, held by the computer and used in processing. Can also consist of one or more programs.

FLOPPY DISK
See Disk. A floppy disk is a small-capacity single-platter disk, normally used in conjunction with microcomputers. It is similar to a 'single' gramaphone record, and is permanently housed in a protective sleeve which has a slot cut in to allow the read/write heads access to it. It is not flexible in spite of its name.

HARDWARE
The actual computer equipment and its related devices, e.g. VDUs, printers magnetic tapes etc.

INPUT
The feeding in of data to the computer, or data waiting to be fed in.

INTERFACE
The point at which two different systems meet, allowing data to flow from one to the other.

LOG-IN
The process of gaining access to the computer and a particular system, e.g. the media system, via the terminal, using the 'HELLO' command.

LOG-OUT
The process, using the 'BYE' command, of telling the computer you have finished using it. It is important to log-out correctly, otherwise the computer will keep checking the terminal for further input, which will slow down its speed of operation and reduce the efficiency of the system as a whole.

MEMORY.
Also called store. The area in which programs currently being run and data currently being processed are placed for access by the central processor. Not to be confused with a 'memory bank', a phrase used inaccurately by the media to denote a permanent store of data. This would in fact be a disk or magnetic tape.

MNEMONIC
An abbreviation used to represent a longer name or idea, e.g. DAMA for Daily Mail. The computer will normally accept either the mnemonic or the full name.

OUTPUT
The results of processing, consisting either of printed information, a display on a screen (VDU), or magnetically stored data, awaiting further processing.

PROGRAM
A detailed list of instructions which tells the computer how to identify and process data, or perform any function at all.

REAL-TIME
The concept of the computer responding instantly to information it receives, and producing its results immediately. This means that the user can feed in data, have it processed and receive the results as one complete operation. The opposite of real-time operation is 'batch processing', whereby the data to be processed is collected and collated manually, i.e. batched, and then fed into the computer. The results produced then have to be divided up for the various users, and transported to them.

RECORD
See File. A file consists of a number of records, each of which is self-contained, e.g. a name and address file contains names, and addresses, some means of uniquely identifying each one, and possible additional information, such as credit limit, balance to date, etc. A complete set of such details pertaining to one person, company, etc. is a record. Individual items within a record, e.g. credit limit, are known as fields.

SOFTWARE
The 'intangible' parts of the system – the actual programs, both those which control the operation of the computer, and those which process the data.

SORT
The process of arranging a file of data into a specified order, e.g. products within clients in alphabetical order.

SYSTEM
A general term which can mean various things, e.g. the computer system as a whole, or a group of programs and files which relate to a specific activity – the media system, the production system, etc.

TERMINAL
A device for receiving information from, and/or sending information to the computer. May be a VDU or a

printer, which types on paper instead of displaying on a screen. A terminal may be linked to a computer either directly by cable, or indirectly via the public telephone network.

TIME-SHARING

Also multi-programming. The ability of the computer to cope with several independent users at the same time.

VDU

Visual display unit. A device with a TV screen for displaying information from the computer, and a typewriter-like keyboard for inputting information to the computer.

Index